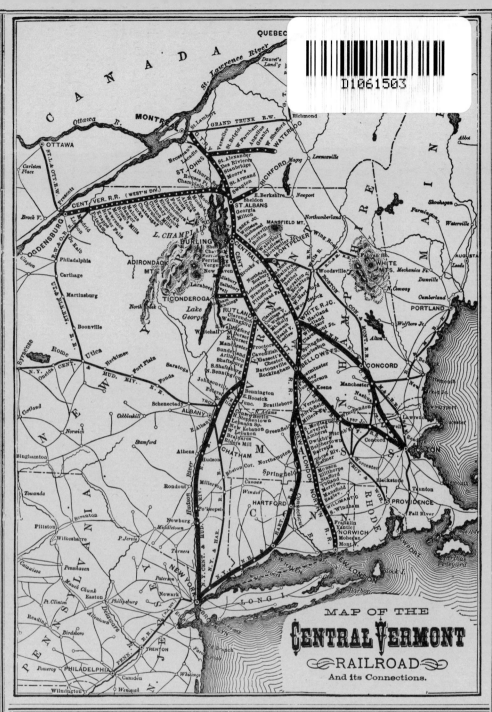
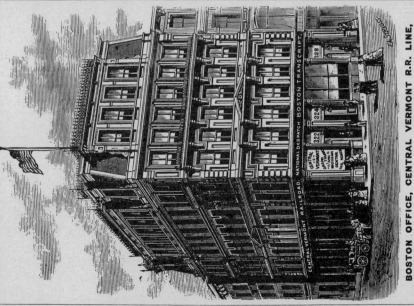

THE
Central Vermont
RAILWAY

This photograph shows one of the first trains to pass through the new tunnel under what was to become North Avenue in Burlington. This passenger train is coming out of the west portal, only a few hundred feet from the shore of Lake Champlain. Details of its construction are covered in Chapter III. (Jim Shaughnessy Collection)

THE
Central Vermont
RAILWAY
A Yankee Tradition
By Robert C. Jones

Volume I

"THE EARLY YEARS, 1830-1886"

SUNDANCE
Books

THE
Central Vermont
RAILWAY

P. O. BOX 597 • SILVERTON, COLORADO 81433

Graphical presentation-
    Sundance Publications, Ltd. Silverton, Colorado
Photolithography-
    Sundance Publications, Ltd. Silverton, Colorado
Typesetting-
    The Silverton Standard and The Miner, Silverton, Colorado
Binding-
    Hawley Bookbinding Co., Denver, Colorado

Editorial Staff-
    Editor - Robert C. Jones
    Supporting Editor - Janet J. Jones
    Assistant Editor - Allen Nossaman
    Production Manager - Dell A. McCoy
    Director of Photography - Steven J. Meyers

Copyright Information-

ISBN 0-913582-27-1
First Printing - September 1981

This Volume is

DEDICATED

TO

My Wife, Janet J. Jones,

In sincere appreciation for her willingness to share me for the past twenty-five years with my second love—railroads—in such an understanding, interested, and helpful way. Without such support, my literary efforts would not have been possible.

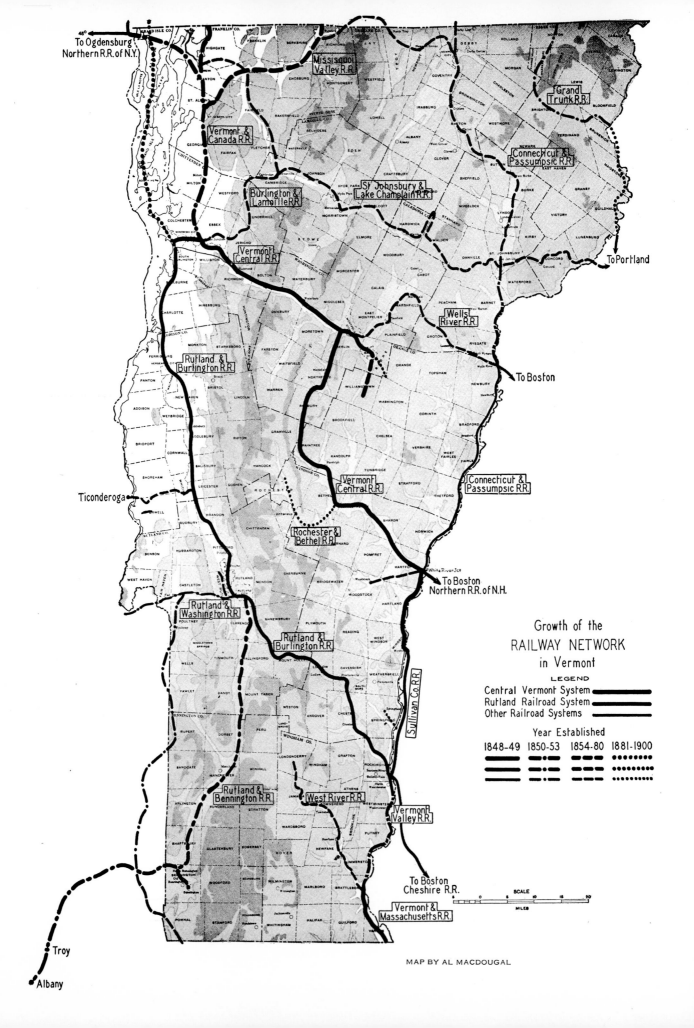

Growth of the
RAILWAY NETWORK
in Vermont
LEGEND
Central Vermont System
Rutland Railroad System
Other Railroad Systems

Year Established
1848-49   1850-53   1854-80   1881-1900

SCALE
0   5   10   15   20
MILES

MAP BY AL MACDOUGAL

PREFACE
AND
ACKNOWLEDGEMENTS

The Central Vermont is regarded by many as one of the "romance railroads" of New England. Its 150-year old history dates back to the very dawn of the railroad era, and this longevity places the Central Vermont in very exclusive company indeed.

The Central Vermont's history is both complex and tumultuous. It is filled with human achievements and failings, heroics and scandals. The road went through its early childhood and adolescence at a time when railroads were planned, built, and operated like pawns in a huge chess game; and the principal figures in this road's history challenged the biggest and toughest opponents that our country's history books have immortalized.

Within a relatively few years, the Central Vermont had grown to become the largest railway system in New England and the seventh largest in the United States. It operated from the Great Lakes to Lake Champlain, and from north of the Canadian border to the southern extremity of Connecticut—all the while somehow missing every metropolitan area in the states it served. The road has survived an untold number of financial panics, a major depression, a Civil War, two World Wars, and several other conflicts of significance. In addition, it has survived the most devastating natural disaster ever to strike New England—the Flood of 1927.

The Central Vermont has promoted or been the victim of virtually every legal maneuver imaginable at one time or another in its history. Yet, it has matured into a railroad that today is modern in every respect. Its roadbed is among the finest to be found anywhere on the continent, its communications systems are second to none, and its equipment and property are judiciously maintained.

The Central Vermont is unique among railroads in that it has operated lake and ocean-going vessels, airplanes, trucks, and buses, in addition to its excellent rail service. Over the years it built many of its own steam locomotives, and it has efficiently utilized both some of the smallest and the largest steam locomotives in New England; and it was an early user of both gas-electric units and diesel power. Further, the Central Vermont's contributions to the railroad industry in

terms of both notable personnel and technical innovations are in a ratio that far exceeds its relative size.

In the pages that follow, some of this history is presented in both words and illustrations. This work is not intended to be the "final word" on the subject. Rather, it is the author's hope that this effort will encourage others to continue the research into the many facets of this intriguing story. There is much more that can be done. It is my hope that any errors found by readers more knowledgeable about the subject than I will be both few in number and inconsequential in nature.

A project such as this can be produced only with the trust, the cooperation, and the contributions of many people. The tremendous amount of support and cooperation that I have received right from the start of the project has been a truly humbling experience. To all who have helped in any way, I publicly express my personal and special thanks.

General Manager Phil Larson and Clerk of the Corporation Gene Olmsted have both been very enthusiastic about the idea and most helpful in making the Company's files and records available during the research phase of the project. I trust that the final product will do their railroad justice.

Alan Irwin has provided the diesel roster, as well as many color photos. Mike McMahon provided the steam locomotive roster and many photographs from his vast collection as well. Gerry Fox made available the material from his years of research on the Burlington & Lamoille Railroad. Albert "Bud" Spaulding provided much of the information pertaining to the road's passenger operations, as well as many photographs from his personal collection. Captain Lynn Bottum supplies much of the information about the road's steamboat operations. The exquisite paintings were done by Bill Gillespie, a retired CV engineer and road foreman of locomotives.

J. Emmons Lancaster was most helpful in providing the fine collection of material in the 470 Railroad Club's archives, as well as photographs from his personal collection. Jim McFarlane opened up his vast personal collection of Central Vermont photos and papers for use in this project—a gesture that is appreciated all the more as Jim had been harboring thoughts for years of doing a book on the CV himself. His letters asking, "Is there anything else I can help you with?" are most appreciated.

Kevin Graffinino, curator of the University of Vermont's Wilbur Collection, made it possible for a number of that institution's photos and rare broadsides to be used. Ed Steele made available the material of the St. Albans Historical Society as well as material from his own collection. Peter Mallette provided access to the holdings of the neighboring Georgia Historical Society. Claire Mullen and Janet Jones made available a variety of items from the Edmunds Middle School Library in Burlington.

Some of the country's finest and best-known photo-

THIS MAP, FROM an early issue of the VERMONT LIFE magazine, clearly illustrates the growth of Vermont's railway network up to the turn of the century. Train service between Windsor and Burlington was inaugurated in December, 1849, with service between intermediate points commencing at earlier dates. Service north of Burlington-Essex Junction on the Vermont & Canada started in the fall of 1850. (VERMONT LIFE Magazine)

graphers have made their material available for use in this series. Their names and their work need no introduction: David C. Bartlett, Philp R. Hastings, Homer R. Hill, Jim Shaughnessy, and Ray Tobey. To a large degree, their outstanding work in years gone by has made this project possible. In addition to his own work, Jim Shaughnessy has provided a number of prints from his classic THE RUTLAND ROAD by Howell-North Books. Through his letters, telephone calls, and visits, Jim has gone out of his way to make sure he could provide all the help possible for this work. It is greatly appreciated.

Large amounts of material were enthusiastically provided from the personal collections of Chandler Cobb, John Gardner, Whitney Maxfield, Armand Premo, Richard Sanborn, and Roger Wiberg. Notable contributions were also made by Lawrie Brown; Lewis R. Brown, Inc., of Brattleboro; Louis Cameron, Glen Davis, Ed Emery, Dick Hoisington, Del Janes, Paul Larner, and Elliott Steward.

Other contributors to whom a sincere "thank you" is due include George Beebe; Gerry Bouchard; Jim Bowler; Paul S. Bugbee; Guy Cambria, Jr.; Jim Concannon; Edwin Dunbaugh; Ed Emery; William E. Ewen, Jr.; Stan Folsom; Nick Frazier; Bill Gove; Ted Hansen, Jr.; Ed Irwin; Bob Yarger; and Rich Yates. Other contributors include Dick Bero, Geraldine Cunningham, Dean Howarth, Fred Maskell, Dick Nelson, Ed Quinn, Neil Raymond, William "Dig" Rowley, Chris Sharrow, Donald A. Somerville, Mrs. Robert Spaulding, Hugh Strobel, Dick and Andy Towle, and Walt Warman. Tom and Carolyn Arey of South Willington, Connecticut, provided hospitality and leads on material during Southern Division research efforts.

I have intentionally put off until now a special mention of my good friend Jim Murphy, both a CV employee and a professional photographer, who has made a major contribution to this series in many ways. He, along with Alan Irwin, conscientiously fostered and promoted the idea of such a project. Jim has made his own extensive CV collection available for use in these books. In addition, he has followed up numerous personal contacts and leads for additional material. His biggest contribution, however, has been his darkroom expertise. Virtually all the illustrative material found between these covers has been processed in Jim's St. Albans darkroom. There is little doubt in my mind that had it not been for him, I would still be thinking, "Wouldn't it be great if someone would do a nice illustrated history of the CV."

To each and every one of the people acknowledged on these pages and to those I may have unintntionally left unnamed, you have my most sincere and personal "thank you." These are really **your** books.

I would be remiss if I did not acknowledge here the tremendous amount of friendly cooperation and professional expertise that have been extended to me by Dell McCoy and his staff at Sundance Publications Limited. Without such a contribution and commitment, these series of books would never have materialized.

A separate acknowledgment section at the beginning of each volume will give credit to the individual contributors to that volume. Those to be so recognized in Volume I include Jim Murphy; Jim McFarlane; Richard Sanborn; Lewis R. Brown, Inc.; Bill Gove; Jim Shaughnessy and Howell-North Books; Donald A. Somerville; and Gerry Fox. Others who have contributed several items for this volume are Louis Cameron, Whitney Maxfield, Albert C. "Bud" Spaulding, Ed Steel and the St. Albans Historical Society, the Wilbur Collection of the University of Vermont, and Roger Wiberg.

Valuable material was also provided by Robert Adams, Jim Bowler, Chandler Cobb, Glenn Davis, the Edmunds Middle School of Burlington, Ed Emery, Dan Foley, Philp R. Hastings, Dean Howarth, Paul Larner, Michael McMahon, Armand Premo, William "Dig" Rowley, the "Vermont Life Magazine," and Rich Yates.

To each person who has helped in any way, you have my personal and sincere thanks.

Enjoy your trip over the Central Vermont!

Robert C. Jones
Burlington, Vermont
July, 1981

FRONT COVER: The first "Governor Smith" simmers away amid considerable attention in front of the White River Junction station. (Bill Gillespie painting)

TABLE OF CONTENTS

Vermont Central Number 32 was built in 1852 by the Essex Company and was named the ''Richmond.'' She exploded on November 11, 1853, and was rebuilt the following year. The engine was again rebuilt in 1869 and renamed the ''B. P. Cheney.'' It was scrapped in 1897. This finds the shining Number 32 heading a southbound passenger train at the St. Albans depot about 1870. (Jim Murphy Collection)

Chapter **I**

The Railroad Era Dawns 1830-1852

*T*HE STEAM ENGINE WAS INVENTED BY JAMES WATT, AN *Englishman, in 1773, and during the next two decades far-sighted thinkers of the day worked on improvements and expanded uses of this invention. History gives credit for the invention of the steam locomotive to Richard Trevithick, an eccentric genius, who put together the first piece of such equipment at his London shop in 1804. But because Trevithick had not mastered the technique of making steam in his mobile machine, it would move only at very slow speeds, and it pulled little more than its own weight.*

During the succeeding years, George Stephenson and his son Robert worked to make the steam locomotive more practicable, and in so doing they invented the steam-blast technique. This enabled them to constantly "blow" the fire in the tubular-boilered "Rocket," thus providing sufficient steam pressure to pull ten passenger cars at the rate of thirty-five miles per hour. Thus, in 1829, one of the world's greatest inventions materialized. For the first time in history, man had the means at his disposal to travel long distances in relative comfort at speeds faster than those attainable by a horse.

The Delaware & Hudson Canal Company imported three locomotives from England in late July or early August, 1829. One of these, the "Stourbridge Lion," was tested on August 8 of that year, and thus earned the distinction of being the first steam locomotive to operate on a track in North America. It wasn't perfect, but a small group of American inventive geniuses clearly saw its potential.

As in projected canals, Vermonters were pioneers in the promotion of railroads. The honor of first suggesting a railroad to connect Boston with Lake Ontario, however, probably goes to John L. Sullivan, a well-known Massachusetts civil engineer. In 1827, letters from Sullivan to a Port Kent, New York, promoter by the name of Elkanah Watson spelled out some of Sullivan's ideas. Basically, he was convinced of the feasibility of building a rail line from Boston to some point on Lake Champlain, where a crossing would be effected by ferry, and then another rail line from the western shore of Lake Champlain across northern New York to the St. Lawrence at Ogdensburgh.

During these early decades of the 1800s, Vermont was experiencing a wave of emigration, with thousands of its people moving westward, looking for the fabled "land of milk and honey." The state's leading men felt that by providing cheaper, dependable transportation they could simultaneously stem the westward movement of human resources and stimulate Vermont's industrial and agricultural production.

By 1830, a sort of railroad fever had been stirred up by newspapers in both Massachusetts and Vermont. Hardly a day passed without an article on the subject appearing in the Montpelier newspapers. And this was four years before the first steam locomotive was brought into New England and five years before the first New England railroad was operational.

Upon hearing that the Massachusetts legislature had reported in favor of a railroad from Boston to Lowell, a group of Montpelier citizens met at the venerable Pavilion Hotel on January 26, 1830, and appointed a committee to report on the subject at a meeting scheduled for February 2.

The committee reported at the appointed time, and their findings favored a railroad from Boston to Ogdensburgh. The report concluded with the adoption of the following resolutions: "Resolved, That the public good requires vigorous and persevering efforts on the part of all intelligent and public-spirited individuals, until by the enterprise of individuals, the cooperation of State Legislatures, or the aid of the General Government, the survey and completion of a route is established for a National Railroad from the seaboard at Boston, through Lowell, Mass., Concord in New Hampshire, and thence by the most convenient route through the valley of the Onion River to Lake Champlain, and thence to the waters of Lake Ontario at Ogdensburgh, New York. Resolved, That the chairman and secretary of this meeting be authorized to call an assembly of the inhabitants of the County of Washington, at such time and place as they may think proper, to consult on this important subject, and to adopt such measures as may be deemed expedient." This document was signed by Lyman Reed, E.P. Walton, and S. Baldwin.

At this meeting, General Parley Davis, Joshua Y. Vail, Araunah Waterman, and Sylvanus Baldwin were appointed to a committee "to prepare a topographical and statistical statement of facts on the subject of a route for a railroad from Boston to Ogdensburgh." The Honorable Daniel Baldwin was appointed as agent to represent the views of the meeting to the Massachusetts Railroad Association. These men were all Montpelier residents.

Lyman Reed prepared the first lectures on the subject for the Montpelier Lyceum. He then elaborated on these lectures in the form of seven lengthy articles that were published in E. P. Walton's newspaper, the **"Vermont Watchman & State Gazette."**

The president of the group, Captain Timothy Hubbard, and the secretary O. H. Smith, immediately called a meeting of citizens of Washington County, which was held at Montpelier on February 17, 1830. At this meeting, a very lengthy report was presented by the committee appointed earlier to study topography and other facts. Information was provided by John L. Sullivan and John McDuffie regarding routes in Massachusetts and New Hampshire, and by engineers from New York on routes in that state. Davis, Waterman, and Baldwin provided information on routes in Vermont.

On February 22, The Vermont Railroad Association was formed at Montpelier, of which all officers were Montpelier men. Timothy Hubbard was elected president; Joseph Howes, vice-president; Araunah Waterman, Joshua Vail, Silas C. French, Ira Owen, and Timothy Merrill, directors; Daniel Baldwin, treasurer; Lyman Reed, recording secretary; and E. P. Walton, Sr., corresponding secretary.

On March 11, 1830, a meeting was held at Keeseville, New York, with Elkanah Watson serving as chairman. The proceedings of the February 17 meeting held at Montpelier were read, including the full report of the study committee. The New Yorkers then resolved "that we cordially concur in the sentiments disclosed in the proceedings of a meeting held at Montpelier, Vermont, on the 17th;" and a committee of which Watson was chairman was "authorized to commence a correspondence with that appointed at the Montpelier meeting, and with any other similar bodies," and "with our national and state authorities." A copy of the proceedings of both the Keeseville and the Montpelier meetings, was sent to Isaac Finch, congressman from New York, who was requested to invite the cooperation of the New York delegation in securing U.S. engineers to make surveys.

Other regional meetings followed in Ogdensburgh on March 23, Concord April 6, and Burlington May 12. At the latter meeting, those present resolved: "That we consider the public much indebted for the patriotic exertions of numerous associations of individuals on the contemplated route, and particularly to the gentlemen of Washington and Orange Counties for their elaborate and able report, and offer them our zealous cooperation in the laudable endeavor to excite attention and diffuse information on the subject."

Perhaps the most important meeting, however, was one held at Malone, New York, on May 26, 1830, of which a former Montpelier citizen, George B. R. Gove, was an active member. The important feature in these proceedings was the suggestion to form a General Railroad Convention, which would consist of delegates from counties on the proposed route in New York, Vermont, New Hampshire, and Massachusetts. The proceedings of this meeting were published in the **"Boston Patriot,"** whose editor approved of

CHARLES PAINE WAS a major promoter of the Vermont Central and served as its first president from 1845 to 1853. (Jim Murphy Collection)

the proposed General Convention which was planned for Montpelier in the fall.

The Railroad Convention was held in Montpelier on October 6, 1830, with 48 delegates from New York, Vermont, New Hampshire, and Massachusetts in attendance. Luther Bradish of Moira, New York, was elected president. The secretaries were Albe Cady of Concord, New Hampshire, and John Johnson of Burlington, Vermont. This was indeed a body of able and earnest men, each of whom was successful in his own right.

Interesting addresses were delivered by Elkanah Watson of Port Kent, New York, and James Hayward, Henry Williams, and David Lee Child of Boston. Hayward was an engineer; Williams, a merchant; and Child, a newspaper editor. A lengthy communication containing much valuable information from John L. Sullivan was read, and the Convention was closed with a speech by Bradish.

Two men destined to be among the most famous pioneer railroad builders in the history of Vermont appeared at this Convention—31-year-old Charles Paine of Northfield, and

Timothy Follett of Burlington. Paine was later to become president of the Vermont Central Railroad and governor of the state, and Follett was to become president of the Rutland & Burlington Railroad.

The main business of the convention was to increase the number of committees for furthering this great project. In forming these committees, the convention went outside of its own group and enlisted eminent men in each state to help promote the project. This scheme to enlist men wielding a strong influence in their home states was an admirable one, but it proved to be inefficient. Getting these men together for meetings became an impossible task. It had been hoped that these influential people would be successful in convincing the state or federal governments to commence the work—at least to conduct and finance the surveys—but such was not to be the case. The idea of government aid was thus soon abandoned, and the promoters came to the sad realization that the project would be completed only through private enterprise.

Nonetheless, many of them persisted, and the first charter for the Vermont section of the road was passed by the legislature on November 10, 1835. This charter officially approved the incorporation of "The Vermont Central Railroad Co." The commissioners for obtaining stock were John N. Pomeroy, Timothy Follett, John Peck, and Luther Loomis of Burlington, John Spalding, Timothy Hubbard, and Johathan P. Miller of Montpelier, Amplius Blake of Chelsea, Chester Baxter of Sharon, and Lewis Lyman of Hartford. The first meeting was held at Montpelier on January 6, 1836, and the books for subscriptions to the stock were first opened the following day.

This attempt failed, as the promoters undoubtedly expected it would. Adequate funds were not secured to even cover the organizational costs as specified by the terms of the charter. However, this effort was significant in that it showed Massachusetts, New Hampshire, and New York that Vermont was ready when the time should come for practical action on their part.

Little more than a year later the nation was the victim of a major financial panic—an event at least partially perpetrated by the country's over-reaction to the new concept of railroads. However, the Vermonters had an idea that they couldn't let go of; and, after biding their time for a few years, they again applied to the legislature for a charter to build a railroad. It was approved on October 31, 1843, and the commissioners were Charles Paine of Northfield, John Peck and Wyllys Lyman of Burlington, Daniel Baldwin and Elisha P. Jewett of Montpelier, Andrew Tracy of Woodstock, and Levi B. Vilas of Chelsea.

This charter stated that the corporation could build a railroad "from some point on the eastern shore of Lake Champlain, thence up the valley of the Onion (now Winooski) River to a point of the Connecticut River most convenient to meet a railroad either from Concord, New Hampshire, or Fitchburg, Massachusetts." One interesting clause in the new charter was a provision that "the stock, property, and effects of the company shall be exempt from taxes."

Another Railroad Convention, consisting of representatives from Vermont and New Hampshire, was held at Montpelier on January 8, 1844. Charles Paine was elected president, Elijah Blaisdell of Lebanon, New Hampshire, General Joel Bass of Williamstown, Simeon Lyman of Hartford, and Joseph Howe of Montpelier, vice-presidents. Oramel H. Smith of Montpelier and Halsey R. Stevens of Lebanon were named secretaries. Charles Paine, Daniel Baldwin, and Colonel Elisha P. Jewett formed a Central Corresponding and Financial Committee, with authority to

JAMES R. LANGDON of Montpelier was very active in railroad promotional activities in Vermont for many years. In 1844 he advanced $10,000 of his own money to cover the costs of a preliminary survey from the Connecticut River to the shores of Lake Champlain. (Jim Murphy Collection)

raise funds and procure a preliminary survey from the Connecticut River to the shore of Lake Champlain. James R. Langdon of Montpelier advanced $10,000 for this purpose, and the work was completed by late fall. A detailed report of the survey was made to the group on November 20, 1844.

The commissioners awaited this information before pressing for subscriptions to the stock. However, a further delay occurred when the directors of the connecting Northern Railroad of New Hampshire had trouble getting their road started. Some of the Vermont Central directors scheduled a meeting at Lebanon, New Hampshire, with directors of the Northern Railroad for April 29, 1845, but the New Hampshire group failed to appear. It happened that a meeting with friends of the then-projected Sullivan Railroad had been scheduled for the following day at Claremont.

Charles Paine, ex-Governor of Vermont, was furious, and he asked Elisha P. Jewett and E. P. Walton, Jr., to attend the Claremont meeting and to pledge the Vermont Central Railroad to a connection with the Sullivan, Cheshire, and

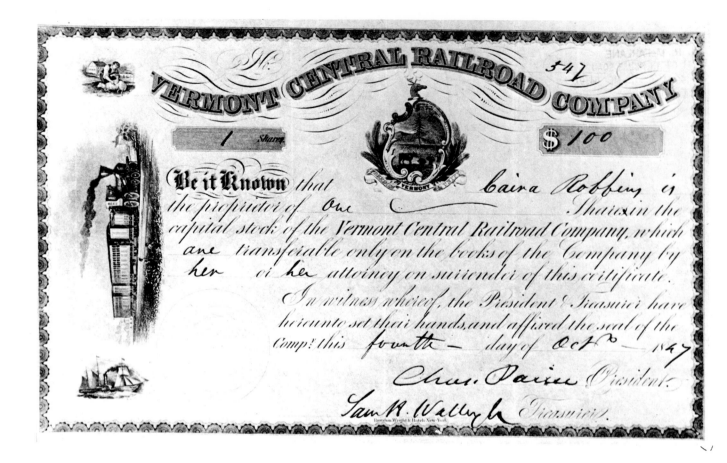

THIS 1847 VERMONT CENTRAL stock certificate was signed by President Charles Paine and **Treasurer Samuel H. Walley, Jr.** (Jim McFarlane Collection)

Fitchburg roads, thus forming a through railway line to Boston. This was done, and it proved to be a masterly stroke. It forced the construction of the Northern road, and ultimately the completion of the Cheshire, Sullivan, Vermont Central, Vermont & Canada, and Northern Railrod of New York. This was the realization of the grand scheme suggested by John L. Sullivan in 1826-27 and vigorously urged all along the line by the action taken in Montpelier in 1830.

Within two weeks of the Claremont meeting, the New Hampshire railroad commissioners reported in favor of permitting the construction of the Northern Railroad from Concord to West Lebanon. On June 4, the directors of the Fitchburg road voted in favor of a connection with the Vermont Central, and a circular to that effect was issued to the officials of the other roads in the area.

On June 10, 1845, the books of subscription to Vermont Central stock were opened in Boston. Thus, suddenly, there were significant forward movements of all the roads involved, principally because of Paine's "flank movement" at Claremont.

One of the first things done upon opening the books for subscription in Boston was the construction of a map, prepared and published by E. P. Walton in his Montpelier newspaper, which showed all the great western lakes and the bordering territory in the United States and Canada. This map was accompanied by a table of tonnage of all the U.S. collection districts on the lakes. This information was taken from the official reports of the U.S. Secrtary of the Treasury, and it revealed the vast internal commerce of the country—tonnage that was greater than that of foreign trade. This information was at first received with considerable surprise and doubt, and it became necessary to confirm the table by placing an official printed copy of the Secretary's report in the **Boston Exchange** for the inspection of the doubters. This was followed for nearly three months by a series of articles in the Boston papers which emphasized that the Vermont Central was a necessary way for Boston to reach not only the local trade of Central Vermont, but also the immense commerce of the mid-Western states and Canada.

The work of obtaining capital in Boston for the Vermont Central was undertaken at a very unfavorable time, as sharp competition had developed for the Boston investment capital among several recently chartered roads in Massachusetts, New Hampshire, and Vermont. The task of selling Vermont Central stock in Boston was assigned to ex-Governor Paine, with help from James R. Langdon and E. P. Walton, Jr. Sales in Vermont were the responsibility of Daniel Baldwin.

The first meeting of the stockholders was held at Montpelier on July 23, 1845, at which time the Company formally organized with a subscribed capital of $2,000,000—the result of six weeks of hard work. Of this amount, $1,500,000 was obtained in Boston and the remaining

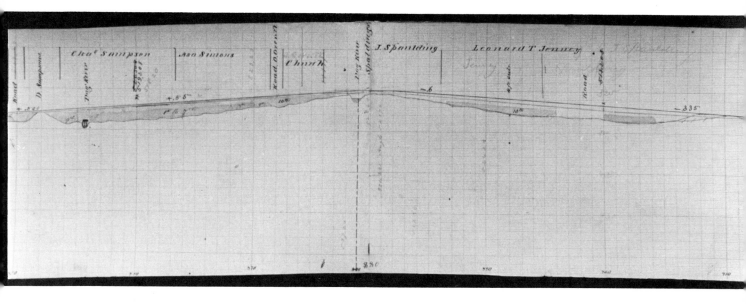

THIS TRACK PROFILE was drawn in 1845 and shows the ruling grade on the entire line between Burlington and Windsor. This segment is the top of Roxbury Mountain. The nearly illegible pencil notations on the profile show the completion dates of the various segments of the line. (Jim Murphy Collection)

$500,000 from Vermont. About $200,000 of the Vermont contribution came from Montpelier. Investors from that town also bought $200,000 worth of bonds in the new road. Montpelier was certainly the leading Vermont community in terms of support for the enterprise; yet, ironically, it was to be ultimately bypassed by the railroad's main line.

At this July 23 meeting, the following directors were elected: Charles Paine, Samuel Lewis of Boston, Daniel Baldwin and James R. Langdon of Montpelier, and John Peck of Burlington. The new board of directors then met and elected the following officers: president, Charles Paine; treasurer, Samuel H. Walley Jr. of Boston; and clerk, E. P. Walton, Jr.

At this time, charters had also been granted simultaneously to both the Connecticut & Passumpsic Rivers Railroad and the Champlain & Connecticut River Railroad. The former was authorized to build northward along the two rivers mentioned in its name, from Vernon or Brattleboro near the Massachusetts border to the international boundary, a distance of about 185 miles. The latter, on the other hand, planned to connect the Connecticut River with Lake Champlain by crossing the Green Mountains between Bellows Falls and Rutland, and then traversing the fertile farmlands of the Champlain Valley.

Timothy Follett—a successful and well-established merchant—was already involved with Lake Champlain shipping, and he saw great promise in building a railroad to connect this traffic with the Cheshire and Fitchburg roads and entry into Boston. With Paine heading the Vermont Central and Follett now his counterpart with the Champlain & Connecticut River (soon to be re-named Rutland & Burlington), the sides had been chosen, so to speak.

Those associated with the Vermont Central did not consider this north-south route on the eastern side of the state to be a threat. However, the plans of the Rutland & Burlington Railroad were another matter. In order to cover his options, Charles Paine met with the directors of the Cheshire and Fitchburg railroads, and they signed a secret

agreement giving the Vermont Central exclusive use of the Fitchburg road into Boston. This, Paine reasoned, would effectively block the plans of Follett's Burlington group. This agreement stipulated that the Vermont Central was not to connect with the Northern Railroad of New Hampshire without the consent of the Fitchburg, while the latter was not to offer aid of any kind to the Rutland & Burlington without the consent of the directors of the Vermont Central.

When learning of this rather clandestine arrangement, Follett figuratively bit his tongue and publicly commented that his road had been "neglected and discarded by those who were expected to have nurtured and cherished it." He was referring, of course, to the officials and backers of the Cheshire and Fitchburg lines, which he was planning to use as his southern connection into Boston.

Despite this agreement, the sympathies of some of the Cheshire's directors remained with Follett's project. They clearly understood that it would ultimately be to Paine's advantage, both from the standpoint of distance and cost, to meet with the Northern Railroad of New Hampshire. They thus had serious doubts that Paine's road would ever make a through connection with their road at Bellows Falls. As time wore on, their doubts and suspicions grew; finally, in October, 1846, they voted to rescind their agreement with the Vermont Central.

For any road planning to build across Vermont, finding a suitable route across the spine of the Green Mountains presented a formidable chore as, topographically, there were few options. The Lake Champlain valley on the west side of the state and the Connecticut River valley on the east side afforded some relatively level terrain, but most everything in between consisted of a ridge or range of the Green Mountains. Basically, the only exceptions were the various river valleys. As the purpose of these early roads was to tie Boston into a through trade route to the Great Lakes and the Midwest, it was understood from the beginning that in all likelihood the route surveyed would follow the river valleys wherever possible.

Paine and his group hoped to build their road from the junction of the White and the Connecticut rivers, up the valley of the White River to or near Montpelier, and then on through the Winooski River Valley to Burlington—the state's largest city—situated on the eastern shore of Lake Champlain. The exact location of the crossing of the Green Mountains, though, posed somewhat of a problem. Some of those in the Paine camp advocated a route through Williamstown Gulf and on through Barre and Montpelier. Others—principally Charles Paine—were in favor of a 5.09-mile longer route which would cross the mountains at Roxbury Summit and then go through Northfield. This route would bypass both Montpelier and Barre, although it was planned that the capital city would be served by a one-mile spur. This line would enter the Winooski River valley about one mile west of Montpelier.

Meanwhile, a man by the name of George Leonard Jr., had been hired in 1844 to survey a line through Williamstown Gulf; and his work showed that the grades would be "generally moderate," with the steepest at Williamstown where, "for two and one-half miles, the road would have to ascend at a grade of forty-three feet to the mile" and "another grade through the Gulf would be five miles at forty feet to the mile."

Despite Leonard's favorable survey, Paine persisted in his desire that the railroad he was heading should go through his hometown of Northfield. Being the shrewd businessman that he was, Paine had been gradually adding to his already extensive land holdings in Northfield so that he would be in a position to resell considerable acreage to the new railroad—if he could get it routed through his town.

In addition to the land, Paine also owned a woolen mill which he had inherited from his father, a farm on which he bred high-grade cattle, a power dam, a hotel, and a beautiful home. He saw the hotel as a potential bonanza as it would be a logical place for passenger trains to stop for overnight accommodations.

For about a year, a great deal of time and money had been spent surveying and resurveying the disputed route through Williamstown Gulf. Although the snow was unusually deep during the winter of 1844-45, the survey crews stayed in the field practically all winter, doing whatever work they could. Progress was slow because of the snow, however, and little work was accomplished on the Northfield Route until late March.

With the controversy simmering between himself and the majority of his directors over the location of the line, Paine sought to lend credence to his demands by bringing in Samuel M. Felton, a highly respected civil engineer and railroad surveyor from Charlestown, Massachusetts, to supervise the location of a preliminary line through Northfield. Under Felton's supervision, T. J. Carter started another line from a point near Chase's Island in Windsor on the Connecticut River. It ascended the White River valley through Hartford, Sharon, Royalton, and Bethel. There the line went up the West Branch through Randolph and Braintree to the summit at Roxbury, some 46.61 miles from the Connecticut River. At the summit, the line crossed the Green Mountains 678 feet above the level of the Connecticut River and 913 above Lake Champlain. From this point, the road was located down the Dog River through Northfield on a steep grade and through a narrow gulf to the Onion (now Winooski) River just west of Montpelier. Here the line picked up the shorter and more direct route that had been run through Williamstown Gulf. The survey then ran through Middlesex, Waterbury, Bolton, Richmond, Williston, Essex, and into Burlington. The latter point was reach-

ed only four weeks after the work had started—quite an achievement. This entire survey, however, followed virtually the same line as those previously done.

Felton's survey showed the line from the center of the village of Windsor to Blin's Wharf at Burlington to be 114 miles. From the mouth of the White River to the same Burlington location it was 99.89 miles. Some 71 miles of this distance was straight, while five-sixths of the remainder consisted of curves exceeding 1,900 feet radii—and one-half of that with 2,800 feet radii or more. There was no curve between Lake Champlain and the Connecticut River of less than 1,432 feet radius. Between White River and Windsor there would be one curve of 1,146 feet radius (about five degrees) and another of 1,432 feet.

On one-half of the line, the maximum grade was 20 feet to the mile, and for 50 of those miles it was 15 feet. On three-fourths of the line the maximum grade would be 30 feet and under; and on one-fourth, the grades would vary from 30 to 40 feet, with one exception. That exception was near Burlington, where for a distance of 1.46 miles it would be 45 feet to the mile. Rail, 56 pounds to the yard, would be laid on tie plates and ties measuring 6 by 7 inches and 7½ feet long. The track would be laid on a bed of sand or gravel throughout the line.

Originally it had been planned that the road would enter the Queen City some two miles south of town and then follow the lake shore to the bustling wharves, warehouses, and steamboat landings located near the commercial heart of the city. However, it was ultimately decided to enter the city from the north—from Essex, through Winooski, and finally through a 350-foot tunnel.

Carter estimated that the cost of grading his survey would be $767,265. This figure would include the one-mile branch into Montpelier, and all masonry necessary on the entire line. He proposed that the track would cost about $8,000 per mile—a total of about $896,000. It was estimated that the initial roster of rolling stock would cost another $110,000, a figure that would include eight locomotives at an estimated price of $5,000 each. Carter added in an estimate for miscellaneous items and also a ten percent contingency. The total estimated cost to cover the building and initial equipping of the line came to $2,204,970.

No one was denying that this figure represented a lot of 1845 dollars! This estimate convinced the directors that the $2,000,000 which the charter authorized them to sell in stock subscriptions would not be adequate to get the road built and equipped, so they voted to increase the amount authorized by the charter to $3,000,000. This amendment to the charter was quickly approved by the General Assembly.

Paine was successful in persuading the directors to adopt the Felton-Carter survey through Northfield. Keenly aware of the strong sentiment by many in favor of the Gulf Route, though, he tried to placate that faction by saying that the engineers felt that it would be extremely dangerous to attempt to operate a railroad through a narrow one and one-half mile pass ranging in depth from four hundred to six hundred feet. They claimed that there would be a constant danger in the winter and spring from slides of snow, ice, earth, and rocks. Felton had also reported that he estimated the Williamstown route would cost $764,867 while the Northfield route would cost $460,825—even though the latter was over five miles longer! Paine made good use of these figures in his arguments in favor of the Northfield route. From this far-off point in time, one can almost visualize the meetings that must have taken place between the president and his hand-picked surveyors and civil engineers.

Paine did pull it off, though, and Northfield was immediately established as the road's headquarters. But getting his way was not without a price. In protest, the directors from Montpelier resigned with great indignation. A route that placed their hometown—and the state capital—on a branch line was both unacceptable and incomprehensible to them. In addition, with the announcement of the route chosen, many Montpelier and Barre citizens defaulted on their stock subscriptions.

John Smith of St. Albans, Vermont, had been instrumental in helping Paine obtain the charter for the Vermont Central. Now that it had been obtained, however, Smith commenced to focus his attention a little closer to home. From the beginning, he had visions of building a railroad through his hometown, and now, while still a Vermont Central director, he started taking active measures to build his railroad.

He formulated these plans with his son's brother-in-law, Lawrence Brainerd of St. Albans, and James Clark of Milton, Vermont. These three men formed a corporation in 1843 and were prepared to invest large sums of their own hard-earned capital. Plans were soon made to survey a line northward from the Vermont Central at Essex Junction, a line that would be called the Vermont & Canada Railroad. Smith felt that Paine no longer had any real need for his active assistance with the Vermont Central, so he, Brainerd, and Clark decided to devote their full energies to building the Vermont & Canada. But more about that later!

On November 25, 1845, Charles Paine engaged Sewall F. Belknap as the general contractor to build his railroad on a cost-plus basis, in return for Belknap's promise to purchase one-fourth of the company's stock issue. Belknap had already gained considerable experience and earned a solid reputation in the New England railroad construction field. He immediately divided the line into three major sections and then sub-divided them into seven sub-contracts. The first section was from Windsor to White River, a distance of 15 miles. The second section of 53.51 miles extended from White River to Northfield, and the third section of 48.21 miles ran from Northfield to Burlington—a total distance of 116.72 miles.

Ground was broken by Belknap's small crew near Windsor on December 15, 1845, as a cold, cruel north wind whipped down the bleak Connecticut River valley. As a small shivering crowd watched, picks and shovels were raised and then forced into the frozen earth. This simple ceremony represented the first tangible evidence of the birth of the Vermont Central Railroad.

On January 28, 1846, Paine organized a second ground-breaking ceremony—this one a more lavish affair on his farm at Northfield, the site on which the road's passenger depot was soon to be built. The day again was cold, but clear and sunny. Promptly at 11 a.m. Paine and Belknap appeared, each carrying a shovel. The site had been cleared of snow and thawed for the occasion. Paine made a few brief and appropriate comments, and then turned three shovels of earth. Contractor Belknap then repeated the ritual, after which everyone moved to a nearby hall for a celebration dinner. After the meal, Paine delivered a well-prepared speech in which he stressed the significance of the occasion.

Effective January 1, 1846, J. C. Chesbro was hired to superintend the construction of the entire road, and Samuel Felton was retained as a consulting engineer on the project. By the first of June, 1846, there were over 2,000 workers on the line. Over one-third million cubic yards of earth and 12,000 yards of rock were moved during the month of June. Some 3,000 yards of masonry abutments and bridges were erected during the same period. Considerable work was also done changing locations of town roads and in opening stone quarries.

Large numbers of Irish laborers had left their homeland, many driven away by the likelihood of starvation following the failure of the potato crop. They had read ads for labor needs in American and had only recently come pouring into the port cities of Boston and New York. Some did not have the price of a ticket to Vermont, so they came to the Green Mountain State on foot.

Paine was, at this time, managing the entire project single-handedly. It was already becoming painfully obvious, however, that contractor Belknap was not financially able to make good on his agreement to purchase and pay for one-quarter of the company's stock. Paine was thus forced to seek capital elsewhere in an amount similar to Belknap's pledge.

Work progressed, however, and by May 25, 1847, the line had incurred construction costs as follows:

From the mouth of the White River to Windsor $189,538
From the mouth of the White River to Northfield 312,485
From Northfield to Burlington   284,755
Total $786,778

Contracts were made with the locomotive building firm of Hinckley & Drury in Boston for ten locomotives, and with Davenport & Bridges of Cambridge, Massachusetts, for passenger and freight cars.

In order to avoid paying large sums for both tolls and damages to the Winooski Turnpike Company on the line between Montpelier and Burlington, the directors decided to make the turnpike company an offer to purchase its business. Undoubtedly, the turnpike owners saw the proverbial handwriting on the wall, and they accepted the railroad's first offer. The Vermont Central Railroad now found itself the owner of a turnpike.

The construction work continued without serious setbacks, and the road was opened for passenger service between White River Junction and Bethel on June 26, 1848—a distance of 25 miles. This service represented the first passenger service in the state of Vermont. Two weeks later, on July 10, the road ran its first freight train over this portion of the line. Depots along the new line were under construction, although the citizens of Royalton were so excited about being served by a road of iron that they insisted on covering the expense of building their facility—an unusual example of Yankee independence.

On September 17, a train was run to the summit at Roxbury, a distance of 46 miles. The first train entered Northfield, seven miles from Roxbury, on the 10th of October, 1848, at 9:20 a.m., with conductor Charles Paine Kimball in charge. At this point, the work was suspended for the winter, and the crews moved south to work on the fourteen miles of line between White River Junction and Windsor.

On February 13, 1849, a passenger train ran for the first time south from White River Junction to Windsor. This train was greeted by an artillery salute and a large crowd of people who were gathered at the station. Assuming his official duties as station agent at Windsor on that day was Abner Forbes, a position he was to hold for the next eleven years.

A long brick passenger station was built at White River Junction in 1848 to serve the Vermont Central, the Connecticut & Passumpsic Rivers Railroad, and the Northern Railroad of New Hampshire. For many years, this union station was a regulr meal-stop for several trains daily from the various roads. Passenger cars carried signs indicating that that particular train would stop for twenty minutes for dinner and lunch in the "new elegant dining hall and restaurant at the depot." The dining room, which later was known as the "Stationhouse Cafe," became famous for its checkerberry candies that were shaped like small switchmen's lanterns.

This facility was renovated a number of times over the years until it burned to the ground in 1911. A "temporary" wood frame building was immediately built on the original foundation, and it served the road until it too was destroyed by fire, in March, 1935.

By mid-February, 1849, regular passenger service over the entire 67.5 miles of the line between Windsor and Northfield had been inaugurated. In a contemporary account, it was reported that the first train consisted of "a locomotive and a few passenger cars."

The first revenue train entered Montpelier on July 4, 1849, and it consisted of a locomotive and ten flatcars loaded with 100 barrels of flour each. Engineer John Danforth was at the throttle of the locomotive "Winooski," and conductor John Hobart was in charge of this historic train. Hobart went on to become general superintendent of the Central Vermont Railroad. Regular passenger service between Montpelier and Windsor commenced on July 23, 1849. This early service consisted of two passenger trains each way daily, in addition to one freight train each way.

At Montpelier, the travelling public had to use a recently completed freight house for accommodations for a few months until the passenger depot was completed and ready for use early in 1850. This first passenger depot was built of brick and measured 50 by 150 feet. It was replaced by a larger structure in 1880.

The following portions of a letter written in 1882 by the then-superintendent John W. Hobart to a Montpelier newspaper reporter reveal many interesting aspects of early Central Vermont operations at Montpelier:

"Well do I remember the interest manifested and the commotion created among the people who came in from the surrounding country to see the first trains in Montpelier. There being a circus upon the meadow near Mrs. Nicholas' house, on the Berlin side, which taken together with the usual 4th of July as a holiday, the town was packed, and we were compelled to send men in advance to clear the way for the train. Every building from which the cars could be seen was covered, every available window occupied, the tops of the buildings were covered if possible, and even the tree-tops were alive with people.

"Warner Hine, who was then master of transportation, was the acting agent at that station during the summer of 1849. In the autumn of that year the road was completed to Waterbury, and Mr. Hine with his force was removed to that station. Mr. J. Edwards Wright was made the first permanent station agent at Montpelier, where he remained until August, 1851, resigning his position at that time to engage in the purchase of wool in Ohio. A.V.H. Carpenter, now the General Passenger Agent of the Milwaukee & St. Paul Railroad, succeeded Mr. Wright, and remained in that position until June, 1862, at which time he was relieved to take another position, and J. W. Hobart was installed as the agent.

"As you are aware, Montpelier is at the terminus of a branch one and one-fourth of a mile in length, and up to October of that year, all the trains passed in and out over the branch. In October, they discontinued running the main line trains into Montpelier, but in place established a branch train, consisting simply of a small engine, fitted up with seats on each side of the tender.

"This engine was called the **Abigail Adams.** It was determined in the course of a very few days that it would be impossible to do the business of the Capital with the facilities then provided. So the President, Governor Paine, ordered a small car built, as the engine had not sufficient capacity to handle a large car, except under the most favorable circumstances. Meantime, however, a large car was provided, and when the business required it, the car was attached to this miniature engine, which in many instances proved unequal to the task, and the conductor, who was none other than the agent at Montpelier, the cars of the branch trains having been added to his duties, the baggage master, and many time the engineer, were compelled to push in aiding the engine the whole distance, and it was not infrequently the case, that the passengers themselves, in response to a request, would aid in furnishing power to move the train.

"In due time the small car was finished, and we had less trouble. This car proved quite a novelty, it having been finished like an omnibus, with seats upon the side. This condition, however, did not last long, as it was found and admitted by the officers, who, by the way, were not over and above friendly to Montpelier, that the facilities were entirely inadequate; so a full and quite respectable train was provided, consisting of an engine called the **Flying Dutchman,** a baggage and a first-class passenger car. Soon after the management changed from Northfield to St. Albans, and Montpelier was evidently improved by the change. James Bowers, who is still there, was one of the engineers who ran the **Flying Dutchman.**

Much of the line between Windsor and Montpelier was still sub-grade, although it was considered satisfactory for regular train service. This proved to be a regular construction practice over the years on virtually all railroads. A new railroad would get its trains running as soon as possible in order to derive some income to cover initial expenses. Refinement on the trackwork would take place as time and resources permitted.

The final grade on the road consisted of an average of 24 inches of gravel. Samuel Felton, the engineer in charge, claimed in his 1849 annual report to the directors that "no other road in New England excels the Vermont Central for the quantity or quality of its grading material. The surface of the roadbed, when finished at final grade, will be sixteen feet in width on embankments, and thirteen feet in width between side ditches in excavations." Timber bridges on the line were built on the "Burr Plan," so named for its inventor, Theodore Burr. Bridges built according to the Burr Plan were more costly, but they were considered more durable.

After the line from Windsor to Montpelier had been brought up to snuff, President Paine ran a by-invitation-only special train over the road to show it off to a party of about 250 influential guests, most of whom had never before ridden on a train, nor even seen a locomotive. The "Governor

Paine Special," as it was known, left Montpelier at 7 a.m. on November 5, 1849, and it arrived in Lebanon, New Hampshire, three hours later. Lebanon, on the Northern Railroad of New Hampshire, was chosen as the destination because White River Junction did not have a hotel large enough to provide a banquet appropriate for the distinguished travelers.

The passenger list included the state officers, members of the legislature, U.S. Senator William Upham, former Governor Horace Eaton, and others. Virtually all the passengers were personal acquaintances of Paine, who had served as Governor of Vermont from 1841-43.

The banquet was hosted by Henry R. Campbell, a great engineer of his day who was responsible for building the huge bridge across the Hudson River at Troy, New York. After-dinner speeches that suitably covered the magnificence of the moment followed the meal. The passengers then boarded the train for the return trip to Montpelier, which was reached without incident. All were agreed that it was a memorable trip on this pioneer railroad—a trip that was most fitting for the occasion. One person who was disappointed about the trip, however, was Paine's sister, Caroline. One account of the trip stated: "She wanted to go with us on our excursion over the road, but as there were no other ladies on the train, she declined."

The following impromptu composition was reportedly written aboard the train by General D. W. C. Clarke and then "sung at least thirty times" enroute:

THE RAILROAD SONG
Written by Gen. Clarke aboard the cars between
Northfield and Bethel.
Tune - "Dearest Mae."

We took an early start to-day,
  And braved a rough old ride,
To reach the place where PAINE, they say.
  Wins people to his side;
The Iron-horse was breathing gas
  In the "sequestered vale,"
And every one ambitious was
  To ride upon a rail!
            Hurrah! Hurrah!
  For Governor PAINE, the Rail-er!
He builds his roads o'er rocks and hills.
  AND GOES FOR GENERAL TAYLOR!

Hurrah! Hurrah! Hurrah!
  If it don't beat all natur'!
To see the "wisdom and the virtu'"
  Of our great Legislatur'
A riding through the hills and vales,
  From Northfield to the river.
On Governor Paine's new-fashioned rails!
  I'never! did you ever?
            Hurrah! Hurrah! &c.

I tell you what it is, old boys,
  this ride we are not loth in,
Especially when we do the thing
  Free gratis and for nothin'!
And when, besides, the dinner comes
  On just such terms again,
I'd like to know who will not sing.
  Hurrah for Governor PAINE!
            Hurrah! Hurrah! &c.

I wish to introduce a bill—
  I offer it quite humbly,
And move its passage through these cars,
  By this 'ere J'int Assembly:
Section I provides that PAINE
  Shall have the right to go
With his old Railroad where he will;
  He'll do it **whether or no!**
            Hurrah! Hurrah! &c.

The 3rd section has a **clause,**
  As sharp as any cat's,
That when old BELKNAP comes along,
  We'll raise our cotton hats,—
Because he has a rough old way
  In that old pate, 'tis said,
Of doing things when he takes hold;
  They call it "GOING AHEAD!"
            Hurrah! Hurrah!
  For BELKNAP, high and low!
He goes ahead because, you see,
  He's got a head to go!

In section 3, it is declared,
  That that 'ere long man, MOORE,
Who straddles this old iron horse,
  And brings us through secure,
Shall be the Chief old Engineer,
  By special legislation,
Of this 'ere J'int Assemble here,—
  As ZACH shall of the nation!
            Hurrah! Hurrah!
  Let's make the echoes roar!
Though other roads are safe enough,
  The Central Road is MOORE!

In section 4, is set down,
  That 'mong these mountain ridges,
The name of CAMPBELL shall resound:
  The HERO OF THE BRIDGES!
And that the man to carry out
  A project very mighty,
And show that "it is bound to go,"
  Is that 'ere same "OLD WHITEY!"
            Hurrah! Hurrah!
  Let's keep the chorus humming!
For word has passed along the line—
  That same old "Campbell's coming!"

As an amendment to the bill
  It's moved to add a section
Which has a tendency to raise
  A rather sad reflection:—
It is that Governor PAINE do seek—
  (Why, what's the man about?)
To keep the family on earth—
  The race must not run out!
            Hurrah! Hurrah!
  For PAINE, the bachelor!
The wonder groweth every day,
  What's he unmarried for?

Amendment 2d is proposed:—
  It is to make provision
That shall our thanks to CAMPBELL show
  With **very nice** precision.

He has a head that's great to plan,
A will that never flinches:
We wish you'd find a bigger man
Than CAMPBELL, of his inches.
                    Hurrah! Hurrah!
For "Whitey," brave and true!
His heart goes fitly with his head?
So say I—what say you?

Now if the President will rise,
And put the thing to vote,
I'd like to know your sentiments
Upon this bill I've wrote;
And so, to end the matter well,
Before we take a glass,
I hope you all will answer "AYE!"
And let the old bill pass.
                    Hurrah! Hurrah!
Please put this vote again;
All you who are affirmative,
Hurrah for Governor PAINE!

I think I may declare the vote—
I'll do it if you will,
And now announce to this J'int House
The passage of the bill:
It is before the Governor—
We care for no **Veto**—
If Governor PAINE won't sign the act,
Our COOLIDGE will, we know!
                    Hurrah! Hurrah! &c.

It now is moved that we adjourn,
And in the usual way:
For plain it is, at this late hour,
We break up "without day,"
And when we reach our homes again,
We'll tell the wondrous tale,
How PAINE has rode this J'int
Assembly on a rail!
                    Hurrah! Hurrah! &c.

As for the title of our bill,
It is decreed to be:—
"An act to lighten public cares,
And aid festivity,"
So now farewell to Governor PAINE,
To BELKNAP, CAMPBELL, MOORE!
This J'int Assembly is dissolved;
T'was **liquorfied** before!
                    Farewell! Farewell!

Rails were laid to Middlesex in August, 1849, and to Waterbury the following month. By now, however, general manager Belknap was in serious financial difficulty, and by the time the construction crews had reached Bolton, his resources were exhausted. He had never honored his pledge to purchase one-fourth of the company's stock issue, and now he was unable to pay his Irish work gangs. In retaliation, they marched on the Jones Hotel in Bolton, which Belknap was using as his field headquarters. Surrounding the hotel, the workers shouted for their pay—the imprisoned contractor and his men all the while fearing that they would be dragged out and lynched.

Even the arrival of the militia, who arrested some of the leaders, failed to make the angry mob disperse. A Catholic priest was brought to the scene, and he was finally able to quell the disturbance. The workers resigned themselves to the fact that they would not be likely to get the wages they had earned, so they eventually all drifted away.

The locale of this incident is a bit ironic, because it was here that 17 of the Irish workers' countrymen lost their lives while blasting the right-of-way through the many rock ledges high above the river.

With the financial failure of the general contractor, the directors were forced to cancel their contract with him and to re-let the rest of the work in short sections to other contractors. Henry R. Campbell was put in charge of seeing the project through to its completion.

Work continued, and the line was finally completed into Burlington in late December. At Burlington the railroad ran diagonally across the city, partially in a ravine and partially on grade with the city streets. The first depot was located at the southwest corner of the present-day Maple and St. Paul Streets intersection. The Vermont Central purchased a large, unfinished brick home and completed it in a manner suitable for use as a pasenger depot. This first line into the city crossed Maple Street at Church Street and then circled back sharply to its passenger depot. This building, which is still standing, now serves as an apartment building and a photography studio.

The Vermont Central, which was not interested in making a physical connection with the rival Rutland & Burlington Railroad, ran its first train into the city on December 31, 1849. Unfortunately, however, Timothy Follett's road had reached town less than two weeks earlier. The latter road located its first station in City Market, now the intersection of Maple and Battery Streets and the northern end of the Vermont Railway yard. Burlington's two passenger stations, thus, were located about three blocks apart.

Perched atop the ravine to the east of the Vermont Central's depot was a newly built Greek Revival home owned by Giles S. Appleton, who served as the first passenger conductor on the line between Burlington and Essex Junction. This building still stands at 194 Maple Street. Appleton later served as the road's ticket agent at the Burlington depot for well over thirty years.

But, the completion of the Vermont Central into Burlington unfortunately was not the cause for celebration. Instead, it proved to be a rather hollow victory, as Charles Paine and his associates were ruined financially. They had used up their personal assets, and finding themselves involved to the point of no return, they had borrowed large sums at high interest rates in order to complete the project. In 1847, delinquent shares with a par value of some $756,000 had to be sold at auction. The following year, a new $1,000,000 issue was offered at 75 percent of par value, but only $62,000 was subscribed.

During the fall of 1849, the company signed a contract with the U.S. Post Office for carrying mail. The contract specified that the railroad would receive $1,000 per month, to be effective upon the completion of the line into Burlington.

In 1849, the Vermont Central had a total of seven locomotives on the roster—three 4-4-0's for passenger service, three of the same wheel arrangement for freight service, and a 4-6-0 for hauling freight. In addition, there was a small 0-4-0, the road's first engine, named **Abigail Adams** for the wife of the nation's second president. This was a rare honor indeed in that long-ago era prior to the recognition of women's rights. This little engine had been a mainstay throughout the construction of the road.

The equipment roster at this time showed "7 eight-wheel

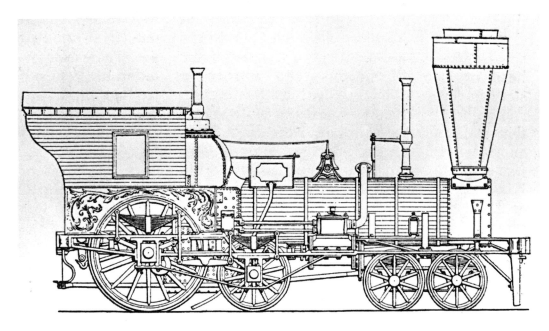

**THE UNIQUE "GOVERNOR PAINE" is described
in detail on this page.** (Jim Murphy Collection)

passenger cars, 1 eight-wheel freight car, 4 four-wheel freight cars, 4 four-wheel platform cars, 20 eight-wheel platform cars, 88 four-wheel gravel cars, 4 four-wheel iron cars, 9 hand cars, 1 snow plough of the largest size, and several of a small size." More cars were being built at the road's shops in Northfield, including two cars to be used for "Post Office, express, and baggage combined," and 25 "eight-wheel freight cars."

Even with the cars under construction, it became obvious almost immediately that more locomotives and rolling stock would be necessary to meet the demand. Within a year, seven more locomotives and ninety freight cars of various types were ordered and added to the roster.

Earlier, President Paine had conceived the idea that passenger service on his railroad should be operated at very high speeds. He sent Henry R. Campbell to Philadelphia even before construction was completed to talk with Matthias Baldwin about the feasibility of building a locomotive that could pull a passenger train through the Vermont hills at sixty miles per hour. Campbell had been authorized by Paine to offer Baldwin $10,000 for the job if the builder thought he could produce such a machine.

Baldwin, confident of his own capabilities, felt that he could produce a machine that could meet these specifications, so Campbell returned to Northfield with a signed contract in his pocket. The exciting new machine was delivered to the Vermont Central on September 7, 1849, and it carried Baldwin's construction number 343. Charles Paine was no doubt both impressed and proud when he first saw his new locomotive, with the name **Governor Paine** emblazoned on her cab panels. Her polished brass glistened and her bright red wheels and green and gold paint scheme made her a sight to behold.

The **Governor Paine** was, however, a somewhat strange looking machine, even for its day. She had one pair of driving wheels, 78 inches in diameter, located behind the firebox. Another pair of smaller and unconnected wheels was placed

directly in front of the firebox. A four-wheel lead truck carried the weight of the front of the locomotive.

The cylinders were 17¼ inches in diameter, with a 20-inch stroke. They were located horizontally between the frames and the boiler near the middle of the boiler. This was done in an attempt to reduce the lateral motion of the locomotive. The bearings on the two rear axles were so contrived that by means of a lever part of the weight usually carried by the wheels in front of the firebox could be transferred to the driving axle.

Paine apparently found this machine to be everything he had hoped for. There are several stories that have come down through the years which tell how fast this engine did run—but how she did so on the track of the day is a source of wonderment today. After a few years, the single-axled locomotive proved to be far too light in the tractive-effort department, so she was eventually rebuilt into a more powerful 4-4-0.

Superintendent James Moore reported at the end of fiscal year 1849 (June 30) that his road had carried 47,095 passengers and 25,075 tons of freight. Gross earnings were $93,610, while expenses were held to $27,484. This resulted in a net income of $66,126. This was a most auspicious start from a fiscal standpoint, considering at the time of this report the road had been open between Windsor and Northfield for only a few months, and for but a few days between Windsor and Montpelier. This income statement, however, is misleading as it did not take into account any maintenance, depreciation, or interest charges.

By the end of June, 1849, the records showed that the Central Vermont had made actual expenditures of $3,325,813 to build and equip the line, and it was estimated that another $830,000 would be required to complete the job. This would figure out to an average cost of $35,795 for the 116-mile project. This was considerably higher than the original estimate used at the time the initial stock subscriptions were being solicited. The directors attempted to

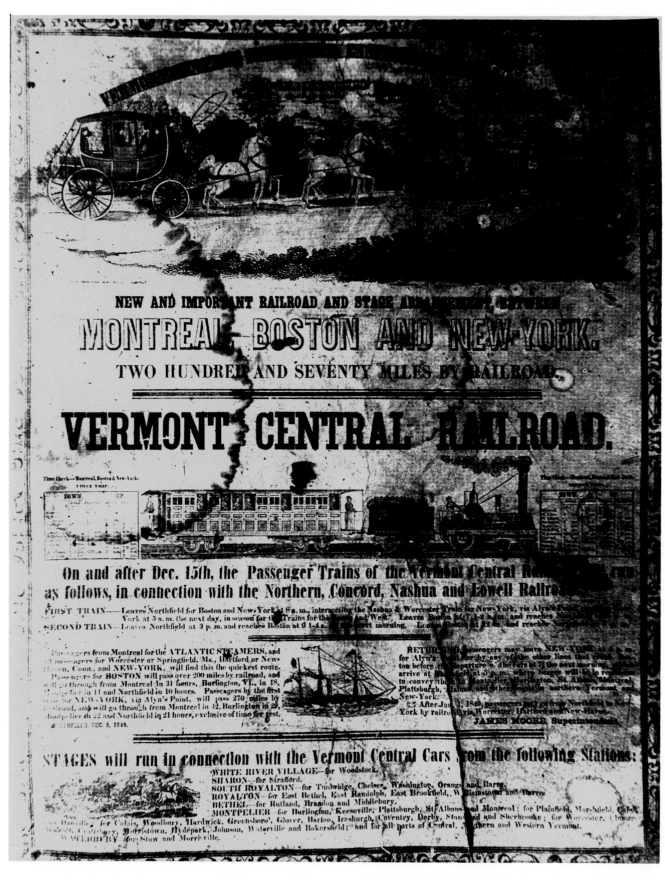

THIS RARE TIMETABLE dated December 5, 1848, is believed to be the first ever issued by the Vermont Central. At this time, train service was available only as far north as Northfield. (Jim Murphy Collection)

justify this difference by explaining in their 1849 annual report that land damages had been considerably higher than anticipated and that the superior construction of the road's bridges caused the original estimate for those structures alone to be exceeded by some $100,000.

The net result of these cost overrides was that the road's construction budget showed a deficit of $276,427 by June 30, 1849. To meet this debt, the directors voted to authorize the issue of new $100 per value stock for $50, to a total of $1,000,000. This offer was well received, as it was soon oversubscribed by $321,000.

What would have been the road's first major accident was narrowly averted on the morning of September 3, 1849. An elderly farmer by the name of Silas Mead had quarreled with railroad officials earlier, and to vent his spite he attempted to wreck the early morning passenger train near his Middlesex farm by piling logs across the tracks. Fortunately, while making a track inspection ahead of the train, a sectionman discovered the obstruction and removed it before any harm was done. Mead was quickly apprehended and held in the Montpelier jail while awaiting trial.

When the road had been opened to Bethel, there was virtually no wood supply along the line that was suitable for locomotive use, so the railroad had to pay $2.00 to $2.50 a cord for good dry wood. However, the company acquired several large tracts of well-timbered land adjacent to the railroad line which had been taken in land-damage settlements. The road's officials fully expected that by contracting cutters to work on these company-owned timberlands, the cost of good, seasoned wood would be reduced to about $1.00 per cord in the following years. The business of supplying railroads with wood gave work to many men and their teams. The timbered hillsides around a major woodyard were always bustling places. Also, many special trains had to be run to keep the various sheds filled.

In these early days of railroading, trains had to stop about every thirty miles to "wood up." Wood stops between White River Junction and Burlington were located at Chase's Cut between Bethel and Randolph, at Tarbell's between Braintree and East Granville, and at Roxbury, Northfield, Montpelier, Middlesex, Waterbury, and Bolton Flats. At each wood stop, all members of the crew would actively assist in this work.

During July of 1850, a freshet put the road out of business for four weeks. Despite such setbacks, however, business continued to grow. During the winter of 1850-51, it was again found that the equipment in service was not sufficient to meet the demand. Consequently, nearly $350,000 was spent to build more locomotives and cars.

In Northfield, the Vermont Central constructed a well-built two-story brick building to serve as the road's depot and general offices. It contained about a dozen rooms for offices in addition to the passenger facilities. President Charles Paine, treasurer Samuel H. Walley, Jr., and clerk E. P. Walton, Jr., as well as various other officials, each had their own office. For the first few years, all personnel assigned to the construction, operating, freight, passenger, and auditing offices reported directly to the president or an assistant. The latter position at various times carried the title of "general superintendent," "general agent," "superintendent," "superintendent of transportation," or "chief engineer."

SULL. RAIL ROAD OPENING TO CHARLESTOWN.

Special Notice.

All those who have been particularly invited to be present on this occasion by the President and Directors of the Sull. R. R. Company, are respectfully requested by the Citizens of Charlestown to partake of a Collation provided at the Town-House.

Tickets of admission to the Collation will be found for each guest at the Con't. River Bank and at S. L. Wilder's Store.

Those citizens who are subscribers will also find a Ticket for each, at the same places.

ENOS STEVENS,

Jan. 4, 1849.   Pres. of the Day.

THE SULLIVAN RAILROAD was one of the southern connections of the Vermont Central. This 1849 broadside announces the opening of the first portion of that line. (Wilbur Collection, University of Vermont)

VERMONT CENTRAL RAILROAD.
TIME CARD.

	1st Pas. Train.				2d Pas. Train.				
	DOWN.		UP.		DOWN.		UP.		Dist. bet. St.
	ARR. H. M.	DEP. H. M.	ARR. H. M.	DEP. H. M.	ARR. H. M.	DEP. H. M.	ARR. H. M.	DEP. H. M.	Miles
Montpelier,		4.20	4.55			10.40	9.30		
Northfield,	5.00	5.45	4.15	4.25	11.10	11.20	8.40	8.50	9.8
Roxbury,		6.03		3.56		11.39		8.20	7.1
Braintree,		6.25		3.36		12.01		8.00	8.5
Randolph,		6.39		3.22		12.15		7.46	5.6
Bethel,	6.54	7.00	3.00	3.05	12.30	12.35	7.24	7.29	7.1
North Royalton,		7.08		2.52		12.43		7.16	3.8
Royalton,		7.12		2.48		12.47		7.13	1.1
South Royalton,		7.18		2.42		12.53		7.08	1.8
Sharon,		7.30		2.29		1.05		6.55	4.9
West Hartford,		7.12		2.16		1.18		6.42	5.6
White River Vil.	7.55	8.01	1.58	2.03	1.30	1.36	6.23	6.30	5.6
White River Junc.	8.05	8.10	1.47	1.55	1.40	1.55	6.13	6.20	1.5
North Hartland,		8.23		1.35		2.06		6.00	5.6
Hartland,		8.33		1.25		2.18		5.50	4.1
Windsor,	8.43			1.15	2.30		5.40		
									75.6

BETWEEN NORTHFIELD AND MONTPELIER.

Leave Montpelier at 4.20 and 10.40 A. M. and 7.30 P. M.
Leave Northfield at 7.30 A. M. and 4.25 and 8.50 P. M.

The freight will be taken by the 4.20 A. M. train from Montpelier by the 8.50 P. M. train from Northfield, and remain over night at Montpelier.

All freight, and irregular trains, will keep out of the way of the Passenger trains, according to the Book of Rules and Regulations.

☞ The first Passenger train up from Boston, will pass the first passenger train down, at W. R. Junction at 1.55 P. M.

The *Conductor* of the *first passenger train down*, will leave his Passenger & Baggage Car at Windsor, and take the cars of the first up train to W. R. Junction, and then attach to his train, the cars from the Northern road.

The *Conductor* of the *second* Passenger train down, will switch off one Passenger and Baggage Car at W. R. Junction, then proceed to Windsor, where he will leave the rest of his train to the Sullivan Conductor, then attach to his engine the cars which were left by the conductor of the first train down.

To commence Monday, July 9, 1849.

JAMES MOORE, Supt.

BY JULY, 1849, the Vermont Central had built its line into Montpelier. This time card announcing that accomplishment contains much interesting information about the early train operations over the line. (Jim McFarlane Collection)

This building was located virtually in the center of the village of Northfield, a busy community of about 2,900 residents. Paine owned the Northfield Hotel, located about a block east of the depot; and he soon made arrangements so that passenger trains were scheduled to "overnight" in Northfield. To conveniently accommodate the passengers, he constructed a spur right to the front steps of his hotel. Tracks came in from the main line on either side of the depot and joined to the east of the depot, forming a wye. The hotel was located on the north side of the tail of the wye, according to an 1857 street map of the Village of Northfield. Across from the depot, to the west, large locomotive and car repair shops were built at this time. They served both the Vermont Central and the Vermont & Canada until they were removed to St. Albans in 1860.

In Burlington, the combination of the rail connections with the water route brought about many physical changes on the waterfront. The Rutland & Burlington alone had taken over 65 acres of land for its yard, and it was continuing to fill in marshy areas along the lake shore for more space for tracks.

Large new wharves and warehouses were finished by 1853 so that Burlington would be better equipped to handle the increasing lake traffic. By the middle of the 1860s, there were nearly 600 ships operating on Lake Champlain. Ten of these were steamers, while there were 25 sloops, 15 schooners, and over 500 canal barges.

By the time the railroads entered the Champlain Valley, the area had been well denuded of its standing timber. However, vast quantities were coming up the water routes from Canada. Burlington was well situated as the best port on the lake with rail connections. Planing mills sprang up along the waterfront, and the lumber industry grew dramatically between the mid-1850s and the early 1870s. In 1855 about 15 million board feet of lumber was received at Burlington, while 15 years later this figure had increased to 110 million board feet.

In 1865, there were twelve wharves in full use, and lumber piles and processing mills occupied every square foot of land not already occupied by the railroads. At this time, some 400 vessels on the lake were engaged exclusively in the lumber trade, and 200 million board feet of finished lumber left the city either on the railroads or the lake. This business flourished until about 1890, at which time a steady decline commenced.

All the while Charles Paine had been actively organizing and building the Vermont Central, John Smith had been busy in St. Albans doing likewise with his Vermont & Canada Railroad. It was intended by both Smith and Paine that the latter road would serve as a northern extension of the Vermont Central. In the spirit of the original concept of building a route between Boston and Ogdensburgh, neither man viewed either road as a rival of the other.

BOSTON, AUGUST 16, 1849.

SIR:

At a meeting of the Directors of the *Rutland and Burlington Rail Road Company*, held at Ludlow on the 15th day of August 1849, the following votes were passed:

Whereas, sundry persons, in whose name the stock of this Corporation stands, are delinquent in the payment of assessments ordered thereon, and whereas, at the meeting of Stockholders on the 20th day of June last, the following resolution was adopted:

" *Resolved*, that the Directors are hereby requested to take prompt and efficient measures for the collection of unpaid assessments upon the capital stock of the Corporation, and, so far as they think expedient, to sell all such shares, as are not paid before the first day of August next;"

Now be it resolved that all stock, on which assessments shall remain unpaid, on the 20th day of September next, shall be, and hereby is, forfeited to the use of this Corporation.

Resolved, that the Treasurer is hereby directed to issue a circular, giving immediate notice of the above vote, to all delinquent stockholders; and that all stock forfeited to the Corporation by virtue of the foregoing resolution, be brought to a public sale, under the direction of the Treasurer; and sold on account of the delinquent stockholders, at such times and places as he shall think expedient; and for any deficiency that may remain unpaid on assessments after such sale, the Treasurer is hereby directed to enforce the collection by a suit at law.

Your **PROMPT** and **IMMEDIATE ATTENTION** to this subject, will, I trust, prevent the necessity of any farther action thereon.

Your obedient servant,

SAMUEL HENSHAW, Treasurer.

THIS PIECE OF 1849 correspondence suggests that the rival Rutland & Burlington Railroad may have been having some difficulty collecting some of its stock subscriptions. (Wilbur Collection. University of Vermont)

THIS RECENT PHOTOGRAPH shows what is believed to be the original Vermont Central depot located near the intersection of Maple and St. Paul Streets in Burlington. This facility is described on page 20 of this volume. (Albert C. Spaulding Collection)

John Smith, like Paine, was experiencing some trying moments financially, but he cleverly calculated a way out. Citing recently enacted legislation which authorized railroads to lease their roads to other corporations, Smith suggested to Paine that the Vermont & Canada would be willing to lease itself to the Vermont Central—subject to certain conditions, of course.

The conditions that Smith stipulated were that the Vermont Central would pay "a clear rent equal to eight percent per annum on the construction cost of the Vermont & Canada," and that "if ever the parent company (the Vermont Central) fails to pay the rent to the Vermont & Canada, the latter company should have the right to take over the parent, manage that company, and run the two properties until all past-due rents should be paid out of net earnings."

Paine presented the idea to the stockholders, and they agreed to accept the conditions as stated—apparently with some illusions of grandeur and expansion of their own operation. However, having the advantage of hindsight, one now must wonder why the Vermont Central stockholders ever agreed to such a one-sided contract. Obviously, they harbored few doubts that their company might some day default on its payments. Regardless, it did. The contract went into effect on January 1, 1850, for a 50-year period, during which time the Vermont Central would pay the Vermont & Canada annual lease payments of $108,000, to be payable in semi-annual installments of $54,000 each. This was undoubtedly the worst agreement the generally shrewd Charles Paine was ever a party to in his entire lifetime. It proved to be the beginning of the end of his ambitions to become a railroad magnate in Vermont.

The money market in 1850 was poor, and it continued to get worse. Finally, in 1852, the road went into receivership and was subsequently operated and managed by a board of directors of the first mortgage bondholders. This receivership was to continue until 1874, although the Vermont Central maintained its corporate existence throughout the period. Annual meetings were held regularly and directors and officers continued to be elected. Trustees who served the road during this 21-year period were:

William Amory	1852-58
James E. Eldredge	1852-58
William R. Lee	1852-58
John Smith	1852-58
Charles O. Whittemore	1852-58
Lawrence E. Brainerd	1858-70
J. Gregory Smith	1858-73
Joseph Clark	1859-70
R. F. Taylor	1861-70
Benjamin P. Cheney	1861-73
Worthington C. Smith	1866-73
James R. Langdon	1867-73
Lawrence Barnes	1870-73

THIS ANNOUNCEMENT OF the commencement of service into Burlington in late December, 1849, was blown up from a very small newspaper ad appearing in a contemporary issue of the ''Burlington Free Press.'' (Edmunds Middle School Library, Burlington)

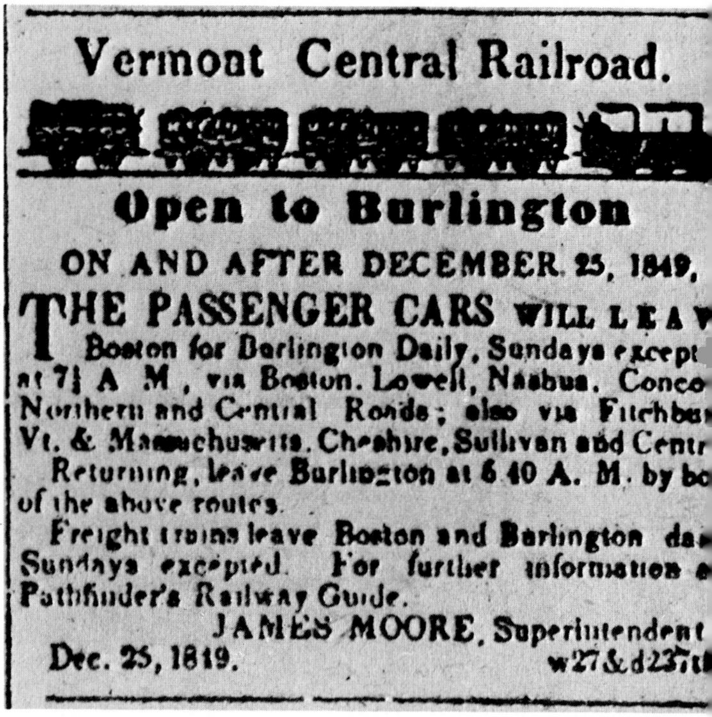

THIS HAND-LETTERED TIMETABLE of the early 1850s shows passenger train service on the Vermont Central, as well as that of the Vermont & Canada which was built to St. Albans in the fall of 1850 and to Rouses Point, N.Y. during the following year. (Jim Shaughnessy Collection)

Vermont Central Railroad.

Open to Burlington

ON AND AFTER DECEMBER. 25, 1849,

THE PASSENGER CARS WILL LEAV[E] Boston for Burlington Daily, Sundays except[ed] at 7½ A M , via Boston. Lowell, Nashua. Conco[rd] Northern and Central Roads; also via Fitchbu[rg] Vt. & Massachusetts. Cheshire, Sullivan and Centr[al] Returning, leave Burlington at 6.40 A. M. by bo[th] of the above routes.

Freight trains leave Boston and Burlington da[ily] Sundays excepted. For further information [see] Pathfinder's Railway Guide.

JAMES MOORE, Superintendent

Dec. 25, 1849.   w27&d23?t[?]

VERMONT CENTRAL AND VERMONT & CANADA RAILROAD

WINDSOR TO ROUSES POINT — Read Downwards | ROUSES POINT TO WINDSOR — Read Upward

FRS From Bos.	MLS Via Lowell	MLS Via Fitch.	P.M.	A.M.	A.M.	Trains	P.M	R.M	P.M.	MLS	FRA
			5 00	7 30		Boston	6 25	8 44	1 00	287	7 30
			8 AM	~~		New York	11 10	—	4 40		9 00
			4½ PM	6 20		Worcester	7 00	—	2 00 PM		
			1 30	7 45		Springfield	6 20	—	11 45 AM		7 45
365	138		6 50	1 25		Windsor	1 10	—	6 55	158	5 10
385	142½		7 02	1 35		Hartland	1 00	—	6 45	153½	5 05
400	146½		7 14	1 45		North Hartland	12 44	—	6 35	149½	5 05
405	142	152	11 10	2 05		White River Junc	12 35	2 25	12 43	144	5 05
415	143½	153½	11 15	2 10		White River Village	12 05			142½	
425	145½	155½	11 20	2 15		Woodstock	12 00	2 15	12 33	140½	4 40
440	149½	159½	11 29	2 24		West Hartford	11 50	1 52	12 22	136½	4 75
460	155	170	11 42	2 37		Sharon	11 36	1 52	12 08 A.M.	131	4 55
480	160	170	11 57	2 50		South Royalton	11 24	1 41	11 55	126	4 35
490	162	172	12 02	2 54		Royalton	11 17		11 44	124	4 25
510	167	177	12 15	3 05		Bethel	11 05	1 25	11 29	119	4 05
535	174½	184½	12 35	3 21		Randolph	10 47	1 10	11 08	112	3 80
555	179½	189½	12 51	3 35		Braintree	10 33	12 58	10 52	106½	3 60
585	188	198	1 15	3 54		Roxbury	10 11		10 20	98	3 30
			1 35	4 12		ar North- field lv	9 53	12 24	10 10		
603	195	205	1 40	4 16	8 25	lv (ar)	9 49	12 09	9 47	91	3 05
630	205	215	2 22	4 40	8 54	Montpelier	9 27	11 49	9 22	81	2 75
630	211½	221½	2 35	4 51	9 13	Middlesex	9 13		9 06	74½	2 50
630	216½	226½	2 50	5 02	9 26	Waterbury	9 01	11 27	8 55	69½	2 30
645	222½	232½	3 12	5 18	9 45	Bolton	8 44	—	8 36	62½	2 05
645	226½	236½	3 20	5 25	9 54	Jones	8 37	—	8 27	59½	1 95
645	229½	239½	3 30	5 32	10 05	Richmond	8 29	10 59	8 18	56½	1 85
650	234½	244½	3 45	5 44	10 19	Williston	8 17	10 47	8 05	52	1 70
650	238½	248½	3 55	5 52	10 28 ar	Essex Junction lv	8 06	10 34	7 55	50	1 55
655	242½	252½	4 15	6 10	10 50	Winooski	7 50	10 20	7 40	48	1 55
			4 25	6 20	11 00 ar	Burling- ton lv	7 40	10 10	7 30		
655	245	255	3 30	5 30	10 10 lv	ton ar	8 30	11 00	8 15	53½	1 55
			3 40	5 40	10 20	Winooski	8 20	10 50	8 05	48	1 55
			4 00	5 55	10 36 lv	Essex Junction ar	8 04	10 36	7 52		
655	245	255	4 11	6 05	10 47	Colchester	7 54	—	7 42	44	1 55
655	252	262	4 28	6 19	11 03	Milton	7 38	10 13	7 26	37	1 45
660	256	266	4 36	6 27	11 12	Georgia	7 30	—	7 16	33	1 30
670	265	275	5 00	6 49	11 37	St. Albans	7 09	9 44	6 54	23	1 05
690	275	285	5 20	7 08	11 58	Swanton	6 49	9 26	6 14	65	
710	280	290	5 38	7 23	12 16	Alburgh Springs	6 33	9 12	5 56	6½	30
720	282	292	5 45	7 30	12 25	Alburgh	6 25	—	5 46	4½	20
730	286	296	5 50	7 35	12 30	West Alburgh	6 20	—	5 40	1	
730	287	297	6 00	7 45	12 40	Rouses Point	6 10	8 50	5 30		
900	331	341	9 15	10 00	4 30	Montreal	—	7 00	3 15		
900	405	415	11 00	12 30	7 00	Ogdensburg	—	4 10	12 20		
FRS	MLS	MLS		A.M.	A.M.	P.M ar Trains lv	A.M	A.M	P.M.	MLS	FRS

Passengers leave Montpelier for South and East at 9.15 and 11.38 A.M. & 9.10 P.M. For North and West at 2.10 and 8.40 A.M and 4.30 P.M

CARS CONNECT at Rouses Point with trains over Ogdensburg and Champlain and St. Lawrence Railroads.

Burlington with Rutland R.R. for Rutland, Whitehall, Saratoga, Troy, Albany and New York City.

Windsor with trains over the Sullivan, Cheshire & Fitchburg R.R.: to Bellows Falls, Keene, Worcester and Boston; and over the Vermont Valley and Connecticut River Railroads to Holyoke, Springfield, Hartford, New Haven and New York.

White River Junction with trains over Passumpsic Railroad to Wells River, St. Johnsbury and the White Mountains, and over Northern Railroad to Concord N.H.: Portsmouth, Portland, Manchester, Lawrence, Salem, Nashua, Worcester, Lowell, Providence and Boston.

The Vermont Central and Grand Trunk, or Potsdam Route and New York Central Lines are the shortest routes from Northern New Hampshire and Vermont to the West, more expeditious than any other route, the fare as low, and is the only route by which the cars pass over Lake Champlain between Vermont and New York or by which Passengers, Baggage and Merchandise can be transported without changing cars.

BAGGAGE IS CHECKED THROUGH

This is the most comfortable and expeditious route between the White and Franconia Mountains or Camels Hump Mt. Mansfield, and the Green Mountains and Burlington and Niagara Falls Montreal, Ogdensburg or Saratoga via Burlington and passing over Vermont Central Connecticut and Passumpsic Rivers and White Mountain Railroads to Littleton N.H. — within 12 miles of Franconia Notch and 18 of Fabyan's House.

Passengers leaving Saratoga by evening train will reach Mt. Mansfield early the next P.M and the White Mountains the next evening. Passengers for Mt. Mansfield and the Green Mountains, leave the train at Waterbury within 10 miles (by Stage over plank road) of the Mansfield House.

A sleeping car is attached to the Express Train leaving Boston at 5 P.M.

G. MERRILL Supt Northern.

Passengers' baggage and freight taken on conditions as found on page 4.

RUTLAND AND BÚRLNGTON RAIL ROAD.

NEW ARRANGEMENT.....DAY AND NIGHT LINE.
Commencing Monday, July 22, 1850.

PASSENGER TRAINS

Leave Burlington daily, (Sundays excepted,) for Boston, Lowell, Worcester, New York and intermediate Stations, at 8 A. M. and 7.30 P. M., arriving in Boston at 6 P. M. and 10 A. M. respectively. Passengers by the 7.30 P. M. Train will lodge at Bellows Falls.

RETURNING,

Leave Boston at 7.30 A. M. and 4.05 P. M. arriving in Burlington at 6 P. M. and 7.30 A. M. Passengers by the 4.05 P. M. Train will lodge at Rutland; those by the Morning Trains will have an hour to dine at Bellows Falls, both ways, connecting with the Morning and Evening Line of Steamers on Lake Champlain.

Passengers for New York, by either of the above Trains, intersect at Walpole with Stages to Brattleboro', thence via Conn. River R. R. to Greenfield, Northampton, *Hartford*, *New Haven* and intermediate Stations; thence via New York, & New Haven R. R. or by Steamer on the Sound to New York—through from Burlington in 21 hours.

ALSO—To New York, intersecting at Fitchburg with Fitchburg & Worcester R. R. to *Worcester*; thence via Worcester & Norwich R. R. to Allyn's Point; thence by Steamer on the Sound to New York —through from Burlington in 21 hours

ALSO—Intersect at Worcester with Providence & Worcester R. R. to *Providence, R. I.* and intermediate Stations—with Boston & Worcester R. R. to Stations east of Worcester, and with Worcester R. R. to Stations between Worcester and Springfield.

ALSO—Intersect at Groton Junction with Worcester & Nashua R. R. and with Stony Brook R. R. to Lowell.

Passengers arriving by Steamboat from Canada, Northern New York or Northern Vermont, will find Cars *at the Steamboat Landing* at Burlington, over the Rutland & Burlington Rail Road, being the shortest and quickest route between Lake Champlain and the Seaboard, and avoiding all coaching and staging. ☞Rates for passengers and freight as cheap as by any other route. **L. BIGELOW,** Sup't.

For Tickets and all necessary information, apply to
M. L. CHURCH, R. R. Office, Burlington,
J. W. CARPENTER, American Hotel, Burlington,
H. D. DOANE, 24 M'Gill St. Montreal.

4722

THIS BROADSIDE OF the Rutland & Burlington road shows in considerable detail its service and connections, including those in the Burlington and Lake Champlain areas. (Wilbur Collection, University of Vermont)

THIS PROMOTIONAL FLYER shows the area served by the Vermont Central shortly after the line was extended northward to Rouses Point, N.Y. (Wilbur Collection, University of Vermont)

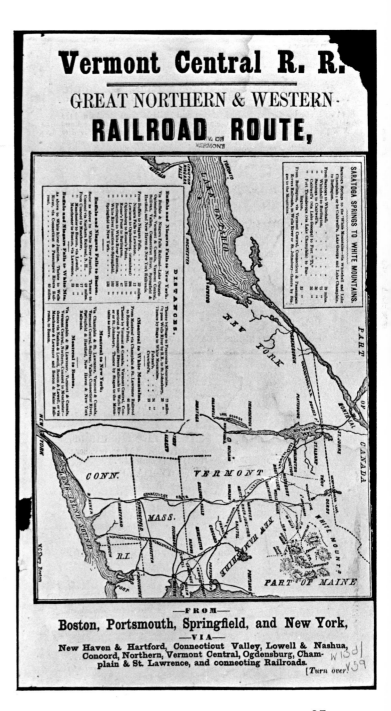

Vermont Central R. R.
GREAT NORTHERN & WESTERN
RAILROAD ROUTE,

—FROM—
Boston, Portsmouth, Springfield, and New York,
—VIA—
New Haven & Hartford, Connecticut Valley, Lowell & Nashua, Concord, Northern, Vermont Central, Ogdensburg, Champlain & St. Lawrence, and connecting Railroads.

[Turn over!

VERMONT CENTRAL RAILROAD TIME TABLE, JUNE 7th, 1852.—NO. 3.

FROM ROUSE'S POINT TO WINDSOR.

Stations.			Mail Train	Pass Train	1st Freight	Burl. F't.	Express F't
Rouse's Pt.			8 00am	6 40 "			
W. Alburgh	0.9	0.9	8.10 "	6.50 "	9.20am		4.34pm
Alburgh	4.0	4.9	8.19 "	6.58 "	a9.45 " 9.55 "		4.56 "
Missisco	2.7	7.6	8.25 "	7.03 "	a10.10 " 10.24 "		5.08 "
Swanton	6.3	13.9	8.38 "	7.14 "	D10.54 m 11.10 ef	M a5.40 m 6.01 m	
St. Albans	9.0	22.9	8.59 "	N 7.32 ef	L 11.55 m 12.47 f	N a6.50 pf 7.34 p	
Georgia	8.6	31.5	9.15 "	7.48 "	a1.27 pm 1.37 "		8.19pm
Milton	4.2	35.7	C 9.24 m ef	7.57 "	1.57 " 2.07 "		8.40 "
Colchester	7.2	42.9	9.38am	8.12 "	a2.42 " 2.53 "		9.15 "
Essex Junc.	4.1	47.0	K a9.44 m 9.54 f	a8.20 " 8.25 "	a3.10 " 3.20 "		a8.33 " 9.43 "
Williston	4.0	51.0	10.02am	8.33 "	3.40 "		10.00 "
Richmond	4.7	55.7	10.11 "	8.43pm	F a4.05 m 4.32 f		10.23 "
Bolton	6.0	61.7	10.24 "	8.54 "	4.58 "		10.49 "
Waterbury	7.0	68.7	10.40 "	9.08 "	a5.28 " 5.38 "		11.20 " 11.30 "
Middlesex	5.1	73.8	10.50 "	9.18 "	6.04 "		11.53 "
Montpelier	6.5	80.3	11.00 "	9.28 "	6.28 "		12.13am
Northfield	9.8	90.1	a11.17 " 11.27 "	9.44pm 5.00am	a7.13pm 3.30am		a12.58pm 3 00am
Roxbury	7.1	97.2	11.42 "	5.15 "	a4.15 " 4.25 "		a3.45 " 3.50 "
Braintree	8.5	105.7	11.59 "	5.32 "	a5.05 " 5.12 "		a4 30 " 4.40 "
Randolph	5.6	111.3	12.10pm	T 5.43 f 1f	T a5.36 ef 5.48 p		a5.06 " 5.15 "
Bethel	7.1	118.4	12.25 "	O 5.58 ef	O a6.21am 6.31 "	O a5.47 ff 6.08 p	
Royalton	4.9	123.3	12.34 "	6.07am	a6.53 " 7.00 "		a6 30am 6.35 "
S. Royalton	1.8	125.1	S 12.40 m ef	6.15 "	a7.19 " 7.40 "		a6.43 " 7.13 "
Sharon	4.9	130.0	H 12.49 f 1f	6.25 "	a8.02 " 8.12 "		a7.33 " 7.43 "
W. Hart'd	5.6	135.6	1.00pm	6.37 "	a8.38 " 8.48 "		a8.08 " 8.43 "
Woodstock	4.0	139.6	1.08 "	6.46 "	a9.06 " 9.16 "		a8.30 " 8.40 "
W. R. Vil.	1.8	141.4	1.14 "	6.55 "	a9.26 " 9.36 "		a8 48 " 8.58 "
W.R.Junc.	1.5	142.9	A a1.18 m 1.48 ef	7.05 "	G a9.46 m 10.30 f		a9.06am
N. Hartland	5.6	148.5	1.59pm	7.16 "	a10.54am 11.00 "		
Hartland	4.1	152.6	2.07 "	7.25 "	a11.17 " 11.27 "		
Windsor	4.3	156.9	a2.15pm	a7.33am	a11.45am		

FROM WINDSOR TO ROUSE'S POINT.

Stations.			Mail Train	Pass. Train	1st Freight	Burl. F't	Express F't
Windsor			12.45pm	6.15pm	9.00am		
Hartland	4.3	4.3	12.54 "	6.23 "	a9.18 " 9.28 "		
N. Hartland	4.1	8.4	1.02 "	6.33 "	a9.46 " 9.50 "		
W. R. Junc.	5.6	14.0	A a1.13 m 1.35 ef	a6.44 f 6.50 "	G a10.15 m 11.00 f		10.15am
W. R. Vil.	1.5	15.5	1.39pm	6.58 "	a11.08am 11.18 "		a10.22 " 10.32 "
Woodstock	1.8	17.3	1.43 "	7.02 "	a11.28 " 11 38 "		a10.41 " 10.51 "
W. Hartford	4.0	21.3	1.51 "	7.10 "	a11.58am 12 08pm		a11.09 " 11.19 "
Sharon	5.6	26.9	2.02 "	7.21 "	H 12.33 m 12.50 ef		a11.46 " 11.56 "
S. Royalton	4.9	31.8	2.12 "	7.32 "	a1.10pm 1.40 "		S 12.17 m 12.50 ef
Royalton	1.8	33.6	2.16 "	7.36 "	a1.48 " 1.56 "		a12.59pm 1.09 "
Bethel	4.9	38.5	J 2.31 f 1f	7.48 "	J a2.20 ef 2 35 "		a1.31 " 1.44 "
Randolph	7.1	45.6	B 2.45 f ef	8.03 "	a3.07pm 3.17 "		B a2.16 ff 2.48 p
Braintree	5.6	51.2	2.56pm	8.15 "	a3.43 " 3.53 "		3.15pm 3.25 "
Roxbury	8.5	59.7	3.13 "	8.32 "	a4.35 " 4.45 "		a4.12 " 4 26 "
Northfield	7.1	66.8	a3.26pm 3.32pm	a8.43pm 4.50am	a5.20pm 5.30am		a5.00pm 4.56am
Montpelier	9.8	76.6	3.46 "	5.04 "	6 03 " 6.05 "		5.30 "
Middlesex	6.5	83.1	3.55 "	5.13 "	6.36 "		5.56 "
Waterbury	5.1	88.2	4.05 "	5 22 "	a7.00 " 7.30 "		a6.17 " 6.44 "
Bolton	7.0	95.2	4.19pm	5.36 "	8.07 "		7.14 "
Richmond	6.0	101.2	F 4.31 m 1f	5.48 "	a8.33 " 8 40 "		7.39 "
Williston	4.7	105.9	4.40 "	5.57 "	9.06 "		8.00 "
Essex Junc.	4.0	109.9	a4.46 " 4.53 "	a6.03 " 6.10 "	K a9.26 m 9.45 ef		a8.16 " 8.22 "
Colchester	4.1	114.0	5.01 "	6.18 "	a10.04am 10.14 "		8.40 "
Milton	7.2	121.2	5.14 "	6.32 "	10.50 " 11.00 "		C a9.10 m 9.25 ef
Georgia	4.2	125.4	5.23 "	6.40 "	a11.20 " 11.30 "		9.45am
St. Albans	8.6	134.0	5.41 "	6.58 "	L 12.15 m 12.50 1f		10.21 " 10.31 "
Swanton	9.0	143.0	M 6.00 m ef	7.15 "	a1.30pm 1.40 "		D 11.08 m 11.15 1f
Missisco	6.3	149.3	6.13 "	7.27 "	a2.10 " 2 20 "		11.45 "
Alburgh	2.7	152.0	6.19 "	7.32 "	a2.34 " 2.44 "		12.00 "
W. Alburgh	4.0	156.0	6.26 "	7.40 "	a3.02pm		a12.20pm
Rouse's Pt.	0.9	156.9	a6.35pm	a7.50am			

Explanation of labels, &c. M T, Mail Train; P T, Pass. Train; E F, Express Freight; 1 F, 1st Freight; 2 F, 2d Freight; B F, Burlington Freight. The small m, meets; p, passes; a, arrives. The large capitals AA, BB, CC, &c., denote meeting and passing of trains. 2d, 3d and 4th Freight Trains will follow preceding Freights and will be announced by flags borne on Engines.

PASSENGERS LEAVE		PASSENGERS ARRIVE AT	
Burlington for Boston, &c. at	9.15 A. M. and 7.55 P. M.;	Winooski from Boston, &c. at	6.15 A. M. and 4.56 P. M.;
Winooski	9.34 A. M. and 8.05 P. M.;	Burlington	6.25 A. M. and 5.06 P. M.;
Burlington for Rouse's Point, &c. at	5.40 A. M. and 4.23 P. M.;	Winooski from Rouse's Point, at	10.00 A. M. and 8.30 P. M.;
Winooski	5.50 A. M. and 4.33 P. M.	Burlington	10.10 A. M. and 8.40 P. M.

REGULATIONS.

1. The Conductor has charge of the Train, and is responsible for his Cars being in proper order. He will run as near card time as possible. He will in no case permit a Train to leave a station before the time indicated on card. The Engineer is responsible for his running time.

2. The Standard Time is the clock in Northfield Depot. Conductors and Engineers must carry a watch which should be compared daily with the Northfield clock.

3. Mail and Passenger Trains take the track in preference to all other Trains, and will not wait for Freight Trains, but will proceed when their own time has expired.

4. Freight Trains will wait indefinitely for Passenger Trains. Wood and Gravel will keep out of the way of Passenger and Freight Trains at least fifteen minutes.

5. Freight Trains must keep fifteen minutes out of the way of Mail and Passenger Trains, unless as directed in this Card; run with care into all stations, and run no risk of meeting or being overtaken by any Train in order to reach regular passing places.

6. A Brakeman must always be stationed on the rear Car of Freight Trains, the brakes of which must be in good order, and the Car designated by a Red Flag by day and a Red Light by night.

7. Regular Trains will in all cases stop at stations as shown on Card, and when one Train is following another, the rear Train will keep at least ten minutes behind the preceding Train and approach stations with caution, so that there shall be no danger of collision with another Train.

8. All Trains will meet and pass at stations designated in Time Table by AA, BB, &c. When either Train is delayed from any cause, the other Train must wait until the absent Train is heard from.

9. Telegraphic despatches must in all cases be twice repeated before the Conductor should suffer his Train to leave, and then proceed with care.

10. When any Train has occasion to stop on the road from any cause, or is behind time at a Station, the Conductor must see that signals are kept at suitable positions at least five hundred yards each way from Train, so as to guard against the possibility of collision.

11. A Red Flag by day or a Red Light by night borne on an Engine shows that a Train is to follow, which must be waited for, the same as the Engine bearing it. A White Flag displayed on an Engine shows that a Train is to follow, but which will keep out of the way of Regular Passenger or Freight Trains. The Engineer and Conductor of Trains bearing a Flag will be particular to call the attention of Conductors of meeting Trains, Station agents and all concerned, and explain the meaning of it to them.

12. No Train shall pass a station without stopping sufficient time for the agent to communicate with the Conductor or Engineer.

13. Station Agents will stop a Train which has been preceded within ten minutes by another Train unless directed in Card.

14. A Red Flag by day or a Light by night placed over the draw at Missisco Bay Bridge shows the Draw to be open, and the Train will stop. All Trains approaching the Draw at West Alburgh must keep a good look-out, always presuming the Draw to be open until it is seen to be right.

15. Freight Trains must pass all Bridges with care—the speed of Train not to exceed ten miles per hour.

16. The speed of all Freight Trains in no case exceed 14 miles per hour.

17. Any signal displayed on the Track indicating danger, will cause the Engineer and Conductor to stop the Train as soon as possible.

18. The whistle sounded once means to apply the brakes; sounded twice, let go the brakes; a quick succession of blasts indicates danger, and the Train be stopped as soon as possible. The whistle will not be sounded in or about the Engine houses or stations only in cases of necessity. It will not be sounded to call conductors or other men to their duty.

19. In stopping at stations the Engineers will shut off steam in season so that the brakeman will have no more to do than to stop his cars.

20. The Engine men must know and inform the Superintendent of motive power, or Master Machinists, of the condition of his Engine.

21. The Engine man on approaching a switch or road crossing, will be careful to see that the switch is right and the way is clear. Should the switch not be seen to be right he will stop his train.

22. All persons working on the Road, and Wood and Gravel Trains, will notice passing Trains, and on seeing a flag displayed on the Engine, will keep the Track clear until the Train announced has arrived, or should repairs be necessary will only make them after placing a signal 900 yards distant from the obstruction. All persons employed on the road will give notice of any obstruction to the passage of trains by exhibiting a Red Flag by day or a light by night conspicuously, at least 600 yards distant from the obstruction in both directions of the road. Engineers and conductors will regard such signals, and proceed with caution until the cause is ascertained.

23. In case of doubt or difficulty as to right to road or safety of proceeding, adopt the safe course. Keep signals far enough ahead to obviate danger to your own or other Trains.

24. Only Engineers are permitted to move Engines. No person is allowed to ride upon the Engine or Tender, except the Road Master or Master Machinist.

25. At 2 o'clock A. M., the right of any Train of the preceding day to the Road ceases, and after that hour will become irregular, and will keep out of the way of Passenger and Freight Trains, but otherwise may proceed to its destined Station.

JOHN CROMBIE, *Supt. Motive Power V. C. R. R.*

VERMONT STATE FAIR

At Rutland, Sept. 1st, 2d & 3d, 1852.

Vermont Central Railroad,
FARE HALF PRICE!

On *Wednesday* 1st, and *Thursday* 2d, only, persons wishing to attend the Fair will be carried *at fare one way*, in each train, by purchasing through tickets, and may return on Thursday, the 2d, & Friday, the 3d, only, in each train. Passengers via Bellows Falls, by the train which leaves Northfield at 5 A. M., reach Rutland at 11.20 A. M., and by the train leaving at 11.27 A. M., reach Rutland at 7.30 P. M.

Passengers via Burlington, by the train leaving Northfield at 4.50 A. M., reach Rutland at 10.30 A. M., and by the train leaving Rouse's Point at 8 A. M., reach Rutland at 1 P. M. Passengers with half price tickets will *not* be allowed to stop at intermediate Stations and proceed in other trains.

PASSENGERS MUST PROCURE THEIR TICKETS AT THE TICKET OFFICES,

Freight Trains leave Northfield, via Burlington, at	5.00 A. M.
" " " Rouse's Point, via "	9.20 "
" " " Northfield, via Bellows Falls, at	3.30 "
" " " White River Junction, via Bellows Falls, at	10.30 "

Those trains by which Stock, &c. to be exhibited at the State Fair may be sent *Free*, at the risk of owners as to connections & loss, will connect with the Stock trains for Rutland, which leave Burlington & Bellows Falls at 4 P. M., Tuesday, August 31st.

Freight Trains for White River Junction & Northfield leave Bellows Falls at 5.50 A. M. *Freight Trains* for Rouse's Point leave Burlington 7.00 A. M.; leave Burlington for Northfield 2.30, or 7.55 P. M.

ONSLOW STEARNS, *Agent.*

Northfield, August 21st, 1852.

AMERICAN RAILWAY GUIDE,

AND

POCKET COMPANION,

For the United States;

CONTAINING

CORRECT TABLES,

FOR TIME OF STARTING FROM ALL STATIONS, DISTANCES, FARES, ETC.

ON ALL THE RAILWAY LINES IN THE UNITED STATES;

TOGETHER WITH A

COMPLETE RAILWAY MAP.

—ALSO—

MANY PRINCIPAL STEAMBOAT AND STAGE LINES
RUNNING IN CONNECTION WITH RAILROADS.

CHARLES COBB, Compiler.

1851.

NEW YORK:

CORRECTED AND PUBLISHED ON THE 1ST OF EVERY MONTH
BY CURRAN DINSMORE & CO.,
PARKER'S JOURNAL OFFICE, 22 SPRUCE STREET.

—GENERAL AGENTS—
Redding & Co., Boston: M. Bussey, Springfield, Mass.; E. Smith & Co.,
Burlington, Vt.; L. Willard, Troy, N.Y.; P. L. Gilbert, Albany; H.
W. D. Brewster, Rochester & Buffalo; J. A. Roys, Detroit, Mich.;
W. W. Danenhower, Chicago, Ill.; R. R. Edwards, Cincinnati, Ohio; R. Hackett, Philadelphia; T. Newton
Kurtz, Baltimore; Henry Taylor, Richmond, Va.;
Gross & Courell, Charleston, and the South.

THIS 1852 EMPLOYEES' timetable contains a great deal of interesting information about train operations of the day. The "regulations" are particularly interesting, the more noteworthy because many of these operating rules are still universally used 130 years later. (Wilbur Collection, University of Vermont)   **OPPOSITE PAGE**

VERY EARLY IN its history, the Vermont Central promoted and ran special trains and offered excursion rates. This broadside illustrates one such example. (Wilbur Collection, University of Vermont)

PAGE 82 OF THE 1851 "American Railway Guide" shows passenger timetable information that must have succeeded in convincing the travelers of the day that travelling by train was considerably better than going by horse. (Jim McFarlane Collection)

VERMONT CENTRAL RAILROAD
Chas. Paine, Pres., Northfield, Vt.   R. H. Campbell, Eng'r, Northfield, Vt.

	Fares	WINDSOR ROUS'S PT.	1st Tr'n	2d Trn	3d Trn		Fares	ROUS'S PT. WINDSOR	1st Trn	2d Trn	3d Trn
		TRAINS LEAVE	PM	PM	PM			TRAINS LEAVE	AM	PM	PM
		Windsor....	12 45	6 15				Rouse's Pt		2 00	
4	15	Hartland....	12 55	6 25		1	5	W. Alburgh..		2 10	
6	50	N. Hartland..	1 04	6 33		5	15	Alburgh....		2 20	
14	45	White R. J...	1 48	6 53		7	20	Missisco....		2 27	
15	50	White R. Vge	1 56	7 05		13	40	Swanton....		2 44	
17	55	Woodstock..	2 01	7 09		23	70	St. Albans..	7 00	3 00	
21	65	W. Hartford	2 11	7 17		32	95	Georgia.....	7 21	3 31	
27	80	Sharon......	2 24	7 29		36	1 10	Milton......	7 31	3 41	
32	95	So. Royalton	2 35	7 40		43	1 25	Colchester...	7 49	4 00	
34	1 00	Royalton....	2 39	7 44		47	1 40	Essex Junc'n	7 59	4 10	
39	1 15	Bethel......	2 55	8 00				Burlin'nt	7 35	3 40	
46	1 35	Randolph....	3 10	8 15		3	5	Winooski..	7 45	3 50	
51	1 50	Braintree...	3 23	8 26		7	20	Arr Essex			
60	1 75	Roxbury.....	3 42	8 42							
67	2 00	Northfield...	4 00	8 AM		51	1 50	Williston...	8 19	4 30	
77	2 25	Montpelier..	4 34	8 24		56	1 65	Richmond...	8 31	4 42	
83	2 45	Middlesex...	4 50	8 40		59	1 75	Jones's.....	8 36	4 47	
88	2 60	Waterbury..	5 10	9 05		63	1 85	Bolton......	8 46	4 57	
94	2 80	Bolton......	5 27	9 22		69	2 05	Waterbury..	9 03	5 04	
98	2 90	Jones's.....	5 32	9 27		74	2 20	Middlesex...	9 23	5 27	
101	3 00	Richmond...	5 42	9 37		80	2 40	Montpelier..	9 39	5 43	
106	3 15	Williston...	5 54	9 49		90	2 60	Northfield..	10 05	5 AM	
110	3 25	Essex Junc'n	6 14	10 09		97	2 85	Roxbury....	10 31	5 17	
		Essex				106	3 10	Braintree...	10 50	5 34	
114	3 40	Winooski	6 42	10 24		111	3 25	Randolph...	11 03	5 45	
117	3 45	Burlin'n	6 32	10 34		118	3 45	Bethel......	11 18	6 01	
120	3 40	Colchester..	6 34	10 19		123	3 60	Royalton....	11 29	6 11	
124	3 55	Milton......	6 42	10 37		125	3 65	So. Royalton	11 33	6 15	
128	3 70	Georgia.....	6 52	10 47		130	3 80	Sharon......	11 49	6 32	
137	3 95	St. Albans..	7 13	11 15		136	3 90	W. Hartford	12 02	6 44	
147	4 25	Swanton....	——	11 31		140	4 00	Woodstock..	12 12	6 52	
153	4 35	Missisco....		11 48		142	4 05	White R. Vge	12 17	6 56	
155	4 40	Alburgh.....		11 55		143	4 10	White R. J.!	12 26	7 06	
160	4 50	W. Alburgh..		12 05		148	4 25	N. Hartland	12 47	7 23	
162	4 55	Rouse's Pt..		12 15		153	4 40	Hartland....	12 56	7 31	
						157	4 55	Ar Windsor	1 09	7 40	

* Connects with Sullivan R. R. at this place, see page 50
† The Connecticut & Passumpsic Rivers R.R. diverges here see page 53 Also, Northern (N.H.) R.R. see page 91.
‡ Connects with Rutland & Burlington R.R. at this point, see page 61.
Trains leave Burlington for Rouse's Point at 6.13 A.M. and 4.53 P.M.
— arrive at Burlington from Rouse's Point at 10.30 A.M. 6.48 P.M.
§ Connects at this point with Northern (N.Y.) R.R., see page 66. Also,
Champlain & St. Lawrence R.R., see page 67.
Stages run in connection with the Central R.R. for all parts of Central, Northern and Western Vermont, New York and Canadas.

THIS 1850's MAP shows St. Albans "Village" at the time the Vermont & Canada was built through the town. Immediately after this map was completed, the railroad facilities were expanded considerably. (Jim McFarlane Collection)

Chapter **II**

A Northern Extension 1845-1851

AS RELATED IN THE PREVIOUS CHAPTER, THE VERMONT GENERAL *Assembly granted charters to both the Champlain & Connecticut Rivers Railroad—soon renamed the Rutland & Burlington—and the Vermont Central Railroad in 1843. The charter of the Vermont Central authorized it to build a railroad from some point on the eastern shore of Lake Champlain, up the valley of the Onion [Winooski] River, and across the Green Mountains to the Connecticut River. Accordingly, the directors of this road claimed the right to build across the Sand Bar to South Hero to connect with a railroad that had been surveyed from Ogdensburgh to Plattsburgh, New York. The directors of the Rutland & Burlington, however, objected vehemently to this, as such a line would be in direct competition with the long-range plans of their projected road.*

It was at this time that John Smith of St. Albans and several of his associates sought to obtain a charter that would permit an independent company to build a railroad northward from Burlington to effect a connection with a road that would eventually be built southward from Montreal. Primarily through Smith's personal efforts, such a charter was granted by the Vermont General Assembly on October 31, 1845, to the Vermont & Canada Railroad Company. The incorporators named were Benjamin Swift, John Smith, Lawrence Brainerd, William O. Gadcomb, Victor Atwood, Abel Houghton, Gardner G. Smith, Romeo H. Hoyt, Samuel W. Keyes, Stephen E. Keyes, Timothy Foster, George Greene, Bradley Barlow, Peter Chase, Jacob Weed, William Greene, Hiram Bellows, Homer E. Hubbell, Isaac P. Clark, Alvah Sabin, Joseph Clark, Albert G. Whittemore, Daniel H. Onion, Oscar A. Burton, Horace Eaton, William Clapp, and Asa Owen Aldis. This was certainly an impressive list of promoters! This charter was granted exactly six weeks before Charles Paine turned the first sod on his Vermont Central Railroad at Windsor on December 15.

The route established in the Vermont & Canada's charter was as follows: "From some point on the Canada line, thence through the village of St. Albans to some point or points in Chittenden County most convenient for meeting, at the village of Burlington, a railroad to be built on the route described in the act to incorporate the Champlain & Connecticut Rivers Railroad Company, and to some point or points in Chittenden County most convenient for meeting a railroad to be built on the route described in the act to incorporate the Vermont Central Railroad Company, and

with the right, and for the purpose, of extending a railroad from any point in the aforesaid route to some point on the western shore of Grand Isle County, passing across the sand bar to South Hero, as the said company may hereafter designate." The charter specified the capital stock could be issued in the amount of $1,000,000, with authority granted to increase this to $3,000,000 if it was deemed necessary.

Both Charles Paine and John Smith considered their roads to be extensions of each other, and not as rival enterprises. Both men had been among the original ten incorporators of the Vermont Central, and Smith had been instrumental in securing the charter for that road. The Vermont Central, in turn, was to lend the Vermont & Canada money for its original survey; and both roads were soon to share a treasurer and civil engineer.

Before the coming of the railroad, St. Albans and all of Franklin County was in a real sense quite isolated economically. The large islands comprising Grand Isle County served to cut Franklin County off from the main channel of the lake, which had historically been the main north-south avenue of travel. In earlier years, those who had occasion to travel to New York City proceeded on horseback to Troy, New York, where they boarded a sloop for the remainder of the trip down the great Hudson River.

Goods had to be freighted from New York to Troy by sloop, forwarded by wagons to Whitehall, and then trans-shipped to lake vessels for the trip to St. Albans Bay. When a line of steamboats was established on the lake, it was only a moderate benefit to the residents of Franklin County, because then a land journey to Burlington was neccessary as that was the nearest port served.

THE REDOUBTABLE JOHN SMITH was the major force responsible for getting the Vermont & Canada Railroad built. There were few men indeed who could match him for business acumen and shrewdness. (Jim Murphy Collection)

When a steam ferry was introduced to Plattsburgh in 1828, little was gained as transshipment at either end was still an unavoidable fact of life. The markets of Boston and the great manufacturing centers of the East were hardly available at all to the residents of Franklin County, and inter-regional trade was virtually non-existent. The coming of the railroad, then, was the primary factor in initiating political, social, and commercial progress in Franklin County.

The connection with the Ogdensburgh road at Plattsburgh was, from the first, regarded as quite impractical by those even slightly acquainted topographically with the area. Nonetheless, John Smith spent some time investigating the feasibility of operating freight-car ferries across Lake Champlain at Burlington and also the possibilities of bridging two sections of the lake near the southern end of South Hero Island. The route across the lake from South Hero Island to Cumberland Head near Plattsburgh was really not much more than a pipe dream. It would have involved bridging a very deep five-mile expanse of open lake or building multiple dock facilities and operating slow and costly ferries. And then what would happen during the four months each year when the lake was frozen solid?

Meanwhile, after considerable deliberation, the promoters of the Northern Railroad of New York had seen the folly of considering Plattsburgh for its eastern terminus. They decided that it would be in the best interests of all to make their eastern rail connections at Rouses Point, just below the International Boundary.

The idea of bridging the lake between South Hero and Cumberland Head had been regarded by many as so preposterous that hundreds of signatures from both sides of the lake poured into the state capitals of Albany and Montpelier—all on petitions expressing indignation at such a scheme. A bill was even introduced at a session of Vermont's General Assembly demanding that if such a route materialized, the county seat be moved from St. Albans to Sheldon, a farming village some ten miles east of St. Albans.

Smith also soon found himself confronted with bitter attempts by lake and canal operators—as well as New York railroad companies—to block the construction of a railroad route across Lake Champlain at any point. The former were interested in retaining the traffic on the waterways, and the latter wanted to divert rail traffic away from Boston and toward New York City.

Despite all the bickering, the books of the Vermont & Canada were opened for stock subscriptions on June 8, 1847, and one month later to the day, the first stockholders' meeting was held. One of the major actions taken at that meeting was the election of the road's first board of directors. Those so named were John Smith, Lawrence Brainerd, and William Farrar of St. Albans; Charles Paine and Heman Carpenter of Northfield; and S. S. Lewis and S. M. Felton of Boston.

THE HONORABLE LAWRENCE BRAINERD, a noted anti-slavery figure and businessman, contributed significant amounts of capital that made it possible for the Vermont & Canada to be constructed. (Jim Murphy Collection)

The directors met on July 20 for the first time and elected the road's initial slate of officers. One should not be surprised to learn that John Smith was elected the first president of the road. Samuel Walley of Roxbury, Massachusetts, became the first vice-president, and Lawrence Brainerd was elected clerk.

With the eastern terminus of the Ogdensburgh road changed from Plattsburgh to Rouses Point, the directors of the Vermont & Canada gave legal warning that an application would be made to the General Assembly for a change in their charter which would give them the right to locate their railroad to the eastern shore of the lake at Alburgh and to build and maintain a bridge from that point to the state's western boundary—which was the middle of Lake Champlain. Accordingly, a bill was introduced and passed, to be effective October 27, 1847. However, the victory did not come easily. An historic debate had taken place in the state's legislative halls, and when the vote was finally called, the amendment to the original charter passed by a simple majority of two votes!

JOSEPH CLARK, THE third of the three principal promoters of the Vermont & Canada along with John Smith and Lawrence Brainerd, owned a number of sawmills and grist mills in the Milton area. He lived to the age of 84, a much loved and respected man. (Jim Murphy Collection)

THIS VERMONT & CANADA Railroad Company stock certificate is dated March 3, 1850, some seven months before the first train ran into St. Albans. It has been co-signed by President John Smith. (Jim Murphy Collection)

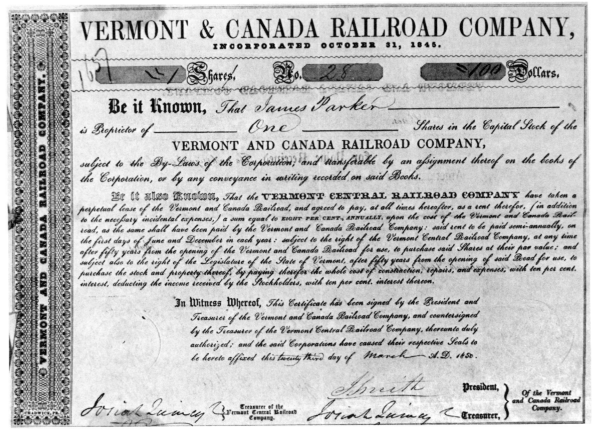

VERMONT AND CANADA RAILROAD COMPANY.

Whereas, many Shareholders of the VERMONT CENTRAL RAILROAD COMPANY have expressed a wish that they might again have an opportunity of subscribing to the VERMONT AND CANADA RAILROAD, under the new guarantee for the payment of dividends on the same—

Notice is hereby given, that, by order of the Directors, the Subscription Books for

TWENTY-FIVE HUNDRED SHARES

of said stock, will be open on WEDNESDAY, the 24th day of July current, at the office of the Treasurer, No. 27 State street, Boston, and at *Bank of Montpelier*, Montpelier, Vt., *Farmers' and Mechanics' Bank*, Burlington, *Ascutney Bank*, Windsor, to Shareholders in the VERMONT CENTRAL RAILROAD COMPANY *only*, who will be required to pay $10 a share at the time of making the subscription.

Should more than said amount be subscribed on the day of closing the Books, the Directors reserve the right of apportioning the same *pro rata*, according to the stock held by the subscribers in the VERMONT CENTRAL.

By order of the Directors,

JOSIAH QUINCY, Jr.,

Treasurer Vermont and Canada Railroad.

VERMONT CENTRAL RAILROAD.

NOTICE is hereby given that all subscribers to new Stock in the VERMONT CENTRAL RAILROAD, who do not pay the instalments on or before the *First day of August next*, will forfeit their right to take the same.

By order of the Committee of Finance,

JOSIAH QUINCY, Jr.,

Treasurer Vermont Central Railroad.

BOSTON, JULY 18, 1850.

BY JULY, 1850, Josiah Quincy, Jr., had become treasurer of both the Vermont Central and the Vermont & Canada roads. He issued this notice as treasurer of both companies, an indication of the confused state these railroads were soon to find themselves in. (Wilbur Collection, University of Vermont)

By now only a little over $100,000 in stock had been received, a figure barely adequate to organize the company. In an effort to obtain Boston capital for the project, John Smith had taken steps to have two wealthy Bostonians elected to the road's first board of directors—Lewis and Felton. Investment dollars from the Boston market, nonetheless, were conspicuous by their paucity.

Fully realizing the importance of obtaining more capital quickly, Smith himself journeyed to Boston to see if a personal approach would bring the desired results. He was disheartened, but not surprised, to find it very difficult to pry any substantial amounts of money away from the Boston financiers. They were only marginally interested in investing in projects in which they were not assured a goodly amount of direct control. In those days, St. Albans, Vermont was a long way from Boston. Perhaps just as important, John Smith's reputation for business acumen and shrewdness had preceded him. The Boston bankers, in fact, were not much interested in even talking about the project until there were assurances that the Vermont & Canada would be part of a road that would cross into New York State and create a through direct connection between Boston and the Great Lakes. Bluntly put, Smith did not have a satisfying trip.

Back on the home front, though, an interesting development was taking place. Timothy Follett, president of the Rutland & Burlington Railroad, viewed the Vermont & Canada's amended charter as a threat to his plans to eventually build north from Burlington to the Canadian border. Follett placed a secret agent in St. Albans to buy up stock subscriptions in the Vermont & Canada. However, the ruse was discovered, and the state voided all subscriptions so purchased on the grounds that they had been made "in a clandestine manner." And so, the first shots of what was to become known as "The Forty Years' War" in Vermont had been fired! It was no longer just a noisy argument.

By now, many of the Vermont & Canada promoters were deeply concerned that enemies of the project might try to influence the session of the General Assembly to repeal the company's amended charter. They felt that it was imperative that tangible action be undertaken at once, so chief engineer Henry R. Campbell was brought in from the Vermont Central to direct the survey of the line. It was decided that the survey would commence at the Vermont Central's line at Essex Junction, some seven miles east of Burlington. From there it would run almost due north through the towns of Colchester, Milton, Georgia, and then into St. Albans. It goes without saying that John Smith would make sure the road's headquarters would be located in his home town.

From St. Albans, the line continued due north to Highgate, a small village near the Canadian border. At that point, it would subsequently be determined how best to continue the line into Canada and also across the entrance to Mississquoi Bay to Alburgh, and then across the narrow northern tip of Lake Champlain to Rouses Point.

Good location techniques would have placed the rail line at St. Albans along the flat plain that borders the eastern shore of the lake. The village itself was situated at a somewhat higher elevation about two miles from the lake shore. The line selected, however, brought the railroad into the center of the village. John Smith saw to that. This meant that forever after trains would have to climb a relatively steep grade into St. Albans from the south and drop sharply downgrade to the north of town. The downgrade, of course, represents a difficult climb for trains coming into town from the north. This particular example of Smith's provincial mein has cost the railroad dearly both in terms of original construction and, more importantly, in operating dollars over the years.

But, as Edward Hungerford wrote in his very informative 1942 treatise on the subject entitled **Vermont Central-Central Vermont** (Railway & Locomotive Historical Society): "The Smiths had willed that the railroad should pass through St. Albans village and they would make the town the headquarters of their railroad. And when the Smiths of St. Albans once willed a thing, it was hard to will it otherwise. So up into the heart of St. Albans the new railroad ascended, and let the other fellow pay the coal bills for climbing up the hills through the years."

Although the road was still under-capitalized, Smith and his fellow directors decided to start construction immediately upon completion of the survey. They awarded the contract for the grading and masonry work to the firm of Balch, Kearney, and Hinch.

Construction activities commenced on a nice fall day in early September, 1848. The first sod is reported to have been turned at a point just north of the village of Georgia, a few miles south of St. Albans. Almost unbelievably, the contractors had a crew of seven men on hand to start this ambitious railway construction project! When the news of this pitifully small work force reached the halls of state government in Montpelier, two very different reactions prevailed. Those sympathetic to the project expressed an attitude of bewilderment, while those opposed to the road broke into disparaging chortling. There were few who were indifferent.

As it turned out, however, there was a reason for this extremely small force of men being on hand. The contractors were finishing a railroad construction project in New Hampshire, and they had not yet moved their large work force and equipment to the site of the new project—the Vermont & Canada. Within a very short time, the New Hampshire road was finished, and men and machines started on the move toward northwestern Vemont. Such a move was an impressive sight—one that a person saw perhaps only once or twice in a lifetime. There were hundreds of men on foot, with large numbers of horses, carts, and road-building machines. Many families of workers who wished to accompany their menfolk from one project to another also helped swell the ranks of this small army.

It was a long, colorful, and dusty parade that moved along the roads and through the villages en route. As the army moved along, news of its coming preceded it from town to town. As the entourage moved through Montpelier, the men of government recessed to the front steps of the capitol in order to see the sight. After its passing, it was said that the disparaging remarks were immediately stilled; for many, a sense of exuberance undoubtedly replaced a sense of bewilderment.

With the arrival of the main construction force, a formal ground-breaking ceremony was held at Essex Junction, near the present-day Maple Street crossing site. Among those present at the ceremony were president John Smith of the Vermont & Canada Railroad, president Charles Paine of the Vermont Central Railroad, and Vermont & Canada directors Lawrence Brainerd and Joseph Clark.

The contractors soon had crews working at various locations on the line between Essex Junction and St. Albans, and good progress was being made. Before the project was half completed, however, the supply of ready capital ran out. Money had been spent on the construction work faster than stock subscriptions were bringing it in. At this critical point in the road's history, directors Smith, Brainerd, and Clark decided on a daring course of action. They borrowed a total of $500,000 on their personal signatures to keep the project from failure. Construction was thus enabled to continue uninterrupted. The individual and collective credit of these three gentlemen proved sufficient to keep the corporation afloat until an arrangement was completed with the Vermont Central whereby that road took sufficient stock to relieve Smith, Brainerd, and Clark of their extraordinary liability.

Long before the Vermont & Canada had been organized, John Smith had earned a reputation for being a shrewd, intelligent, egocentric, hard-nosed Yankee; and his activities during the remaining eleven years of his life served only to enhance this image. The Honorable John Smith was born in Barre, Massachusetts, on August 12, 1789. When eleven years of age, his father purchased a farm in the southwestern part of St. Albans. The family had been settled on the property for only a short time, however, when the farm was lost because of a faulty deed. With this development, Samuel Smith moved his family into St. Albans village. There, John took advantage of the limited educational opportunities available locally to young people of his day. He then embarked upon the study of law in the office of his brother-in-law, Roswell Hutchins. Subsequently, he continued this study in the office of the Honorable Benjamin Swift. Smith was so engaged for the next seventeen years,

THIS IS THE FIRST station at St. Albans shortly after it was built. It is located at the intersection of Champlain [soon to become Lake] Streets. One of the recently completed shop buildings may be seen across the tracks to the west. (Michael McMahon Collection)

during which time the law firm developed an enviable reputation for soundness and ability.

John Smith, meanwhile, had become very active in politics. He represented St. Albans in the state legislature for nine consecutive terms, and in 1826 he was elected state's attorney—a position he held for the next six years. In 1831-33 he was speaker of the General Assembly, and from 1839-41 he served as Vermont's representative in Congress. Between 1842-46 he left public office and resumed his legal practice, but in the latter year he commenced in earnest his activities which resulted in the formation and construction of the Vermont & Canada Railroad.

The Honorable Lawrence Brainerd was for many years a prominent anti-slavery figure. He was a descendent of William Brainerd, an early missionary to the Indians. Brainerd was born in East Hartford, Connecticut, on March 16, 1794. When a boy of nine, he moved to Troy, New York, to live with an uncle. In 1808, Brainerd moved to St. Albans, where he attended public schools and subsequently taught in them for a short time. He left the teaching profession for a job as clerk for N. W. Kingman of St. Albans. In 1816, he started his own mercantile business, and he succeeded in building up a large trade. Brainerd soon became prominently identified with the navigation enterprises on Lake Champlain, and in 1847 he built the first upper cabin steamer on the lake, the "United States." Brainerd became president of the first bank in St. Albans, a position he held at the time he became involved in the Vermont & Canada Railroad.

Brainerd had long had a strong dislike for slavery, and he had been active publicly on this issue. In 1854, after the death of U.S. Senator William Upham, Brainerd was unanimously chosen by the state legislature to serve out Upham's term in Congress. He, thus, became the first state senator ever sent to Washington on an anti-slavery stand. Subsequently, Brainerd received a unanimous nomination for governor of the State of Vermont, but he declined. He also served as chairman of the national delegation that nominated Abraham Lincoln for the presidency. Brainerd passed away in St. Albans on May 12, 1870, but the effects of his long and useful life were not soon forgotten.

Joseph Clark, the third of the three principals behind the Vermont & Canada Railroad, came to the Milton area from Addison County, Vermont, in 1815 at the age of 20. He settled in West Milton and with H. G. Boardman acquired timber rights to vast acreages of virgin woodlands. He made his money cutting pulpwood, cordwood, and long timbers, the latter being sent to England for use in the British navy.

In 1830, Clark moved a few miles into Milton Village, where he built a new home, sawmills, and grist mills in the ensuing years. He was thus engaged when he became involved in his railroad promotion activities. He died in 1879 at the age of 84, a very much loved and respected man. Tradition has it that as long as Clark lived, every Vermont & Canada train was to stop in Milton. If such was a fact, before he died he saw a minimum of two daily freight trains, eight passenger trains, a special daily milk train, and a weekly

THIS PHOTOGRAPH OF THE first St. Albans depot and general office buildings was taken a little later and from a slightly different angle than the one on the previous page. It appears as though another shop building has been built to the west of the depot. (Jim Murphy Collection)

butter train, as well as numerous extra freight trains stop at the Milton depot, which was located only about a block from his home.

In late 1849, as the grade moved ever closer to St. Albans, a group of interested citizens of that town pledged sums of money ranging from $5 to $400—a total of $1,475—to the Vermont & Canada if it would build its depot on the "south side of the Lake Road on the same pieces and parcels of land this day bounded by Abel Houghton, Gardner G. Smith, and John Watson." The original hand-written document containing this pledge is in the company files to this day.

Throughout 1850 the rails moved northward. Finally, by mid-October, 1850, rails had been laid over the entire main line from Essex Junction to St. Albans. The last rails were laid on October 17, and on the following day the first passenger train entered the town over the new road. It consisted of a passenger train from Montpelier, and had on board the directors and officials of both the Vermont Central and the Vermont & Canada roads, as well as members of the legislature from Franklin County, who at the time were attending the annual session of that body in Montpelier.

This historic train was received with the blowing of whistles and the ringing of bells, amid loud cheers from the large crowd that had gathered at the depot. The diminutive "Abigail Adams" pulled the train, and she aroused much curiosity on the part of everyone in attendance. This event had to be at the top of the list of many great achievements

that John Smith had accomplished in his successful and productive lifetime.

The depot and general office building at St. Albans was to serve as the headquarters of the road. It was a large brick structure that contained about twenty rooms that were to be used as offices by the trustees, managers, and officials. The passenger depot portion consisted of a train shed with two through tracks, as well as the normal waiting room and ticket facilities. In addition, a one-story brick ell also housed offices.

By this time, a decision had been reached to cross into New York State by means of a bridge over the narrow foot of Lake Champlain at a point were the Richelieu River joined the lake. A line was surveyed north from St. Albans to Swanton, then northwesterly from Swanton across the entrance to Missisquoi Bay to Alburgh. The latter village was located a short distance from Rouses Point, New York, where the Vermont & Canada would connect with the Ogdensburgh road. The route that had earlier been surveyed to Highgate and on to the International Boundary was not pursued further at this time.

Construction crews worked through the fall and into the winter, and Alburgh was reached on January 10, 1851. The entrance to Missisquoi Bay was bridged by a 4,200-foot pile trestle, and both passenger and freight trains commenced operating immediately. This 23.9-mile segment from St. Albans to Alburgh made St. Albans the exact mid-point on the line between Essex Junction and Alburgh. However,

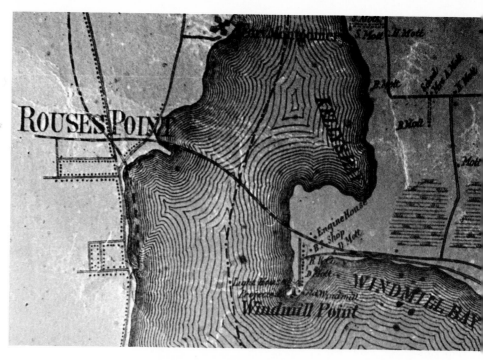

THIS 1858 WALLING'S MAP of Franklin County is interesting in that it shows the original Alburgh yard on Windmill Point on the shore of Lake Champlain—nearly three miles west of the village. A much larger yard was soon constructed on the edge of Alburgh Village. This map shows the crossing of the lake by the rail line to Rouses Point, New York. (Jim Murphy Collection)

when the rails finally reached the shore of Lake Champlain at the point where the navigable Richelieu River and the lake, join, the trouble began.

The steamboat interests on the lake who had heretofore enjoyed a freighting monopoly bitterly opposed the bridging of the lake, claiming such a structure would seriously impede, if not curtail, water traffic between the states and Canada. Legislatures convened and there was much oratory—both pro and con. When the issue ultimately came to a vote, however, the Vermont & Canada was denied permission by the State of New York to bridge the one mile of open water. Meanwhile, from January 10 until the lake thawed in April, both passengers and freight were carried across the lake on the ice. After the ice went out in the spring, this segment was covered by steam and tow boats. The "Ethan Allen" was the first ferry boat so engaged. Such movements, however, were not only costly, they were also dangerous.

But the ingenious civil engineer of the Vermont & Canada, Henry R. Campbell, and the superintendent of the Northern Railroad of New York, C. L. Schlater, saved the day for the railroads—at least to a degree. They jointly conceived the scheme of building trestles from each shore towards the center of the lake. A 100-foot channel, which would provide adequate room for the passage of the largest lake vesels, would be left open. This expanse would then be covered by a "ferry" which was actually nothing more than a long barge with rails laid on its deck. A steam boiler and winch were placed on the barge, and the vessel was attached to the main bridge structure by cables running through blocks. This whole affair could then be winched into position in a matter of minutes to permit trains to pass. This device went into operation in September, 1851, and although it wasn't perfect, it was sufficiently funcional to serve the roads for seventeen years. The original trestlework cost $40,000 and the floating section and its mechanism cost another $20,000.

In 1868, a more costly conventional swing span was constructed with the approval of the New York legislature, and Congress subsequently established a railway mail route across the lake on this line. The original structure, however, was the final link in an all-railroute connecting Boston with Ogdensburgh. A dream had finally become a reality.

In 1851, the Vermont & Canada officials deemed that

twelve miles per hour was a "proper" rate of speed for freight trains. Fifteen miles per hour was regarded as the optimum for "express freight trains," while passenger trains were permitted to travel at thirty miles per hour. Freight shipments could cover the 284 miles from Rouses Point to Boston in thirty-six hours, including regular terminal stops.

The cost of construction of the line from Essex Junction to Alburgh was about $1,350,000, of which $619,450 had been provided by subscriptions and notes from Smith, Brainerd, and Clark. The remaining $730,550 represented a debt to the corporation, with little likelihood of the directors successfully finding a way to pay it off through normal means. But then we must not forget that John Smith was not your normal financier. From the beginning he had been acutely aware of the fact that his project was badly under-capitalized, and it was in August of 1849 that he had started his efforts to persuade Charles Paine of the Vermont Central to lease the Vermont & Canada for fifty years at $108,000 per year. As mentioned earlier, not only did the Vermont Central directors agree to the idea, they also signed the lease which included a clause that gave the Vermont & Canada the right to take over control of the lessee if the Vermont Central defaulted on a semi-annual payment and to retain control until such time as the back payments were made up from net earnings. The deal that Smith's nimble mind concocted and sold to another shrewd Yankee entrepreneur is almost mind-boggling.

Meanwhile, to the west, the 118-mile Northern Railroad of New York had opened for service in late October, 1850. When the Vermont & Canada and the Northern Railroad solved the dilemma of bridging the lake, and the through route between Boston and Ogdensburgh had become a reality, it was only fitting that an appropriate celebration be held. Of course, as the railroads were being built, local celebrations were held at various points along the line, but it was for Boston to stage the celebration to end all celebrations. That Boston should do so, however, is a bit ironic, as its capitalists had not exactly distinguished themselves with their financial backing of the project.

This three-day affair started on September 17, 1851, and was attended by no less personages than United States President Millard Fillmore, the Governor General of Canada, Lord Elgin, and the featured speaker for the event,

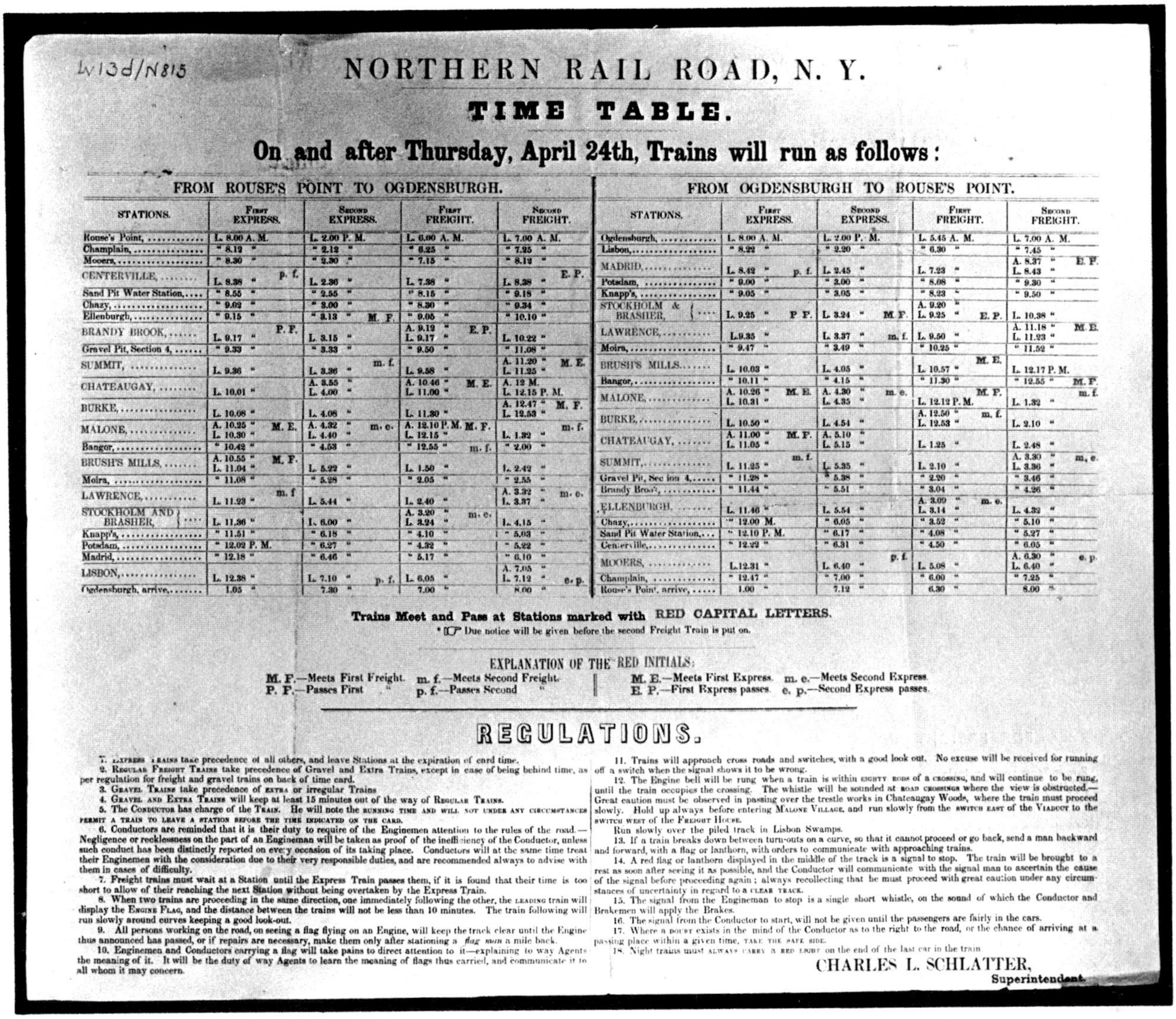

NORTHERN RAIL ROAD, N. Y.
TIME TABLE.
On and after Thursday, April 24th, Trains will run as follows:

STATIONS.	FIRST EXPRESS.	SECOND EXPRESS.	FIRST FREIGHT.	SECOND FREIGHT.
Rouse's Point,	L. 8.00 A. M.	L. 2.00 P. M.	L. 6.00 A. M.	L. 7.00 A. M.
Champlain,	" 8.12 "	" 2.12 "	" 6.25 "	" 7.25 "
Mooers,	" 8.30 "	" 2.30 "	" 7.15 "	" 8.12 "
CENTERVILLE,	L. 8.38 "	L. 2.36 "	L. 7.36 "	L. 8.38 "
Sand Pit Water Station,	" 8.55 "	" 2.55 "	" 8.15 "	" 9.18 "
Chazy,	" 9.02 "	" 3.00 "	" 8.30 "	" 9.34 "
Ellenburgh,	" 9.15 "	" 3.13 "	" 9.05 "	" 10.10 "
BRANDY BROOK,	L. 9.17 "	L. 3.15 "	A. 9.12 " / L. 9.17 "	E. P. 10.22 "
Gravel Pit, Section 4,	" 9.33 "	" 3.33 "	" 9.50 "	" 11.06 "
SUMMIT,	L. 9.36 "	L. 3.36 "	L. 9.58 "	A. 11.20 " / L. 11.23 "
CHATEAUGAY,	L. 10.01 "	A. 3.55 " / L. 4.00 "	A. 10.46 " / L. 11.00 "	A. 12 M. / L. 12.15 P. M.
BURKE,	L. 10.08 "	L. 4.05 "	L. 11.30 "	A. 12.47 " / L. 12.53 "
MALONE,	A. 10.25 " / L. 10.30 "	A. 4.32 " / L. 4.40 "	A. 12.10 P. M. M. F. / L. 12.15 "	L. 1.32 "
Bangor,	" 10.42 "	" 4.53 "	" 12.55 "	" 2.00 "
BRUSH'S MILLS,	A. 10.55 " / L. 11.04 "	L. 5.22 "	L. 1.50 "	L. 2.42 "
Moira,	" 11.08 "	" 5.28 "	" 2.05 "	" 2.55 "
LAWRENCE,	L. 11.23 "	L. 5.44 "	L. 2.40 "	A. 3.32 " / L. 3.37 "
STOCKHOLM AND BRASHER,	L. 11.36 "	L. 6.00 "	A. 3.20 " / L. 3.24 "	L. 4.15 "
Knapp's,	" 11.51 "	" 6.18 "	" 4.10 "	" 5.03 "
Potsdam,	" 12.02 P. M.	" 6.27 "	" 4.32 "	" 5.32 "
Madrid,	" 12.18 "	" 6.46 "	" 5.17 "	" 5.10 "
LISBON,	L. 12.38 "	L. 7.10 "	L. 6.05 "	A. 7.05 " / L. 7.12 "
Ogdensburgh, arrive,	1.05 "	7.30 "	7.00 "	8.00 "

STATIONS.	FIRST EXPRESS.	SECOND EXPRESS.	FIRST FREIGHT.	SECOND FREIGHT.
Ogdensburgh,	L. 8.00 A. M.	L. 2.00 P. M.	L. 5.45 A. M.	L. 7.00 A. M.
Lisbon,	" 8.22 "	" 2.20 "	" 6.30 "	" 7.45 "
MADRID,	L. 8.42 "	L. 2.45 "	L. 7.23 "	A. 8.37 " / E. F.
Potsdam,	" 9.00 "	" 3.00 "	" 8.08 "	" 9.30 "
Knapp's,	" 9.05 "	" 3.05 "	" 8.23 "	" 9.50 "
STOCKHOLM & BRASHER,	L. 9.25 "	L. 3.24 "	L. 9.25 "	L. 10.38 "
LAWRENCE,	L. 9.35 "	L. 3.37 "	L. 9.50 "	A. 11.18 " / L. 11.23 "
Moira,	" 9.47 "	" 3.49 "	" 10.25 "	" 11.52 "
BRUSH'S MILLS,	L. 10.03 "	L. 4.05 "	L. 10.57 "	L. 12.17 P. M.
Bangor,	" 10.11 "	" 4.15 "	" 11.30 "	" 12.55 "
MALONE,	A. 10.26 " / L. 10.31 "	A. 4.30 " / L. 4.35 "	L. 12.12 P. M.	L. 1.32 "
BURKE,	L. 10.50 "	L. 4.51 "	A. 12.50 " / L. 12.53 "	L. 2.10 "
CHATEAUGAY,	A. 11.00 " / L. 11.05 "	A. 5.10 " / L. 5.15 "	L. 1.25 "	L. 2.48 "
SUMMIT,	L. 11.25 "	L. 5.35 "	L. 2.10 "	A. 3.30 " / L. 3.36 "
Gravel Pit, Sec ion 4,	" 11.28 "	" 5.38 "	" 2.20 "	" 3.46 "
Brandy Brook,	" 11.44 "	" 5.51 "	" 3.04 "	" 4.26 "
ELLENBURGH,	L. 11.46 "	L. 5.54 "	L. 3.14 "	L. 4.32 "
Chazy,	" 12.00 P. M.	" 6.05 "	" 3.52 "	" 5.10 "
Sand Pit Water Station,	" 12.10 P. M.	" 6.17 "	" 4.08 "	" 5.27 "
Centerville,	" 12.22 "	" 6.31 "	" 4.50 "	" 6.05 "
MOOERS,	L.12.31 "	L. 6.40 "	L. 5.08 "	A. 6.30 " / L. 6.40 "
Champlain,	" 12.47 "	" 7.00 "	" 6.00 "	" 7.25 "
Rouse's Point, arrive,	1.00 "	7.12 "	6.30 "	8.00 "

Trains Meet and Pass at Stations marked with RED CAPITAL LETTERS.

Due notice will be given before the second Freight Train is put on.

EXPLANATION OF THE RED INITIALS:

M. F.—Meets First Freight.	m. f.—Meets Second Freight.
P. F.—Passes First "	p. f.—Passes Second "
M. E.—Meets First Express.	m. e.—Meets Second Express.
E. P.—First Express passes.	e. p.—Second Express passes.

REGULATIONS.

1. EXPRESS TRAINS take precedence of all others, and leave Stations at the expiration of card time.
2. REGULAR FREIGHT TRAINS take precedence of Gravel and Extra Trains, except in case of being behind time, as per regulation for freight and gravel trains on back of time card.
3. GRAVEL TRAINS take precedence of EXTRA or irregular Trains
4. GRAVEL AND EXTRA TRAINS will keep at least 15 minutes out of the way of REGULAR TRAINS.
5. The CONDUCTOR has charge of the Train. He will note the RUNNING TIME AND WILL NOT UNDER ANY CIRCUMSTANCES PERMIT A TRAIN TO LEAVE A STATION BEFORE THE TIME INDICATED ON THE CARD.
6. Conductors are reminded that it is their duty to require of the Enginemen attention to the rules of the road.— Negligence or recklessness on the part of an Engineman will be taken as proof of the inefficiency of the Conductor, unless such conduct has been distinctly reported on every occasion of its taking place. Conductors will at the same time treat their Enginemen with the consideration due to their very responsible duties, and are recommended always to advise with them in cases of difficulty.
7. Freight trains must wait at a Station before the Express Train passes them, if it is found that their time is too short to allow of their reaching the next Station without being overtaken by the Express Train.
8. When two trains are proceeding in the same direction, one immediately following the other, the LEADING train will display the ENGINE FLAG, and the distance between the trains will not be less than 10 minutes. The train following will run slowly around curves keeping a good look-out.
9. All persons working on the road, on seeing a flag flying on an Engine, will keep the track clear until the Engine thus announced has passed, or if repairs are necessary, make them only after stationing a flag man a mile back.
10. Enginemen and Conductors carrying a flag will take pains to direct attention to it—explaining to way Agents the meaning of it. It will be the duty of way Agents to learn the meaning of flags thus carried, and communicate it to all whom it may concern.

11. Trains will approach cross roads and switches, with a good look out. No excuse will be received for running off a switch when the signal shows it to be wrong.
12. The Engine bell will be rung when a train is within EIGHTY RODS of a CROSSING, and will continue to be rung, until the train occupies the crossing. The whistle will be sounded at ROAD CROSSINGS where the view is obstructed.— Great caution must be observed in passing over the trestle works in Chateaugay Woods, where the train must proceed slowly. Hold up always before entering MALONE VILLAGE, and run slowly from the SWITCH EAST of the VIADUCT to the SWITCH WEST of the FREIGHT HOUSE.

Run slowly over the piled track in Lisbon Swamps.
13. If a train breaks down between turn-outs on a curve, so that it cannot proceed or go back, send a man backward and forward, with a flag or lanthorn, with orders to communicate with approaching trains.
14. A red flag or lanthorn displayed in the middle of the track is a signal to stop. The train will be brought to a rest as soon after seeing it as possible, and the Conductor will communicate with the signal man to ascertain the cause of the signal before proceeding again; always recollecting that he must proceed with great caution under any circumstances of uncertainty in regard to a CLEAR TRACK.
15. The signal from the Engineman to stop is a single short whistle, on the sound of which the Conductor and Brakemen will apply the Brakes.
16. The signal from the Conductor to start, will not be given until the passengers are fairly in the cars.
17. Where a DOUBT exists in the mind of the Conductor as to the right to the road, or the chance of arriving at a passing place within a given time, TAKE THE SAFE SIDE.
18. Night trains must ALWAYS CARRY A RED LIGHT on the end of the last car in the train

CHARLES L. SCHLATTER,
Superintendent.

THIS NORTHERN RAILROAD of New York employees' timetable shows the schedules of both "Express" and freight trains and their connections with the Vermont & Canada during the first years of operation. The "Regulations" for operating employees make interesting reading. (Wilbur Collection, University of Vermont)

---

the renowned orator Daniel Webster. Webster spoke literally for hours to a large audience at the State House, but somehow he managed to never once mention railroads! His comments for the occasion apparently were on a much more nebulous theme. Nonetheless, all accounts of the celebration seem to agree that the famous orator was never in finer form—never mind the content of his remarks.

There were spectacular parades featuring an impressive array of marching units, floats, and the latest in railroad equipment, all accompanied by much flag waving and cheering. An express wagon loaded with ten barrels of flour made its way along the winding parade route, draped with a white and beige banner that proclaimed the real reason for the celebration:

WESTERN VIRGINIA FLOUR, VIA OHIO RIVER, GREAT LAKES, OGDENSBURGH, AND VERMONT RAILROAD. 772 BARRELS FROM ONE MILL—CONSIGNED TO LYMAN REED & COMPANY, BOSTON.
DISTANCE OF TRANSPORTATION 1,000 MILES
TIME OF TRANSPORTATION 12 DAYS

FREIGHT PER BARREL $1.05 PER BARREL FROM THE OHIO RIVER TO BOSTON

Clearly one of the most spectacular features of the parade, though, were two locomotives, each being hauled through the streets of Boston behind sixteen Percherons. One was a 17-ton locomotive named the "Potomac," which had just been completed by the Globe Locomotive Works. The other was a Boston Locomotive Works product, the "Elvira," which was escorted by an army of 350 boilermakers, machinists, and others who had been involved in its construction.

During the three days, there were fireworks everywhere. On the evening of the last day, the festivities were capped off with a great dinner that was served to a throng of 3,600 people in a pavilion on the Common that had been erected especially for the event. The meal was followed by more speeches, and then the great Boston Railroad Jubilee was history. But for those in attendance, it was not quickly forgotten.

THIS UNUSUALLY SHARP photograph from the 1850s shows the Malone shop facilities on the Northern Railroad of New York. At least 48 shop men have taken time out from their labors to pose for the photographer. (Jim Shaughnessy Collection, from THE RUTLAND ROAD)

Chapter III

The Early Years 1850-1862

JOSIAH QUINCY, JR.—A BOSTON ARISTOCRAT, FORMER MAYOR OF *that city for three terms, and an established railroad financier—came to the Vermont Central as its treasurer in 1850. Charles Paine was impressed with Quincy's credentials, and he was given virtually unlimited powers and authority to do almost anything he desired with the road's finances and property.*

In this regard, the Vermont Central directors voted at their August meeting that Quincy's signature would be binding upon the corporation and that he might be authorized to "pledge any of the company's bonds or scrip as security for its debts and as security for any debts or liabilities which he shall incur in his private capacity for the use or benefit of the corporation." A few days later the directors of the Vermont & Canada—Paine, Smith, Brainerd, and S.S. Lewis—voted him virtually the same powers. The acquiescence of these men in handing over their powers to a relative stranger was incredible enough in itself, but the conditions by which they agreed to do so made it even more unbelievable.

Quincy made it clear from the start that he planned to conduct virtually all of his work from his Boston office. He did not demand an annual salary, but he did insist on the right to purchase unlimited quantities of future stock issues of either road at 50 percent of par value. He wasted little time in exercising this option.

In May, 1850, Quincy announced an offer of 50,000 shares of Vermont Central stock. He didn't wait for the public to react to the offer—he immediately subscribed to over 10,300 of these shares himself, giving in payment over $300,000 in personal notes and only a negligible amount of cash.

Harlow, in his classic **Steelways of New England**, states that by November, 1851, Quincy was "no longer able to raise funds, either on his own private notes or on the company's, and certain irregularities had come to light which shocked the business world. He had made extensive use of the company's bonds for his private ends, had sold 1,240 shares of stock belonging to the company, and had sold 3,462 shares that did not yet exist. In justification, Quincy asserted that he had been made sole judge of what was best for the company, and that by the directors' act, he had a perfect right to use the name or the securities of the corporation in any manner he deemed advisable."

One of the directors, Thomas Gray, stated later during court proceedings against Quincy, that "the directors understood so perfectly that we had given absolute power to Mr. Quincy to do what he pleased that we did not feel authorized to step behind his counter to look at the Corporation's books, or to ask what he was doing." It was estimated at the time that Quincy's financial misdeeds had probably cost the railroad at least a half-million dollars.

The financial irregularities and mismanagement by Quincy, of course, soon became common knowledge in the financial circles of the Northeast. The net effect of these monetary indiscretions was that the credit of the Vermont Central was ruined. In July, 1852, the trustees under the first mortgage bonds took possession of the railroad. Their first action was to appoint a committee to investigate the management of the railroad during the past two years. It wasn't long before they found things to cause their hair to figuratively, if not literally, stand up straight!

Correspondence was found indicating that the directors were aware of Belknap's questionable financial standing at the time he was awarded the contract to build the road with the condition that he purchase one-fourth of the initial stock issue. When he failed with the road built only to Bolton, he was unable to pay his bills, including his obligations to his subcontractors and workers alike.

The president of the Vermont Central, Charles Paine, came under chastisement. The investigators disclosed that Paine's annual salary was $5,000, with such a figure to be paid for a period of seven years. This figure was approximately three times that paid any other Vermont railroad president of the day. At the end of seven years, provisions were found whereby the salary was to be renegotiated. In addition, Paine had received considerable capital gain on the acreage he sold to the railroad for its headquarters and facilities in Northfield.

It was also revealed that Paine had received profits from

THIS IS THE Vermont Central's "Montpelier" as built by the Boston Locomotive Works in April, 1852. **It was rebuilt in late December, 1858.** (Collection of Donald A. Somerville)

the car-building activities of the road in his Northfield shops, and that in 1852 alone he had been paid $43,619 for "incidental claims" above and beyond income received in the form of salary, commissions, and land damages. It was further learned that the year before, in addition to his salary, Paine had received over $37,000 from such things as endorsing notes, interest, director's fees, and rentals of land and buildings.

This all came at a time when the Vermont Central's financial picture was changing dramatically. The road had enjoyed a marvelous operating ratio of 38 percent in 1850-51, but that comparison of income with expenses had sky-rocketed to 118 percent for the fiscal year 1852. In other words, the company was now suddenly operating at a deficit. It was costing $1.18 to earn each dollar of revenue!

When all of this information became public in the spring of 1853, the trustees voted Paine out of office. He was replaced by W. Raymond Lee, who was hired away from the Rutland & Burlington Railroad, where he had been filling a similar position. Lee's stay was short, however, as a year later he moved on to the presidency of the Northern Railroad of New York.

After being forced out of office, Paine left his Northfield home and settled in Waco, Texas, where he again involved himself in railroad promotion activities. Within a few months, however, he contracted dysentary and passed away twenty-six days later on July 6, 1853, at the age of 54. His passing, particularly under such circumstances, was most unfortuante. This hard-nosed native Vermonter had, for most of his adult life, done much for his town and his state—both of which he was fiercely proud.

In his home town of Northfield he had been owner of a woolen mill for many years, operated a hotel, and owned large amounts of land. In the political arena, he had served in the state's highest office—that of the governor. His early railroad activities, of course, had been instrumental in getting the first railroad built in the state.

Paine, a Harvard graduate, had donated land for what later was to become Norwich University. He also provided money for equipping the school. Although not a church-goer, Paine provided funds to build a Congregational church in the village. He also gave the Catholic church land for a new church and cemetery. Paine was an animal lover, and he appreciated good cattle and horses. His well-kept 135 by 165-foot fish pond on his hotel grounds in the center of the village was long a Northfield landmark. However, his greatest monument was the railroad that he had been so responsible for building.

Not long after Paine left the Vermont railroad scene, the Vermont Central trustees signed a contract with the newly formed firm of Smith, Brainerd & Company to build and repair Vermont Central freight cars at the Vermont & Canada's St. Albans shops. This firm was comprised of Worthington C. Smith and J. Gregory Smith—sons of John Smith—and two Brainerds. Both of the younger Smiths were to acquire top positions on the Vermont Central and the Vermont & Canada roads in 1858, following the death of their venerable father.

Trustees were now operating both roads, and John Smith saw this as his golden opportunity to secure complete control of railroad operations from Alburgh to Windsor. There were times when any means seemed to justify the

THE "RIDEAU" WAS built by the Essex Company in 1851 for the Northern Railroad of New York. When that road was renamed the Ogdensburgh & Lake Champlain, it became the O&LC's Number 3. (Jim McFarlane Collection)

end. With both roads suffering from turmoil at this time, a small group of stockholders succeeded in securing a court order granting them permission to examine the books of both roads. Almost immediately after this court order was issued, the records at Alburgh, Northfield, and Windsor all were destroyed in a series of mysterious fires.

The Vermont Central's first southern connection toward Boston was the Cheshire Railroad, but in 1853 this situation changed considerably. A gentleman by the name of Onslow Stearns, who was president of the Northern Railroad of New Hampshire which ran between White River Junction and Concord, New Hampshire, became both a director and the superintendent of the Vermont Central. Needless to say, he soon did everything in his power to see that traffic between Boston and the north and mid-west was routed over his road through New Hampshire. This, of course, greatly upset the directors of the Cheshire Railroad. The following year saw an agreement signed between officials of the Northern Railroad of New Hampshire, the Vermont Central, and the Ogdensburgh road requiring exclusive interchange of traffic. It is remarkable that president W. Raymond Lee signed for both the Vermont Central and the Ogdensburgh road, while Onslow Stearns affixed his signature as president of the Northern of New Hampshire and as director of the Vermont Central.

Meanwhile, there was feuding and unrest within the Vermont Central-Vermont & Canada hierarchy. The lease payments for the Vermont & Canada had been paid according to the 1849 agreement until December 1, 1854. However, the Vermont Central defaulted on the next $54,000 semi-annual payment, and president John Smith of

the Vermont & Canada immediately notified the Vermont Central that his road would take control of both roads as provided for in the contract. As might be expected, the trustees of the Vermont Central refused to hand over their line. Smith wasted little time in going to the courts with the matter, which predictably ruled in his favor. The Vermont Central trustees were ordered to deliver their road to Smith, which they did on July 2, 1855. The trustees continued their fight in the courts, and in 1856 the decision was reversed.

Violent quarrelling on another issue was going on at this same time. Four of the seven Vermont & Canada directors were outraged about the road's contract with the car-building firm of Smith, Brainerd & Company. The three directors not so inclined were Smith, Brainerd and Joseph Clark, the Vermont & Canada's three leading lights. Hoping to protect their own interests, the four outraged directors refused to attend board meetings. Smith, Brainerd, and Clark found themselves unable to hold legal meetings, as a quorum was never present. The three, however, were not stymied for long. They decided to act in their capacity as trustees for the first mortgage bondholders, and in May, 1856, they petitioned the court for permission to repossess the railroad on the legal ground that the directors of the railroad had not fulfilled the firm's financial obligations—the major item being the settlement of a bill for 100 boxcars built by the firm of Smith, Brainerd & Company. Considering these three were directly involved in all facets of the controversy—as directors and trustees of the railroad and with the car-building firm—one may be astounded at how far legal manipulations were permitted to go.

ENGINEER EMERSON RANDALL stands by the tender of the "Deer" in front of the Northern Railroad of New York's Malone roundhouse. This engine was built by the Kirk Company of Cambridgeport, Massachusetts, in 1850. (Ed Steel Collection)

The other four directors immediately obtained an injunction which was intended to prohibit the trustees from using the funds of either company to pay the bill for the cars. However, a week later the injunction was overruled by a court order, and the four realized they had been out-maneuvered. Thereupon, they decided to settle, and a compromise of sorts was reached. The bill for the 100 new cars would be paid, and an order for 200 additional cars would be cancelled, but a penalty of $35,000 would be invoked for the cancellation of the order, and the railroad would take over the physical property and operation of the car-building firm at a cost of $210,000.

In 1857, the two roads operated a total of 42 wood-burning locomotives; 29 passenger cars; 10 baggage, express and mail cars; and 753 freight cars. There were 88 grade crossings and 30 crossings located above or below grade between Alburgh and Windsor. Crank-type switches were being used, and there were some 90 main line switches in operation. Rail size ranged from 54 to 64 pounds per yard, and there were an average of 2,058 hemlock and tamarack ties per mile. The main line consisted of 85 miles of straight track and 34 miles of curved track, with a minimum radius of 1,146 feet. The maximum grade on the line was 45 feet to the mile, which figured out to about 1.2 percent.

It is interesting to note the quantity and variety of structures along the line for this period. The 1857 annual report to the railroad commissioners listed the following: 28 passenger houses, 17 freight houses, 10 engine houses, 2

repair shops, 31 water stations, 7 dwellings, 39 wood sheds, 5 turntables, 2 car houses, and 4 ice houses. The 10 engine houses contained a total of 42 stalls.

Injury and death had been a part of railroad work right from the beginning. In 1857, two employees were killed by being thrown from cars, and four others were killed while walking or standing on the track. Five other persons, including a young boy, were killed by trains while trespassing on railroad property.

During the first few months of 1858, heavy repairs were made to a structure spanning a small brook in Roxbury, and to the long bridges spanning the entrance to Missisquoi Bay and extending from the shore to the middle of Lake Champlain at Alburgh. The commissioners were upset that such repairs had not been attended to sooner, but they were relieved that they had been finally taken care of.

A continuing issue with both the travelling public and the railroad commissioners was the awkward and unpopular change of cars at Essex Junction required of all passengers bound to or from Burlington. The charter of the Vermont & Canada required that road to form a connection with the Rutland & Burlington within 13 years from the date of its incorporation—October, 1845. No such connection had been formed by 1858, and the officials of the railroad did not seem particularly sympathetic to the complaints of the public nor to the directives of the commissioners.

However, on January 19, 1858, the directors authorized the president to have a new route surveyed for a direct

Continued on page 51

THE OGDENSBURGH & Lake Champlain's "St. Lawrence" was built by Hinkley in October, 1849. (Whitney Maxfield Collection)

THIS CIRCULAR CLEARLY indicates that the abuse and misuse of railroad passes began at an early date. (Wilbur Collection, University of Vermont)

THIS VERMONT & CANADA timetable of July 23, 1855, shows all regular trains operating between the shore of Lake Champlain at West Alburgh to the Connecticut River at Windsor. (Wilbur Collection, University of Vermont)

CIRCULAR.

...ractices under the system of Free Passes on the Vt. Central, Rutland & Burlington and Ogdensburgh Railroads, ...ome so extended, that no restraint less than limiting the authority of granting free tickets, to the President and ...endent of each road, is believed to be sufficient to correct what has become a serious abuse. The following in... ...s have accordingly been issued to Conductors.

FREE PASSENGERS.

Instructions to Conductors.

...asses signed by the President, a Trustee, or the Superintendent, will be respected during the time for which they ...l.

... Passes, verbal or written, of officers charged with duties, which extend over the road including different points, ...espected for one passage, the pass, if written, to be taken up, and written or verbal to be reported to the Super-

... persons named in the following list will be passed till further notice. No pass will be considered to include ...y of the recipient, unless especially named.

... general passes will terminate on the 1st day of July, each year.

...ductors will daily report names of "free passengers" under special and annual passes, to the Superintendent, ...n no account, except in cases of charity, deviate from these orders.

...ases of emergency, such as accidents, Rule 2 may be modified at the discretion of Conductors, to pass parties, in ...e of the Corporation or Trustees.

...irectors of the Companies above named, are respectfully requested to conform to the foregoing instructions, in ...g from giving free passes to others than members of their families.

...rs of families are understood to mean persons actually resident with the head, to whom the ticket is issued.

W. RAYMOND LEE,
President.

...RY 2d, 1854.

VERMONT & CANADA RAILROAD TIME TABLE,
MONDAY, JULY 23, 1855.—NO. 1.

Down Trains—from Rouse's Point to Windsor.   Up Trains—from Windsor to Rouse's Point.

No. 1. Mail.	No. 2. Acc'n.	No. 3. Express.	No. 4.	No. 5. Freight.	No. 6. Freight.	No. 7. Night Fr.	No. 8. Freight.	STATIONS.	Dist. S. St.	Total Dist.	No. 9. Mail.	No. 10. Acc'n.	No. 11. Acc'n.	No. 12.	No. 13.	No. 14. Freight.	No. 15. Freight.	No. 16. Night Fr.
6.00	3.50	7.55						Rouse's Point.			7.30	2.10	7.45					
6.07	3.55	8.00			3.30	4.30		W.Alburgh	0.9	0.9	7.25	2.02	7.41			6.00		2.30
6.14	4.07	8.07			3.43	4.45		Alburgh	2.5	3.4	7.18	1.52	7.34			5.45		2.18
6.22	4.16	8.16			3.57	5.00		Alburgh Springs	3.3	6.7	7.09	1.42	7.26			5.30 5.25		2.00 1.56
6.35	4.21	8.31			4.25	5.40		Swanton	7.2	13.9	6.53	1.25	7.11			4.45		1.15
6.54	4.42	8.49			5.29	7.10		St. Albans	9.0	22.9	6.35	1.00 12.05	6.51			5.45 3.36		12.30 12.22
7.19	5.11	9.11			6.14	8.00		Georgia	9.6	32.5	6.18	11.44	6.27			2.55 2.45		11.30
7.26	5.18	9.18			6.40	8.25 8.34		Milton	3.2	35.7	6.06	11.33	6.20			2.30 2.20		11.10
7.42	5.33	9.33			7.28	9.20		Colchester	7.2	42.9	5.51	11.18	6.01			1.50		10.30
7.54 7.58	5.42 5.59	9.43 9.48			7.55 8.05	10.15		Essex Junc.	4.1	47.0	5.44 5.34	11.10 11.01	5.52			1.30 1.25	9.34 9.18	10.02 9.52
8.08	6.02	10.14			8.30	10.40		Williston	4.6	51.0	5.23	5.40				1.00	9.00	9.30
8.28	6.14				1.30 1.38	11.20 11.25		Richmond	4.7	55.7	5.10	10.39 5.30				12.55 12.25		
8.31	6.24				1.54 2.05	9.18	11.45	Jones	3.0	58.7	5.03	10.26				12.10	7.54 7.37	8.25 8.15
8.39	6.35				2.19	9.30	12.30	Bolton	3.0	61.7	4.56	10.20				11.20 11.12	7.22	8.00
8.56 9.00	6.56 7.00				2.56 3.10	10.10 10.15	1.10 1.15	Waterbury	7.0	68.7	4.43 4.40	10.00				10.35 10.25	6.42 6.35	7.10
9.15	7.15				3.35 3.40	10.44	1.40 1.45	Middlesex	5.1	73.8	4.29	9.44				10.07 10.00	6.14 6.10	6.29
9.30	7.30 7.33				4.00 4.15	11.15	2.05 2.10	Montpelier	6.5	80.3	4.14	9.30 7.14				9.50	5.45 5.40	6.03
9.52 9.57	7.52 7.57			5.20	3.30 3.50		2.55	Northfield	9.8	90.1	3.49 3.45	8.59 8.56					5.00 5.40	
10.15	8.15				6.10 6.20	4.35 4.40		Roxbury	7.1	97.2	3.29	8.40						
10.39	8.39				7.08 7.20	5.30 5.34	5.45	Braintree	8.5	105.7	3.08	8.14				2.55 2.30	4.10 4.05	
10.54	8.54				7.54 8.05	6.00 6.05	6.20	Randolph	5.6	111.3	2.54					2.00 1.55	3.35 3.25	
11.12	9.12				8.50 9.00	6.58 6.46	7.00	Bethel	7.1	118.4	2.40	7.44				1.15 1.10	2.55	
11.25	9.25				9.26 9.35	7.08 7.30	7.30	Royalton	4.9	123.3	2.25	7.31				12.45	1.55 1.50	
11.30 11.34	9.30 9.34				9.41 9.55	7.25 7.40	7.40 7.48	S.Royalton	1.8	125.1	2.20 2.18	7.27				12.35 12.20	1.40 1.15	
11.46	9.46				10.25 10.35	8.10 8.35	8.08	Sharon	4.9	130.0	2.08	7.14				11.12 12.15	12.46 12.36	
12.00	10.00				11.00 11.14	8.45 8.53	8.45	W.Hartford	5.6	135.6	1.54	7.00				11.00	12.15 11.55	
12.11	10.11				11.34 11.56	9.15 9.22	9.08	Woodstock	4.0	139.6	1.44	6.50				10.35 10.30	11.36 11.32	
12.16	10.16				11.54 12.00	9.30 9.50	9.18	W. R. Vil.	1.8	141.4	1.39	6.45				10.18	11.20 11.18	
12.20	10.20				12.10 12.42	9.50	9.25	W.R.Junc.	1.8	143.2	1.33	6.40 7.17				10.14	11.10 10.05	
1.52	6.47				1.14 1.30			N.Hartland	5.6	148.8	1.19	7.03					9.30 9.25	
2.02	6.57				1.54 2.10			Hartland	4.1	152.6	1.09	6.54					9.00 8.52	
2.10	7.10				2.30			Windsor	4.3	156.9	1.00	6.40					8.30	

Significations of Initials & occ'l figures at table, &c., the number of the Train. Fr., Freight; m. main; r. passes; c. action. Full Fare Figures denote meeting and passing of Trains. * Montpelier Junction.

PASSENGERS LEAVE		PASSENGERS ARRIVE AT
BURLINGTON for South & East		BURLINGTON from East and West
WINOOSKI		WINOOSKI from East and West
BURLINGTON for North & West 5.30 A.M. 10.45 A.M.		WINOOSKI TEN MINUTES earlier than the above.
WINOOSKI 5.40		
LEAVE MONTPELIER for South and East		LEAVE MONTPELIER for North and West

SPECIAL DIRECTIONS.

1. When a white flag or red flag is carried by an engine, at night, indicating that another engine or train is following, the engine bearing such flag must stop at every station, and at Montpelier Junction, and the Engineer must explain to the Station Agents and switchmen, and to the Engineers of other Engines and Conductors of other trains upon the road, the full meaning of the flag.

2. Freight Trains, must take the side track at Stations where a Passenger Train is expected.

3. No. 2 and 10 Trains will stop to leave passengers, at Falls Village and for Passengers, when flagged so to do. The Mail Train will not stop.

4. At 3 o'clock A. M. the right of any Train of the preceding day to the road ceases, and after that hour they will become irregular, and will keep out of the way of Passenger and Freight Trains, but otherwise may proceed to their destined points.

5. Observe strictly, the printed Rules and Regulations of March 1, 1854, for running Trains.

6. The rate of speed indicated above, must be strictly adhered to, and no effort will be made to recover lost time.

7. Mondays, No. 8 will take all live stock north of Northfield.

8. When regular trains are following each other out of time, or extra trains are not over the road, they must never leave a station less than TEN minutes after the preceding train, and then a close watch must be kept ahead by the Engineman and Fireman to prevent the possibility of a collision.

9. The Engineman on approaching a switch, will direct his eye to it as soon as it may be seen, and is not to attempt to pass it without being certain that the Target is right for his train, and is to have his train under such command as to stop it instantly if wrong. It will not be regarded as an excuse for the Engineman (if within his view) that the switch is wrong.

10. Trains No. 1, and 9, will proceed after waiting at meeting places five minutes, and take the road expecting to meet the opposing train at some way station.

11. Trains must keep off of their time. No. 3 Express Train will not stop at way stations Monday nights only.

12. Conductors will have charge of the Trains, and in no case permit a train to leave a station before its time. Enginemen will be equally responsible with the Conductor for keeping off the time of other trains.

13. No. 14 Conductor will have charge of the train. When north of Northfield, will have the right of road over Freight Trains Monday nights only.

14. Any prior special directions are revoked.

R. SHERBURNE, Supt.

THIS ARTIST'S SKETCH shows the Brattleboro, Vermont, station of the Vermont & Massachusetts Railroad as it looked in 1856. This area later became an integral part of the Central Vermont's north-south main line to the coast. (Lewis R. Brown, Inc., Collection)

THIS IS ANOTHER artist's sketch of the Brattleboro railroad facilities of the 1850s. (Lewis R. Brown, Inc., Collection)

THESE WOODBURNERS ARE carefully posed on the stone bridge of the Vermont Valley Railroad at **Brattleboro, probably in the 1860s.** (Both photos, Lewis R. Brown, Inc., Collection)

CONNECTICUT RIVER RAILROAD ENGINE 14 poses in the snow at Brattleboro. (Lewis R. Brown, Inc.)

NOTE THE UNUSUAL crossing sign extending between the two buildings at Brattleboro. Business seems to be good at the mill. (Lewis R. Brown, Inc., Collection)

1857 Vermont Central Line. 1857

OTIS KIMBALL, Agent, 108 State St., Boston.

WESTERN CONSIGNEES.

Chamberlin, Crawford & Co. Cleveland.	Hale, Barclay & Co. - Milwaukee.
E. R. Mathews, - - - Detroit.	Mather & Co. - - Chicago.

Watson's Press. 25 Doane St.

Boston, *Aug 4* 1857.

Duplicate.

RECEIVED in apparent good order, the following packages, contents and value unknown:

Tootle & Hanna

Plattsmouth

W R Howard N. T.

St Louis 86

757

Two Cases Mdse

V. C. Line.

RATES PER 100 POUNDS.

First Class ....Cents.

Second Class ....*Contract*........Cents.

Third Class ....Cents.

Fourth Class ....Cents.

Special ....Cents

As per Classification on back.

Marked and numbered as in the margin, which the VERMONT CENTRAL, OGDENSBURGH, and other Railroads agree to forward to Ogdensburgh, N. Y. and the NORTHERN TRANSPORTATION CO. agrees to forward thence by Steam, and deliver to their Agents in *St Louis* upon payment of freight therefor, as noted in the margin.

☞ The conditions of this contract are, that the dangers of fire, navigation, collisions, breakage of looking-glasses, and leakage of oil, molasses, liquors and other liquids are at the risk of the owner, and should a loss of any of said goods occur on the lakes or rivers, the charges to and at Ogdensburgh shall be paid by the owners of the goods, and in case of loss or damage for which the Line may be liable, it shall have the benefit of any insurance effected by or for account of the owner of the property so lost or damaged, and that the Line shall not be held accountable for any deficiency in contents of packages, if such packages are receipted for in good order by the consignee at the point contracted to. Goods in bond subject to Custom House regulations and expenses. Acids, Burning Fluid, Turpentine, Varnish, and similar combustibles, cannot be shipped by steam vessels, and if sent must be at the risk of the owner, until an opportunity offers for shipping by sail.

Otis Kimball Agent.

A Culum

THIS RARE 1857 Vermont Central paper covers a small shipment under a "contract" rate. The conditions stated in the last paragraph make interesting reading. (Philip R. Hastings Collection)

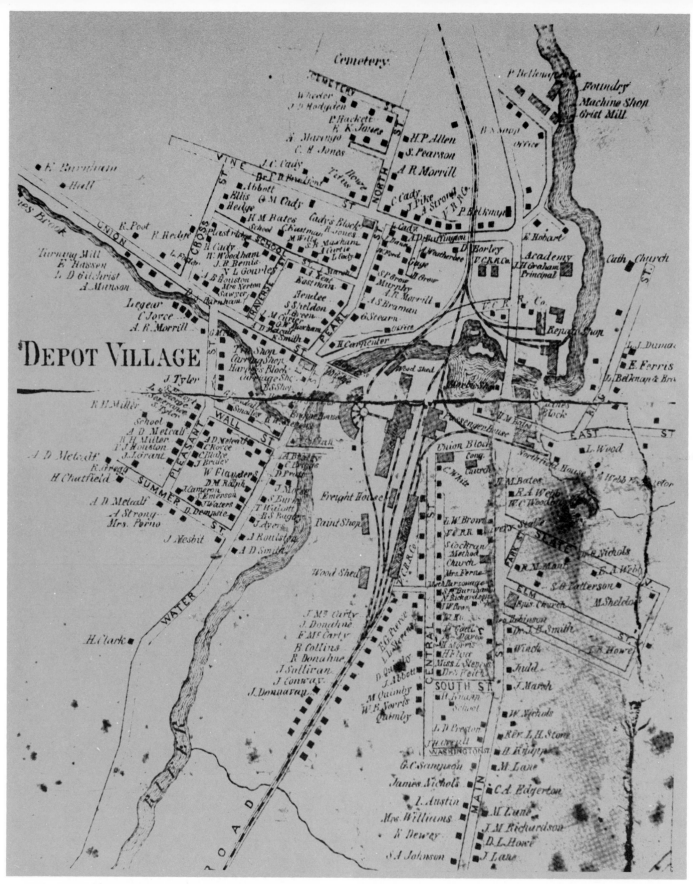

THIS 1858 WALLINGS MAP of Northfield clearly shows the Vermont Central trackage and facilities. Two things are particularly noteworthy—the track shown extending from the turntable to the rear of the machine shop; and the Northfield House built by Charles Paine for the accommodation of overnight passengers. During the very early operations passenger trains did not run at night and they were scheduled to "overnight" at the front steps of the hotel. (Jim Murphy Collection)

Vermont & Canada line into Burlington. The work was started on February 23, and the preliminary survey was completed within a month. Subsequently, a special meeting was held at Northfield at which a committee was appointed to make contracts for building the new line. This group was able to make contracts "upon very favorable terms for the construction of the whole work." Then, about six weeks later these same stockholders held another special meeting at which they inexplicably rescinded the earlier vote and the directors were instructed to terminate all plans for the construction of this line.

In 1858, the ambitious John Smith died at the age of 69. He had made the necessary arrangements, however, for his two sons—J. Gregory and Worthington C—to succeed him in the management of the two roads. John Gregory Smith became president of the Vermont Central and Worthington C. Smith ably filled this position with the Vermont & Canada for the next ten years. The latter road continued to be operated between 1858 and 1873 under receivership by trustees and managers, the chief of which was J. Gregory Smith.

J. Gregory inherited and developed many of the traits of his father. He possessed his father's untiring energy and fortitude, and he was intelligent, shrewd, ruthless, and arrogant. He was in love with his work, and at the same time was both a pragmatist and a dreamer. As a railroad executive, he dreamed of an empire much bigger than that which was now his. He could see expansion to Montreal, New York, and even to the Pacific Northwest. He was already the master of what lay before him, and serving simultaneously as president, trustee of the bondholders, and receiver in bankruptcy, his control was virtually absolute.

J. Gregory Smith, like his father, adopted the profession of law, being admitted to the bar in 1841. Like his father, he relinquished his active practice of law to engage himself in the railroad field. Smith served as governor of his native state in 1863-64, a position that reflects the prestige and honor which he had earned through his legal and executive abilities and reputation. His house and grounds, located on the corner of Smith and Congress Streets in St. Albans, were among the finest in the state. They afforded a view of the surrounding lake and mountain scenery that was virtually unsurpassed.

The Honorable Worthington C. Smith held a wide range of elected and appointed offices, both in government and in the private sector. He was owner of the St. Albans Foundry, president of the Vermont & Canada from 1858-1868, president of the Vermont Atwood Merino Sheep Club, and held many other positions over the years. He was born in St. Albans on April 23, 1823, was graduated from the University of Vermont in 1843, and studied law like his father and brother. After a short while, he gave up law and went into the iron manufacturing and distribution business. In 1863, he was elected local representative to the state legislature. During 1864-65, he was elected to the State Senate, serving in the latter year as president of the Senate. The following year he was elected as Vermont's representative to the Fortieth Congress of the United States.

In an unusual accident, engineer William Shattuck was killed on July 17, 1858. While handling the throttle of the mail train, he somehow fell from the locomotive cab while running at speed and was instantly killed.

At this time, it was standard practice to have the section men examine the track early every morning before the first trains passed, and in the winter this was frequently done before the passing of every passenger train. At Northfield all cars were inspected and passenger equipment was cleaned. Clergymen were allowed to travel at half fare, and a few mileage or commutation tickets were being sold.

THIS 1857 BROADSIDE shows how far one could travel by rail in this country at this relatively early date. (Wilbur Collection, University of Vermont)

The art of train order dispatching had not yet been refined to the degree it was to achieve in later years, and there were undoubtedly many strange orders issued which have been lost to history. One such order, however, is in the collection of W. R. Rowley of Richford, Vermont. It is dated October 7, 1859, and was addressed to "Frank Clatur, engineer: Dear Sir, You will please follow No. 9 mail train this P.M. to Rouses Point with engine Mohegan. The engine on the mail

which was supported on two cross ties placed close together. The joint between the rails was positioned over the space between the ties and the chair was firmly fastened to each rail. When this was done properly, both lateral and longitudinal movement of the rails was prevented; yet, there was said to be sufficient elasticity in the chair so as to cushion the joint from the shock of the passing wheels. Each of these chairs cost about sixty cents, and the officials, as well as the railroad commissioners, were convinced they were worth it.

During the year, the long bridge over the White River at West Hartford was rebuilt. It was a double lattice with arch beams on the side of each truss, and was considered to show excellent workmanship. Another long structure over the Winooski River at Williston was also rebuilt, as another lattice was added to each truss. The superstructures of all the major bridges on the line at this time were covered.

The Vermont & Canada's awesome bridge over the Lamoille River at Georgia was also rebuilt at a cost of $65,000. This, too, was of the double lattice type with arch beams on each side of the truss. The railroad commissioners were concerned by the fact that possibly these large structures contained too much timber, which would result in unnecessary weight and also increase the liability of decay.

In 1860, the Vermont Central and Vermont & Canada had a combined roster of 42 locomotives, 33 of which were in a weight range of 25 to 30 tons. These locomotives consumed 23,395 cords of wood during the year, and the stations and shops used another 4,518 cords. There were now 35 passenger cars of various types and 774 freight cars in service. Receipts for the year totaled $775,600 and expenses were $647,800.

On a wintry night in late January, 1860, a watchman at Ridley's Bridge was killed when a freight engine backed

J. GREGORY SMITH and Worthington C. Smith very successfully guided the destinies of the Vermont Central and the Vermont & Canada roads for many years upon the death of their father, John Smith, in 1858. (Both photos, Jim Murphy Collection)

train will carry red flag for your engine, which they will carry to the Point and you will carry a red flag for engine Winooski, which will follow your engine to the Point and return tomorrow on freight. You be careful to keep safe distance from the train and notify all concerned what your flag is for. You will return tomorrow on freight. Yours, E.F. Perkins, M.M." Engineer Clatur must have handled this personal but confusing message satisfactorily, because he was later to become the road's locomotive foreman.

The winter of 1859-60 was not a harsh one as Vermont winters go, and there was an unusually minor amount of damage to the railroad bed during the spring thaws. One problem that was plaguing the railroads at this time (and which plagues railroads to this day) was the excessive amount of wear on rail ends at the joints. It was at this time that it became common practice to stagger the joints and to always have solid ties supporting each joint. In addition, many roads were starting to use fishplates—heavy straps of steel about two feet long placed on both the inside and outside of the rails at all joints.

The Vermont Central, however, pioneered another technique. This made use of a newly invented cast iron or wrought iron device known as a "Howe chair." The rails rested on the bottom of this chair which had a wood base

THIS DAMAGED PHOTOGRAPH shows the steam-boat dock at Rouses Point, N.Y., in 1860. Trains ran **into the building, part of which served the travelling clientele as a hotel.** (Louis Cameron Collection)

over him during switching movements. In May, a track worker was found dead on the tracks in Northfield one morning. The report to the railroad commissioners stated that the deceased "was probably intoxicated and was run over by a train in the night."

Ties were being cut from hemlock, tamarack, spruce, birch, beech, and maple, but tamarack had been found to be the most durable by this time. The Vermont Central was treating its new ties against decay by a process known as "burnetizing." This treatment cost about eleven cents a tie and all ties were now being so treated before being put into place. The railroad invested in the equipment necessary for this treatment at a cost of $8,000, and company employees handled this work. Operating procedures now consisted of dividing the railroad into sections four or five miles in length, and the sectionmen were required to pass over the track before the first train in the morning and "frequently during the day." Each station agent was required to report to the superintendent the time of arrival and departure of each train. In case of accidents or delays on the road, the conductor of the train was required to have signals posted not less than 1,500 feet in each direction to guard against collision with approaching trains.

Construction was started on the new line between Winooski Bridge and the terminus of the Rutland & Burlington on the Burlington waterfront on February 16, 1860. The project was completed in May, 1861. This project, however, was undertaken by the railroad company rather

reluctantly. The travelling public had become more and more exasperated and vocal at the lack of direct connections at Burlington between the two roads, and they finally secured the backing of railroad commissioner Perkins Marsh in their quest to have something done about it. In time, a legislative mandate ordered that the work commence. It stated that "all passengers passing over the road between Rouses Point, or any intermediate Station, and Burlington, should be carried without delay and without change of cars, except in case of accident or emergency."

The survey, which was directed by the road's chief engineer, Daniel C. Linsley, completely bypassed the hill section of his native Burlington. It followed the southern edge of the marshy Intervale to a mountainous ridge of wind-blown sand that had formed near the lakeshore over the centuries. From there, the line headed south along the lake to a depot site at the corner of College and Lake Streets.

A great amount of fill had to be brought in to raise the grade an appropriate distance above the Intervale. This work progressed well, however. The real trouble was encountered when the 100-foot high ridge of sand was reached. Although it appeared quite stable, when the digging commenced it was found to be like quicksand. For each shovelful taken out, one or two more slid in. Engineer Linsley decided the only hope would be to tunnel a line through. Because of the nature of the material, however, this proved to be an ingenious and unique process.

THIS PHOTOGRAPH CLEARLY shows the North-field depot and offices, the shops, and the large roundhouse. The wye track leading to the Northfield House in the foreground have been removed. (Jim Murphy Collection)

First, a vertical wooden shield was sunk into the sand. Holes in the form of a semi-circle were bored in this, and wooden poles were driven through the holes to form an arch. The sand was then removed underneath, and the process was repeated over and over again. As soon as the half-circle heading was completed, the workers dug down the sides. Nearly 700,000 feet of lumber went into the wooden framework necessary to hold up the sand as the excavating inched forward. As soon as there was room, a brick arch two feet thick and side walls four feet thick were built. The 350-foot long brick arch was horseshoe shaped, 19 feet high at the center and 16 feet wide at the widest point. The bricks were made several miles away and were carted to the site, while the hammer-dressed black limestone used in the approaches was quarried about twenty miles away at Isle la Motte.

About 85 men worked on the project, most of them natives of Ireland. Half worked by day and half by night as the work was pushed through the cold winter months. A small gas apparatus gave light and stoves furnished some heat. Ventilation was provided by lengths of one-foot pipe, which was connected to a chimney. Progress through the treacherous sand, on a four-degree curve, averaged three feet per day. With the completion of the project in May, 1861, the Vermont Central directed its attention toward putting the finishing touches on the new union depot at College and Lake Streets.

Landslides kept occurring around the east portal, so the old ravine route was kept in standby service for two years until the spring of 1863 when it was finally abandoned and the rails removed. During the summer and fall of 1861, it was found necessary to bring in additional fill as the unstable roadbed through the large swamp deteriorated dangerously. At this time, a large culvert was installed near the center of the fill to permit the free flow of water from one side of the grade to the other. During this time, the old route had to be used.

In 1861, a new double-lattice bridge was built north of the Northfield station. Also, improvements were being made steadily, if not rapidly, in the construction and appointments of passenger cars. Gas was coming into use for lighting the cars, and whale oil and candles were on their way out.

After an 1861 inspection over the Vermont Central, the commissioners reported that the alignment of some of the curves was causing an "inconvenient side motion of the passenger cars." The railroads were at this time continuing their efforts to improve their trackage, but the commissioners recommended that all such curves be "flattened" from one hundred feet to three hundred feet at each end "so as to make the entrance upon, and the departure from, the curve less abrupt and more easy."

The Vermont Central's mainline mileage at this time was 119 miles, while that of the Vermont & Canada stood at 55½ miles. Passenger and freight trains accumulated a total of 700,000 miles on this trackage in 1861, while work trains and wood trains ran another 26,000 miles. Some 176,000 passengers were carried at an average speed of 23 miles per hour, and 242,000 tons of freight were also handled.

On February 14, 1861, a passenger train derailed near Middlesex when it ran over a broken rail. One trainman and three passengers were injured, although not seriously. A few days later, a track worker was killed by a train while he was at work at Montpelier.

The decision to move the Vermont Central's shops from Northfield to St. Albans was an important event in the history of the shire town of Franklin County, as it marked the beginning of a period of great growth and prosperity for the community. However, with St. Albans functioning as headquarters for both the Vermont Central and the

THE CURVED TUNNEL at Burlington, built with so much difficulty in 1860-61, is still in daily use. The brick-lined tunnel is 342 feet long and was started on November 1, 1860 and finished the following May 17. E. J. Morrison was the general contractor, and D. C. Linsley was the chief engineer. (Jim McFarlane Collection)

Vermont & Canada, office space soon became in short supply. The old building was remodeled and additions were made, but it was obvious that within a few years an entirely new structure would have to be built.

Early in 1862, the officials purchased additional land for new shop buildings just west of the depot. Construction on the machine shop, roundhouses, and the necessary auxiliary buildings was started immediately. By the summer and early fall of 1863, all were completed and ready for service. Included in the complex were a machine shop and blacksmith shop, a passenger car house, and two roundhouses containing 38 stalls. The machine shop and blacksmith shop consisted of a main building 200 feet long and 78 feet wide, with two wings, each 200 feet long and 62 feet wide. The passenger car house was 400 feet long and 29 feet wide. One enginehouse measured 350 feet in length, while the other was 250 feet long. Both were 62 feet wide.

All of these new buildings were solidly constructed of brick. Some of them, fortunately, still stand today. In addition to these brick structures, the company built a wood frame freight depot. The main building measured 232 feet long and 30 feet wide. To this building, a 120 by 30 foot wing was attached. Nearby a frame paint shop 132 feet long and 50 feet wide was also constructed at this time. By the early 1860s these facilities required a payroll of 360 persons—and the railroad became St. Albans' largest employer, a situation that was to remain in effect for the next one hundred years.

The new shop complex served to point out how inadequate the passenger depot and main office facilities had become. The Smiths decided that a new, larger structure would have to be built, and work was started in the summer of 1866. A year later St. Albans boasted a very impressive three-story brick building that was 120 feet long and 70 feet wide that housed the general offices. Attached to it was a brick structure 263 feet long and 27 feet wide containing a waiting room, baggage room, ticket, express, and telegraph offices, and other facilities. The entire building contained 46,000 square feet of floor space, more than twice the office space of the original building.

In addition, a 350-foot-long covered trainshed ran the length of these buildings, through which trains ran on four through tracks. The main building still serves as the headquarters of the Central Vermont Railway although, unfortunately, the massive trainshed was razed in 1963. It seems eminently fitting that this structure still serves the railroad today, as it thereby continues as a living memorial to the three generations of Smiths and the contributions they made to their home town. Occupancy of these buildings took place in the fall of 1867, and the management decisions of the railroad have been made here continuously in the ensuing 114 years.

Along with the improvement in the line into Burlington, a new and larger depot opened for service at Essex Junction about the first of October. Also, a considerable amount of heavy bridge work was done during the year. A major rebuilding of the long pile bridges across the Missisquoi Bay entrance and across the lake between Rouses Point and Alburgh was undertaken. A new bridge was completed across the Jewett Brook in St. Albans, as was one across the White River at Sharon. A 600-foot structure across the White River at Royalton was rebuilt at about the same time, also.

Freight shipments were heavy during 1861 and 1862, and the officials decided to lay about 1,500 tons of new iron rails and install 75,000 new ties.

During the 1850s and 1860s, Vermont railroads generally observed some rather reasonable and prudent operating procedures and regulations. As a matter of interest, some of those related to the movement of trains are listed, many of which are still appropriate and in use today:

REGULATIONS

1. No train will leave a station under any circumstances before its time, as specified in the time-table.
2. Gravel and extra trains will keep at least fifteen minutes out of the way of regular trains.
3. Any extra train following a passenger or freight train will proceed with great caution, keeping at least one mile in the rear of it.

     *   *   *   *   *   *

6. On approaching all stations and road-crossings, the whistle must be sounded.
7. The bell must be rung eighty rods before crossing any road, and must be rung until it is passed. Any omission will be sufficient for a discharge.

Vermont Central, and Vt. & Canada Railroads.

Notice to Station Agents.

In consequence of an increased demand for cars, it is very important that the **utmost exertions** be made to have them **loaded and unloaded** with as little delay as possible.

Do not send off cars partly loaded if it can possibly be avoided, but when necessary to forward small lots of freight, load it into some car in the train.

If cars are detained at your Station in consequence of any delay on the part of the shippers, or consignees, more than **twenty-four hours**, notify the parties interested that the same will be **unloaded at their expense**, if convenient, if otherwise, a charge of two dollars per day for **each days detention** will be made for **each car**, and collected with the freight bill. A Report of the same should be made to this office, of all such collections on a common daily report.

Conductors of Freight Trains must keep as well informed as possible, as to **where the cars are**, and **where they are wanted**, and do all in their power to supply the Agents with them, and assist them so far as they can, in the forwarding of freight.

Station Agents of **connecting Roads**, will confer a special favor by **returning** all cars belonging to this line as **early as possible.**

J. W. HOBART, M. T.

St. Albans, Dec. 12, 1862.

PER DIEM DEMURRAGE RATES designed to encourage prompt unloading of cars by customers have been in effect for a long time, as this 1862 circular attests. (Jim McFarlane Collection)

8. A white flag posted on the track, denotes a bad place, which must be passed cautiously. If a red flag is shown, the train must stop.
9. No extra engine or train shall be run except by orders of the superintendent, or in his absence, the master mechanic.
10. Cross all roofed bridges without steam when practicable, and never exceed ten miles per hour. The speed of the train should be reduced to its minimum, and the brakes let off before entering upon the bridge.
11. Section men will at all times when the track is obstructed, (by taking out rails or otherwise) send a red flag in each direction, so that any extra or regular trains aproaching, will have ample time to stop.
12. No train must be run faster than time-table time, without special instructions.

     *   *   *   *   *   *

14. Approach all stations slowly, pass all switches cautiously, and be sure the switch is seen by its lever to be right. No excuse will be received for running off a switch when the lever shows it to be wrong.
15. A flag or lantern, raised across the track, is a signal for stopping trains.
16. All night trains must carry a light in front, and a red light on rear of train.
17. The position of brakemen on passenger trains when in motion, is on the platform of the cars. The position of one

WE ARE LOOKING at an early view of the first Montpelier depot, with a train emerging from the north end of the train shed. This structure was built in 1850 and replaced in 1880. (William Gove Collection)

THIS IS A VIEW of the Taylor Street side of the first Montpelier depot. Trains entering the building for the convenience of the patrons have badly smoked up the wall above the entrance. (William Gove Collection)

THE ORIGINAL MONTPELIER DEPOT was built at a cost of $7,000 in 1850 on the site of an old hotel. The building on the left is the former Vermont Mutual Fire Insurance Company office, which was razed in 1869. A northbound train stands at the trainshed entrance, the engine spotted outside so its smoke will not fill the building. (William Gove Collection)

THIS CIRCULAR CONTAINS information pertaining to a very early pioneer telegraph service. (Jim Murphy Collection)

brakeman on freight trains when in motion, is on the rear car; and when running at night, he will in all cases, see that a red lantern is on the rear end of the train.

18. Freight trains will in all cases keep entirely out of the way of all passenger trains, never leaving a station unless it has full time to arrive at the next station ten minutes before the time of arrival of passenger trains.

19. If it shall be found impracticable from any cause, for a train, in passing from one station to another, to reach the station to which it is proceeding in season, and another train is expected, then the conductor will send a man in the direction of the approaching train with a flag by day, or two lanterns by night, (that he may have a spare one in case one gives out,) to give notice of his position, and should it be necessary to back a train, a man must be sent in advance around the curves, and a sharp look-out observed.

*   *   *   *   *   *   *

21. All accidents or detentions will be reported at the superintendent's office immediately on arrival.

CHEMICAL TELEGRAPH.
VERMONT AND BOSTON LINE.
OFFICE AT DEPOT.

FROM SO. ROYALTON TO		FROM SO. ROYALTON TO		FROM SO. ROYALTON TO	
Boston,	30—2	Bellows Falls	25—2	Essex	25—2
Lowell	30—2	Brattleboro'	30—2	St. Albans	40—3
Nashua	30—2	Greenfield, Mass	30—2	Swanton	40—3
Manchester	30—2	Northampton, "	30—2	Rouse's Point, N. Y.	50—3
Concord	30—2	Sprngfield, "	30—2	Chateaugay	50—3
Franklin	25—2	Woodstock, Vt.	25—2	Malone	50—3
Enfield	25—2	W. Randolph	25—2	Potsdam Station	50—3
W. R. Junction	25—2	Montpelier,	25—2	Potsdam	50—3
Windsor	25—2	Waterbury	25—2	Canton	50—3
Claremont	25—2	Burlington,	25—2	Ogdensburg	50—3
Springfield, Vt.	25—2				

Connecting with other Lines for North, South, East and West.

New York	60—5	Vergennes	50—4	Brockville	75—5
Middlebury	55—4	St. Albans	50—4	Prescott	60—3
Bennington	55—4	St. Johns	65—5	Hartford, Ct.	60—4
Manchester Vt	55—4	Montreal	85—5	Portsmouth	60—4
Rutland	50—4	Quebec	100—8½	Portland, Me	60—4
Castleton, Vt.	50—4	Toronto	100—10	Bangor	85—5
Whitehall	50—4	Kingston	100—10	Halifax	185—11
Orwell, Vt.	50—4				

All messages strictly confidential. No abbreviations or figures used in the body of a message. Office hours from 8 A.M. to 8 P.M..

W. F. BLAKE, Operator.

THREE YOUNG LADS play in Battery Park, Burlington, in 1870, as we get a good overview of the Vermont Central's yard, the union passenger depot, and the Champlain Transportation Company's facilities. In the distance, about five miles beyond Burlington Harbor, is Shelburne Bay. (Collection of Jim Shaughnessy, from THE RUTLAND ROAD)

Chapter IV

Expansion 1862-1873

WITH THE LINE INTO BURLINGTON FINALLY COMPLETED AND THINGS *functioning rather well over the entire line, J. Gregory Smith looked toward other horizons.*

In 1852, a rail line some 34 miles in length had been completed between Rouses Point, New York, and St. Johns, Quebec, on the Richelieu River. This road connected with the 16-mile Champlain & St. Lawrence Railroad for entry into Montreal, Canada's largest city. In 1859, the Champlain & St. Lawrence bridged the mighty St. Lawrence River with the remarkable Victoria Bridge at St. Lambert. The 25 long spans of this structure were prefabricated in Newcastle, England, and shipped to Canada for erection.

In the spring of 1861, the nation was embroiled in the early weeks of the great Civil War. While the roles of the Canadian government and its waterways in this conflict had not been determined by either words or deeds, the Smiths foresaw the possibility of some financial gain. They felt strongly that the current route between their road and the city of Montreal via Rouses Point and the Champlain & St. Lawrence road was too circuitous, and it also placed the Vermont Central interests in a much too dependent role.

Accordingly, in May of 1861, the Smiths revived an inactive charter granted earlier by the Canadian government to the Montreal & Vermont Junction Railway Company. This charter authorized the construction of a railroad from the Canadian border to a connection with an existing road into Montreal. The charter authorized the company to issue $250,000 in stock for this work. About $70,000 was raised immediately, but this was quickly used up.

The original charter of the Vermont & Canada authorized the construction of a railroad to the international boundary, and the first survey had laid out such a line as far as Highgate a number of years earlier. The new road left the main line to Alburgh two miles south of Swanton to a point known as Swanton Junction (later, Fonda Junction). It then headed almost due north for 10.8 miles through Highgate to the border. The line crossed into Quebec at St. Armand, and then followed the east bank of the Richelieu River to a point two miles south of St. Johns, where it connected with the Stanstead, Shefford & Chambly Railroad. Trackage rights were obtained by the Montreal & Vermont Junction over this two miles of track and also over the SS&C's trestle across the Richelieu.

A contract was signed with D.C. Linsley of Burlington on June 23, 1863, to do the final surveying, grubbing, grading, masonry, bridging, tracklaying, ballasting, and to build all the depots, wood sheds, and water tanks on the 22 miles of this line in Quebec. The agreed upon price was $440,000, and the contract specified that all work was to be completed by December 1, 1868.

Linsley started work promptly and good progress was made along the flat terrain. However, there was a great difference between the U.S. and Canadian currency during the summer and fall of 1864, and Linsley soon found this situation almost impossible to deal with. He abandoned the contract for this reason just before the snow started to fly in late 1864. At this time the grading had been nearly completed and about one-half of the track had been laid, with the track laying progressing from the northern end.

In the meantime, the Vermont & Canada had done more than two-thirds of the work on the Vermont segment. Several consultations were held to decide what to do about finishing the Canadian portion, and Joseph Clark and J. Gregory Smith ultimately agreed to provide the capital to pay off Linsley's debts, which amounted to about $25,000, and to provide for the completion of the line.

This agreement stipulated that when the line was completed, the Vermont & Canada would take the new road off Clark's and Smith's hands. When such time came, however, there was considerable reticence on the part of some of the Vermont & Canada's directors to do so. The matter was settled, at least for a time, with the agreement that Clark and Smith should receive $50,000 rental per year for the line.

The first revenue train operated over the road on November 18, 1864, and a new through line to Montreal was thus established. A large amount of freight and passenger traffic soon developed over this route. In order to facilitate the movement of this traffic across the international boundary, President Abraham Lincoln in 1865 declared the customs port of St. Albans to be entitled to bonding privileges for goods transported to and from the Canadian provinces. This did much to encourage additional growth in

61

ENGINE NUMBER 34, prominently displaying the nameplate of ''The Stranger,'' waits outside the south portal of the St. Albans trainshed for passengers to load about 1868. This engine was built by Taunton in 1852, and was sold to the Vermont Central's Rutland Division in 1871, where it was renamed ''Ticonderoga.'' (Donald A. Somerville Collection)

trade relations between the two countries over the following decades.

This new route now gave the Vermont Central and the Vermont & Canada a choice of two routes between the East and the West—one via Ogdensburgh and the other via Montreal. A meeting of representatives of all the roads forming this line was conducted, and a new traffic agreement of freight commodities was made. This new road became the main line of the railroad until 1946, when through trains between St. Albans and Montreal were routed via East Alburgh and Cantic over the Canadian National.

Ultimately, Clark and Smith bought the securities of the Montreal & Vermont Junction Railway, then leased this road to themselves as trustees of the Vermont & Canada Railroad for 50 percent of the new road's gross receipts. There is evidence that the Vermont & Canada officials listed the mileage of the new road as 35 miles rather than the actual 24 miles, and until this situation was discovered some six years later, a goodly sum of excess receipts had been received. The 11-mile difference in mileage was the amount of the extension that was located in Vermont between Swanton Junction and the border.

Meanwhile, at the southern end of the system, two options for a route into Boston had been available right from the start. Traffic could be routed either to the Northern Railroad of New Hampshire at White River Junction or to the Sullivan Railroad at Windsor. The latter was a 26-mile connecting road between the Vermont Central and the Cheshire, the Vermont & Massachusetts, and the Fitchburg roads into Boston.

The Sullivan Railroad was opened for business in February, 1849, whereupon it was almost immediately taken over by its creditors and placed in receivership. It was operated in this manner for about ten years, during which time most of the traffic from the Vermont Central had been routed to Boston by way of the Northern Railroad and the Boston & Lowell. The Northern Railroad was largely controlled by its president, Onslow Stearns—a man not particularly well liked by the Smiths.

By the early 1860s Smith took steps to increase his independence from the actions of these foreign roads. Although the route to Boston was a bit shorter via Stearns' road, in September of 1861 J. Gregory Smith signed a lease agreement with the officials of the Sullivan Railroad. The Vermont Central immediately proceeded to route virtually all of its traffic over the newly leased line, as one would naturally expect. In 1866, the Sullivan Railroad was reorganized as the Sullivan County Railroad.

About this time, Vermont Central officials were becoming very embarrassed by the number of thefts committed on the line. Thieves were getting into the freight cars, not only on the Vermont Central, but on their southern connections as well. There was concern over both the cost of the claims and also about the adverse publicity that could result. A "Special Service Fund" was established, and detectives were hired in an attempt to put an end to the looting.

Meanwhile, J. Gregory Smith was seeking to add to his growing railway system. Part of this desire was purely a case of "expansionism," while part of it was to thwart the threat of real or imagined competition. The Stanstead, Shefford & Chambly Railroad had built eastward from St.

RAILROADS USED TREMENDOUS quantities of lumber in many different forms in the course of their daily operations. This circular indicates some of the items the Vermont Central was looking for in the fall of 1862. (Jim Murphy Collection)

Johns to Waterloo, Quebec, and pending further capitalization, it was planning to continue eastward through the Eastern Townships to Magog, Sherbrooke, and possibly all the way to the Maritimes.

At this same time, the Connecticut & Passumpsic Rivers Railroad had been expanding northward until now its rails had reached Newport on the southern end of Lake Memphremagog, just south of the international boundary. Over 80 percent of this large body of water was in Canada, with Magog at its northern end. Smith was concerned that this road might build around the lake, and then make a connection with the Stanstead, Shefford & Chambly or continue its own line into Montreal. J. Gregory Smith didn't like the possibility of this competition for the lucrative Montreal traffic one bit.

So, in the summer of 1864, he personally purchased the Stanstead, Shefford & Chambly Railroad for $364,000. He immediately leased it as trustee to the Vermont Central, a transaction by which he predictably made a significant profit. This line had been incorporated on April 22, 1853, by a group of five Waterloo citizens—Moses Colby, Stephen S. Foster, John Gilman, Alexander Kilborn, and Ichabod Smith. These men had dreamed of building a railroad from the City of Montreal through the agriculturally rich Eastern Townships, but as was invariably the case, sufficient capital had been hard to come by. After the charter was granted, it had been nearly five years before construction could be started.

Bonds totaling $910,553, bearing interest at seven percent, were issued to the public on August 27, 1858. The Vermont Central eventually acquired about $755,000 of these bonds. The bonds were defaulted on December 31, 1860, and an agreement was reached later between some of the bondholders and the Vermont Central Railroad Company whereby the bonds were deposited in the Bank of Montreal together with bills of exchange issued by the Stanstead, Shefford & Chambly Railroad company. The Vermont Central was given the right to purchase the bonds and bills of exchange for $154,000 so long as it paid interest at the rate of five percent per annum.

The 13-mile portion between St. Johns and West Farnham was opened for traffic on February 15, 1859. The line was extended from West Farnham to Granby, 15 miles, during the remainder of that year, and was opened for service on December 31, 1859. The terrain covered was virtually as flat as a table top, and the construction had been easy. The final section of 14.4 miles between Granby and Waterloo was through much more hilly terrain, however, and construction was slower and more difficult.

Local legend has it that the citizens of Waterloo offered the promoters a significant financial contribution "if the whistle of a locomotive can be heard in town before Christmas Day of 1860." As the track was still several miles to the west as this date drew near, the ingenious promoters came up with a scheme. A small construction locomotive was loaded onto a stout sledge and hauled into the center of

THE V&C'S "VERMONT" and the "Saguenay" were involved in a spectacular wreck near Bingham's Crossing, about one and one-half miles north of St. Albans, on May 20, 1864. It is not known whether any of the crew members were killed, but judging from the carnage, it would be a miracle if there were no fatalities. (Jim Shaughnessy Collection)

Waterloo by oxen. There she was steamed up and the whistle blown for all to hear. The story generally concludes with the point that the town folk were so impressed—both with the locomotive and the means by which it arrived there—that they immediately made good on their pledge.

In any case, when the Stanstead, Shefford & Chambly became part of the Vermont Central, the Smiths either owned or controlled a rather impressive piece of railroad property:

	Mileage
The Sullivan County Railroad	26
The Vermont Central Railroad	117
The Vermont & Canada Railroad	58
The Montreal & Vermont Junction	24
The Stanstead, Shefford & Chambly	43
	268

And much more mileage was to be added in the next few years.

Fatal accidents occurred with regularity during these early years. The most frequent victims were brakemen and conductors, and large numbers of trespassers lost their lives on railroad property as well. Passengers were not ignored completely in this regard either. Within a period of about sixteen months in 1861 and 1862, four brakemen lost their lives either by falling from the top of moving trains or by slipping when attempting to get on moving trains. A trespasser was killed when run over by a freight train in St. Albans yard, and a few weeks later another man was killed instantly while trying to illegally board a moving train near Montpelier Junction. On a warm spring day in late April, a drunk was run over and killed by a passenger train while he was walking the tracks between Alburgh and West Alburgh.

In 1863, the combined rosters listed 42 locomotives, 46 passenger cars, and 841 freight cars, three-fourths of which were "covered freight and 8-wheel cattle cars." The remainder of the freight car roster was comprised of flat cars and gravel cars. Six of the locomotives weighed 20 to 25 tons, while the remaining 36 weighed between 25 to 30 tons. The passenger coaches of the day weighed an average of 12 tons, while other types of passenger equipment averaged about 10 tons. The boxcars weighed in at about 7½ tons and the flat cars were listed at 6 tons.

Within the next few months, two locomotives, five passenger cars, and 160 freight cars were added to the roster. Ten of the older freight cars were scrapped and eight pieces of passenger equipment were retired. Non-revenue equipment consisted of five "Crane cars," one paymaster's car, and four iron snowplows.

Buildings owned and used by the roads included the

THIS INTERESTING STATION scene has proven to be somewhat of an enigma, as it has been variously identified as both Richford, Vermont, at the end of the Missisquoi Railroad; and also as Waterloo, Quebec on the St. Johns-Waterloo line, which was acquired by the Vermont Central on the first day of 1865. Positive identification has not yet been possible, but may be forthcoming upon publication of this photograph. (Armand Premo Collection)

A WESTBOUND TRAIN pulls into the Granby, Quebec, station, in the 1860s. The Yamaska River flows behind the depot. (Jim McFarlane Collection)

THE "OTTER CREEK" was built by Hinkley & Drury in 1854, for the Rutland & Burlington, later rebuilt, and scrapped in 1892. She was originally named the "Know Nothing" and served well during the Vermont Central's lease of the Rutland Railroad. Note the unusual way in which her number is painted on the cab panel. (Armand Premo Collection)

THE ORIGINAL VERMONT Central station is the large brick structure at the right. The second Pavilion building is on the left, and the third home of the National Life Insurance Company is in the center. This picture was taken prior to 1870. (William Gove Collection)

THIS STOCK CERTIFICATE shows that George F. Edmunds invested $300 for three shares of Vermont & Canada capital stock on October 14, 1865. (Jim Murphy Collection)

following: 35 passenger stations, 23 freight stations, 5 engine houses, 3 repair shops, 28 water stations, 13 dwellings, 48 woodsheds, 4 turntables, 3 car houses, and 5 ice houses.

A major accident occurred near St. Albans on June 30, 1864, when a passenger train and a work train collided head-on. Engineer James Allen of the work train was killed, and the engineer of the passenger train, A.E. Shattuck, received a broken leg. Passenger brakeman M. J. Strothers was severely injured, while two passengers were slightly hurt.

In 1864, New England suffered the only Confederate infringement on its soil—the much-written-about St. Albans Raid. In mid-October, a band of Confederates slipped over the border from Canada two or three at a time, registered in St. Albans hotels, and then busied themselves learning the marketing habits of the community. They learned that Tuesday was market day, the day on which farmers came to town from the outlying districts bringing freshly made butter for shipment to Boston. They quickly found that the bustle of market day was followed each week by a comparatively dull day business-wise. Consequently, the group's leader—Bennett Young—planned his raid for Wednesday, October 19. Upon a pre-arranged signal—the striking of the town's clocks at 3:00 p.m.—the group forced townspeople off the streets, out of the banks, and onto the Green.

The Confederates then stole $200,000 from three bank vaults, shot a man who refused to be driven to the Green, mortally wounded another man with a wild shot, commandeered horses from the town's livery stables, and escaped across the border. A posse was immediately formed, but it could not catch the fleeing band. However, their close pursuit did cause the plunderers to drop about $80,000 of the stolen money.

J. Gregory Smith was in Montpelier tending to his duties as governor at the time of the raid. When Mrs. Smith was informed of the raid, she reportedly armed herself with a hand gun and made her way to the telegraph office in the railroad depot. She had the following message transmitted to the governor in Montpelier: "Southern raiders are in town, robbing banks, shooting citizens, burning houses." After sending the message, the telegrapher locked his office and went out to see for himself what was going on. It was some time before the frantic governor could get a reply through to his hometown.

As the months went by, the accidents continued. On a wintry night in February, 1865, a freight train derailed and brakeman Charles Rock was thrown from the top of a boxcar and instantly killed as his train derailed. In another accident, veteran conductor William White fell between two cars of his moving freight train at White River Junction and sustained fatal injuries.

Engineer James Harrington jumped from his engine as it

ENGINES "JOHN CROMBIE" on the left and "St. Lawrence" on the right are being used to test the rebuilt Harlow Bridge near Northfield in 1867, along with an inexplicably tenderless engine in the middle of the span. This is the site of the train disaster in which 15 workmen lost their lives and 38 others were injured. (Richard Sanborn Collection)

was pulling into the station at St. Albans, but he fell across the track and was killed. In an unusual accident, a track worker was killed near South Royalton when he was run over by the rear part of a freight train. The train had broken apart and the victim apparently didn't realize that the entire train had not passed by him. He stepped onto the tracks to resume work and was struck by the rear part that was running free.

On the night of April 13, 1866, the express train plunged through a small bridge which had mysteriously burned only a short time before. The engineer was unable to stop, and in the ensuing crash one passenger was killed and several were badly injured. In yet another incident, a brakeman was riding the top of one of the cars in his train when an axle broke on the car on which he was riding. The car left the rails and the brakeman was thrown to the ground and killed in the smash-up. On December 6, 1866, the northbound night mail train was hurrying out of White River Junction when the locomotive derailed and hurtled down an embankment. The lifeless bodies of engineer Charles Hayden and fireman Vincent Chamberlin were pulled from the wreckage.

Almost exactly one year later, on December 11, the most serious tragedy the road had yet experienced claimed the lives of 15 men and injured 38 more. About 60 bridge builders, carpenters and laborers, who were engaged in rebuilding the Harlow Bridge about two miles from the Northfield depot, boarded their work train after eating a noon meal at the Northfield House. Francis B. Abbott, a 15-year veteran of the Vermont Central, was at the throttle of the train, which consisted of only the locomotive and one passenger car. Abbott had been reprimanded for returning late from lunch, and his orders were to "hurry up" and deliver the men to the work site and then return to Northfield for the remainder of the workers.

Angered by his reprimand, Abbott opened the throttle, and the train started backing to the work site. However, he had soon accelerated far beyond the normal speed limit, and—as though in a trance—he did nothing to start slowing the train as it approached the bridge. The fireman yelled at him and reportedly threw a piece of wood at the engineer's head in a desperate attempt to wake him from his trance. However, it was too late.

The passenger car derailed and went off into the deep gorge at the work site. The car struck a rock ledge about 25 feet down, and this split the car open. One part remained on the ledge, while the other plunged another 60 feet or more to the bottom of the abyss. The tender followed, and it crashed onto the portion of the car on the ledge, crushing to death nearly all the men in that portion of the car. The engine stopped before it, too, went over, although a report of the accident stated that "the rear drivers overhung the abutment by exactly four feet when it came to rest."

Among those killed was Almon Wetherbee, the foreman of the bridge gang. The other 14 men killed were track workers, bridge builders and laborers. In all, six of the fifteen men killed and three of the thirty-five injured were from Northfield.

Abbott was discharged by the railroad, but no charges were brought against him. He retired to a small farm in a remote section of Northfield, where he lived in poverty as a recluse for the rest of his life. He rarely left his home for fear that relatives of some of the accident victims might try to seek revenge.

In 1865-66, the Vermont Central installed 153 miles of new telegraph line which, with its instruments, cost the road a little over $10,000. Nine new locomotives were purchased at an average cost of $20,000. Six new passenger cars were added to the roster for $21,000, and 20 new double-decked

THIS VIEW OF the J. Gregory Smith estate in St. Albans was taken from Aldis Hill on the east side of town in the mid-1860s. (St. Albans Historical Society Collection)

stock cars were purchased for $1,000 each. An order of 54 new boxcars arrived and were immediately put into service. These cars cost the company $900 each.

Butter and cheese shipments had increased markedly in the period of years that the Vermont Central had been handling this merchandise. In 1851, for example, 60 tons of butter and 275 tons of cheese had been shipped from St. Albans. Fourteen years later, 1,514 tons of butter and 587 tons of cheese were shipped. The quotations for butter and cheese at St. Albans on market-day—Tuesday of each week— affected the market price of these commodities throughout the Eastern United States.

The lumber business at Burlington had become an extremely big business for both the railroads and the freighters on Lake Champlain. In fact, by 1868, Burlington had become the third largest lumber port in the country—behind only Chicago and Albany. Huge quantities came up the lake from Canada to Burlington, where it was dressed and then shipped to eastern markets. By 1869, the firm of Shepard & Morse had become the largest local operation, with a payroll of over 300 in Burlington and a like number employed at other locations. Some six million board feet were dressed (planed) and transshipped here each month by this firm, which had some 4,000 feet of dock frontage that could accommodate 30 to 35 vessels at a time. It was said that this one firm produced over 30 tons of shavings every day.

The peak year for lumber traffic over the railroads and waterways at Burlington was 1873, at which time five large planing mills were in operation. In 1891, however, the boom was over and the traffic started to decline. The first significant production on the West Coast and a $2.00 tariff on all lumber entering the country from Canada had an adverse effect on this business locally.

The following 1865 employment roster and pay schedule is of interest, as we look back to the way things used to be over 115 years ago:

Number of Employees and Compensation

9	Conductors of passenger trains,	$50 to 66.67 per month
25	Conductors of freight trains,	40 to 50 per month
2	Conductors of wood and gravel trains	50 per month
1	Master mechanic,	2,500 per year
2	Road masters, both,	150 per month
276	Men in repair shops,	1 to 3.25 per day
16	Enginemen of passenger trains,	3 per day
20	Enginemen of freight trains,	2.25 to 3 per day
2	Enginemen of wood and gravel trains,	3 per day
39	Fire men	1.30 to 1.50 per day
4	Baggagemen,	40 to 45 per day
20	Switchmen,	1 to 1.5 per day
38	Section men, (foreman,)	1.65 to 1.75 per day
211	Section hands,	1.25 to 1.35 per day
31	Watchmen,	20 to 45 per month
33	Station agents,	10 to 90 per month
306	Other laborers,	1 to 2.50 per day
3	Clerks connected with passenger business	205 per month
6	Clerks connected with freight business	466.67 per month

69

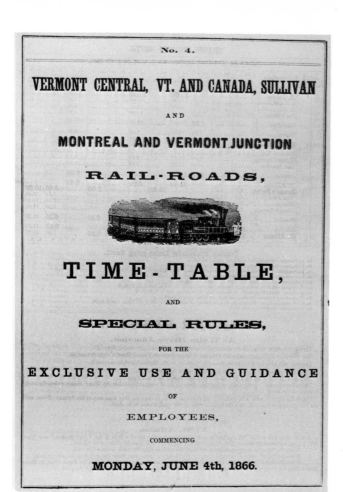

No. 4.

VERMONT CENTRAL, VT. AND CANADA, SULLIVAN

AND

MONTREAL AND VERMONT JUNCTION

RAIL·ROADS,

TIME-TABLE,

AND

SPECIAL RULES,

FOR THE

EXCLUSIVE USE AND GUIDANCE

OF

EMPLOYEES,

COMMENCING

MONDAY, JUNE 4th, 1866.

To express his frustrations about the necessity of having to change cars as well as the inconvenient schedules on the railroads serving the Burlington and Essex Junction area, the Honorable Edward J. Phelps wrote a poem which became widely circulated. Phelps was born in Middlebury, Vermont, in 1822, was graduated from Middlebury College at the age of 18, and studied law at Yale University. He later was Minister to England from 1885 to 1889. One day Phelps left Burlington on the so-called "Shuttle" train, with intentions of going to Boston via Essex Junction. At the latter point, he got off the "Shuttle" and stepped inside the depot to await the arrival of the main line train. The usual shifting of cars and trains took place, and Phelps got aboard a train which he anticipated would take him to his destination. Much to his chagrin, however, he soon found he had boarded the "Shuttle" and was enroute back to Burlington. Upon his arrival there, he wrote the poem which he entitled "The Lay of the Lost Traveler:"

With saddened face and battered hat
And eye that told of black despair,
On wooden bench the traveler sat,
Cursing the fate that brought him there.
"Nine hours," he cried, "we've lingered here,
With thought intent on distant homes,
Waiting for that elusive train,
Which, always coming, never comes:
Till, weary, worn, distressed, forlorn,
And paralyzed in every function,
I hope in hell, their souls may dwell
Who first invented Essex Junction!"

THIS PORTION OF the 1866 timetable covers scheduled train operations over the Northern Division between St. Albans, Vermont, and St. Johns, Quebec. (Both photos, Jim McFarlane Collection)

TRAINS MOVING SOUTH.
NORTHERN DIVISION.

STATIONS	No. 1 PASSENGER A.M.	No. 3 FREIGHT A.M.	No. 5 St. DAY EXPRESS A.M.	No. 7 DAY EXPRESS A.M.	No. 9 FREIGHT A.M.	No. 11 FREIGHT A.M.	No. 13 FREIGHT P.M.	No. 15 MIXED P.M.	No. 17 NIGHT EXPRESS P.M.	No. 19 NIGHT EXPRESS P.M.	No. 21 FREIGHT P.M.
St. Johns			6.45	10.00		10.50				4.50	
S. S. & C. June.			6.52	10.07		11.05				4.57	
St. Alexandre			7.07	10.20		11.45				5.10	
Des Rivieres			7.22	10.38		12.20				5.28	
Stanbridge			7.32	10.45		12.45				5.35	
Moores			7.42	10.55		1.05				5.45	
St. Armand			7.50	11.02		1.20 1.40				6.02	
Province Line											
Highgate Springs			8.00	11.12		2.10				6.14	
East Swanton			8.08	11.23		2.20				6.22	
Junction			8.15	11.30		2.50				6.30	
St. Albans			8.30	11.45		3.20				6.45	
Rouse's Point	4.30	4.35			10.45			2.00		5.45	10.20
West Alburgh	4.40	4.45			10.52			2.10		5.54	10.30
Alburgh	4.46	4.55			10.57			2.20		6.00	10.40
Alburgh Springs	4.58	5.20			11.05			2.35		6.08	11.00
Swanton	5.20	6.00			11.25			3.10		6.35	11.35
Junction	5.30	6.20			11.35			3.20		6.45	11.50
St. Albans	5.50	6.50			11.50			3.50		7.00	12.20
	A.M.	A.M.			A.M.			P.M.		P.M.	A.M.

Crossing Stations for Trains going South.

No. 1.—PASSENGER—Swanton June. meet 2 ; St. Albans, meet 4, 6, 8.
No. 3.—FREIGHT—Swanton Junction, meet 2, 4, and 6 ; St. Albans meet 8
No. 5.—PASSENGER—Des Rivieres, meet 6 ; Stanbridge, meet 2 ; Swanton Junction, meet 8.
No. 7.—PASSENGER—St. Johns meet 4, and 2 ; Swanton Junction, meet 6, 10. St. Albans, meet 12
No. 9.—PASSENGER—Rouse's Point, meet 4, and 2 ; Swanton Junction, meet 6.
No. 11.—PASSENGER—St. Johns meet 6, and 2 ; Swanton Junction, meet 12 ; St. Albans, meet 14, 16, 18, 20, 22
No. 15.—MIXED—Rouse's Point, meet 6, 19 ; Swanton meet 22 ; St. Albans, meet 14, 16, 18, 20, 22
No. 17.—PASSENGER—Swanton Junction, meet 14, 16 ; St. Albans, meet 18, 20, 22.
No. 19.—PASSENGER—Rouse's Point meet 2 ; Swanton, meet 14 ; Swanton Junction meet 16 ; St. Albans, meet 18, 20, 22.
No. 21.—FREIGHT—Rouse's Point, meet 22, 18.

DANGER SIGNALS.
At White River Junction.

The signals on the pole, will be red balls during the day, and red lights during the night.
One red ball or light gives trains from the north on the Vermont Central Road, a right to come in.
Two red balls or light gives trains from the Northern N. H. Railroad, a right to come in.
Three red balls or lights, gives trains from the South a right to come in.
If no signal is visible, no train will have the right to come in until it is signaled.
Trains from the north going south, or drawing down to set off must not go below the Water House, unless the track is known to be clear.
Unless the signal is seen to be right for train from the North to come in, they must stop at the SIGNAL POST, and not run the Engine below it, until the signal is right, or the track known to be clear.

At St. Albans.

A Red Arm with a Red Ball attached to each end, placed at the top of a Pole, is the "DAY SIGNAL," and Two Red Lights, one attached to each Ball, is the "NIGHT SIGNAL," and must be observed as follows:
1. When the Signal is in a perpendicular position, the track is clear for trains to enter the yard.
2. When the Signal hangs at an angle of Forty Five Degrees, trains must enter the yard with GREAT CAUTION.
3. When the Signal is placed in a horizontal position, trains must come to a dead stop at the Signal Post, 50 Rods distant from the Danger Signal, and remain there until the Signal is set right for them to enter the yard.

TRAINS MOVING NORTH.
NORTHERN DIVISION.

STATIONS	No. 2 FREIGHT A.M.	No. 4 NIGHT EXPRESS A.M.	No. 6 NIGHT EXPRESS A.M.	No. 8 FREIGHT A.M.	No. 10 MIXED A.M.	No. 12 FREIGHT P.M.	No. 14 DAY EXPRESS P.M.	No. 16 DAY EXPRESS P.M.	No. 18 MAIL P.M.	No. 20 PASSENGER P.M.	No. 22 PASSENGER P.M.
St. Albans	6.00		7.30	10.55		2.30	5.10		8.25		7.50
Junction	6.15		8.00	12	2.50	6.25			8.40		8.20
Swanton	6.25		8.15 8.20	11.50	3.05 3.10	6.35		8.50			8.35 8.50
Alburgh Springs	6.42		9.00	12.25	3.55	6.52		9.10			9.25
Alburgh	6.53		9.15	12.45	4.20	7.10		9.18			9.45
West Alburgh	7.03		9.25	12.55	4.35	7.15		9.23			9.55
Rouse's Point	7.15		9.35	1.05	4.45	7.25		9.30			10.05
St. Albans	4.50	6.05							6.15	8.30	
Junction	5.25	6.20							6.30	8.35	
East Swanton	5.45	6.30							6.37	8.43	
Highgate Springs	6.05	6.40							6.47	8.53	
Province Line											
St. Armand	6.35 6.55	6.50							7.00	9.08	
Moores	7.05	7.00							7.05	9.16	
Stanbridge	7.32	7.12							7.15	9.28	
Des Rivieres	7.42	7.22							7.22	9.34	
St. Alexandre	8.18	7.37							7.40	9.51	
S. S. & C. Junc.	8.45	7.52							7.53	10.05	
St. Johns	9.00	8.00							8.00	10.15	
	A.M.	A.M.	A.M.	A.M.	P.M.	P.M.	P.M.	P.M.	P.M.	P.M.	P.M.

Crossing Stations for Trains going North.

No 2.—FREIGHT—Swanton June. meet 1, 3 ; St. Armand, 5 passes ; Stanbridge, meet 7 ; St. Johns. meet 7 and 11.
No. 4.—PASSENGER—St. Albans meet 5 ; Swanton Junction, meet 2.
No. 6.—PASSENGER—St. Albans meet 5 ; Swanton Junction, meet 2. St. Armand, pass 2 ; Des Rivieres meet 5 ; St. Johns meet 7, 11.
No. 8.—FREIGHT—St. Albans, meet 1, 3 ; Swanton June. meet 3 ; Rouse's Point, meet 5.
No. 10.—MIXED—St. Albans, meet 3 ; Swanton June. meet 7, 9 ; Rouse's Point meet 15.
No. 12.—FREIGHT—Swanton Junction, meet 11 ; Swanton meet 15 ; Rouse's Point meet 19.
No. 14.—PASSENGER—Swanton June. meet 17 ; Swanton, meet 15 ; Rouse's point, meet 19.
No. 16.—PASSENGER—Swanton Junction, meet 17, and 19.
No. 20.—PASSENGER—St. Albans, meet 17, 19 ; Swanton pass 22 ; Rouse's Point, meet 21.
No. 20.—PASSENGER—St. Albans, meet 17, 19.
No. 22.—FREIGHT—St. Albans, meet 17, and 19 ; St. Albans, 18 pass ; Rouse's Point, meet 21.

At Swanton Junction.

The Signals on the pole, will be Red Balls during the day, and Red Lights during the night.
One red ball or light, gives trains from St. Albans a right to go via Swanton to Rouse's Point.
Two red balls or lights, gives trains a right from St. Albans to go over the Montreal & Vt. Junction Railroad.
Three red balls or lights, gives trains a right from Rouse's Point to St. Albans.
Four red balls or lights gives trains a right from St. Johns to St. Albans.
If no Signal is visible, no train will have the right to pass the Switch, until it is signaled.
All trains will run with great care between Swanton Junction, and St. Albans,—the leading train in case of detention, sending back and the following train keeping a good look out ahead.

At S. S. and C. Junction.

The Signal is an arm at the top of a Pole.
When in a Horizontal position, trains on the Montreal & Vt. Junction Railway, have a right to proceed.
When in a Perpendicular position, trains on the S S. & C. Railway have a right to proceed.

"Here Boston waits for Ogdensburgh
And Ogdensburgh for Montreal,
And late New York tarrieth
And Saratoga hindereth all!
From far Atlantic's wave-swept bays
To Mississippi's turbid tide,
All accidents, mishaps, delays
Are gathered here and multiplied!
Oh, fellow man, avoid this spot
As you would plague or Peter Funk shun!
And I hope in hell
His soul may dwell
Who first invented Essex Junction!

And long and late conductors tell
Of trains delayed or late or slow,
Till e'en the very engine's bell
Takes up the cry, 'No go! No go!'
Oh, let me from this hole depart,
By any route, so't be a lone one,
He cried with madness in his heart,
And jumped aboard a train, the wrong one,
And as he vanished in the smoke
He shouted with redoubled unction
I hope in hell
His soul may dwell
Who first invented Essex Junction!"

Some years later, an Essex Junction native wrote a fitting response. The Phelps poem is very well known, but the Lonergan response has not been widely circulated.

REPLY TO THE LOST TRAVELER

By Postmaster Alfred P. Lonergan of Essex Junction, Vermont

Some years ago, a senator, I believe Phelps was his name,
Sojourned in Essex Junction while waiting for a train,
Inclined to be poetic to pass the time away,
In rhyme real pathetic had quite a lot to say;
Condemning Essex Junction in English not so swell—
In fact, he hoped its founders were shoveling coal in Hell.

The writer has sojourned here nigh on to thirty years—
To diagnose: the senator had brains with wheels and gears
That needed oiling badly to open up his eyes
To find he'd erred quite sadly and should apologize.

The writer finds the Junction a pleasant place to live;
Its people and its founders the best that God could give;
A haven that was founded in our Green Mountain State
By pioneers that rounded among the good and great.

Those pioneers have come and gone—I've stood beside their biers,
They seemed to whisper "Carry on; waste not your time in tears."
Somehow, in kin they left behind, the spirit seems to last.
The Mill will never grind with the water that is past.

The trees will cease to bloom and flower unless you give them sap;
The mighty streams will lose their power unless you fill the gap.
Their names engraved on monuments, their pens have ceased to function,
But they have written history for good old Essex Junction.

Their pens were swords at Gettysburg—also at Valley Forge—
Their inks were drops of human blood that flowed down through the gorge;
That followed good old Sherman from Atlanta to the sea:
That made the good old U.S.A. a land of liberty.

That C.V. station stands erect were sat the famous Phelps
To criticize those gallant men between his groans and yelps,
Because the gears were all gummed up that God put in his brains,
And clogged the art of reason when it came to catching trains.

He couldn't tell if Montreal was way down south or north;
He didn't know but Santa Claus came round on July Fourth.
And so he boarded the wrong train, and had to hike it back—
In other words, our famous Phelps was clean way off his track.

With saddened face and battered hat, on wooden bench the poet sat,
Trying to clear his muddled brains—all mixed up on C.V. trains.
With mighty pen—without compunction—assailed the Village of Essex Junction.
His poem sojourns as an aftermath, and these words are written in epitaph:
Here lies a poet whose muddled brain sent him to Hell on a C.V. train:
Since he has passed the Great Divide, his mistakes and delays have multiplied.
His mighty pen has ceased to function; he shovels coal for lack of gumption.
Not hide nor hair can he find there "who first invented Essex Junction."

THE NEW LONDON Northern's Number 15, the "W. W. Billings," is shown at Thamesville, Connecticut, shortly after she was delivered by the Manchester Locomotive Works. She was scrapped in 1906. (Lewis R. Brown, Inc., Collection)

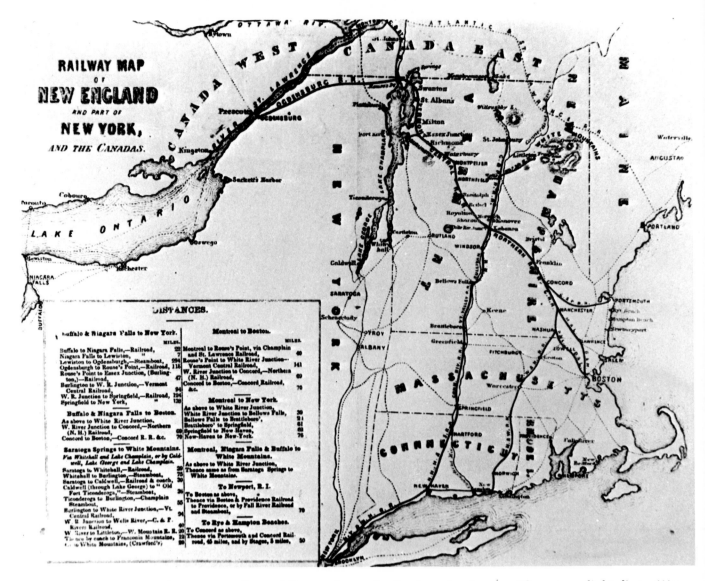

THIS MAP DEPICTS the Vermont Central line and its connections around 1870. It is interesting to note that the line's major rival in Vermont, the Rutland & Burlington, is shown with a very light line. (Jim McFarlane Collection)

During the latter half of the 1860s, J. Gregory Smith rather incredulously was named to the presidency of the Northern Pacific Railroad, and his time and interests became at least somewhat divided for a while. It happened this way.

In the early 1850s, a Boston theater owner by the name of Josiah Perham had achieved considerable success operating a unique mechanized travelerama. Bostonians flocked in large numbers to Perham's Panorama to see the wonders of various rivers, lakes, falls, mountains, and cities. But Perham was shrewd enough to realize that it would only be a matter of time before his local market became exhausted. He hit upon the idea of bringing people into the city by train just to see his production.

He talked with officials of various railroads in Massachusetts about the possibility of running excursions with reduced rates. The reaction of the railroad officials to this idea could at best be described as "cool." Perham persisted and finally one or two of the roads agreed to try offering the special rates. This idea caught on with the public to a much greater degree than had ever been expected by either Perham or the railroads. Thus, the excursion business in this country was born!

Perham, however, excited by his success with the excursion business, now had acquired a rather severe case of "railroad fever." He envisioned a grandiose scheme of building a railroad from the Great Lakes to the Pacific Northwest, an idea that came to obsess him. He meticulously studied everything he could find about other transcontinental railway schemes, and Perham's mind produced some unusual new ideas. He initially called his proposed railroad the "People's Pacific Railroad," and he believed that it could be financed by asking one million men to invest $100 each in cash, with no one being permitted to own more than $100 worth of stock. He also envisioned this road being granted a large land subsidy by the federal government.

Perham's first visit to Congress where he outlined his plans in considerable detail was a complete failure. He came back with no charter and no land grant. Again Perham persisted. Finally, in 1864, he persuaded Congress to issue him a charter for this monumental project, and he obtained a land grant totaling some 47,000,000 acres besides!

THE "ST. LAWRENCE" is shown in front of the Northfield shop building in the 1860s. This engine was built by Baldwin in 1851, rebuilt in 1858, and re-named "Berkshire" in 1871. She was scrapped in 1876. Flat cars of both the Vermont Central and the Northern Railroad may be seen in the foreground. (Donald A. Somerville Collection)

Flushed with success, Perham quickly opened offices in Boston, New York, Philadelphia, and other major cities for the purpose of selling stock subscriptions at $100 per share. But success proved to be fleeting. The Civil War was at its height, and for that and other reasons, response to the stock issue was very disheartening.

Perham had used his own capital in getting his project to this point, but he was now scraping the bottom of the proverbial barrel. It was at this point that several well-known tycoons and financiers stepped forward, and among them was J. Gregory Smith. Smith and the others saw vast potential with the charter and the land grants that Perham had obtained, so their involvement in the project at this point clearly was not for benevolent reasons.

Smith and his associates offered to pay off all the personal debts that Perham had incurred in return for his charter and land grants. Perham was not only in critical financial straits, but his health was broken virtually beyond repair, so he agreed to the proposition with little or no deliberation.

Smith's railroad experience and reputation had definitely preceded him, and his colleagues elected him as the second president of the Northern Pacific Railroad. Now, with the opportunity firmly in his hands to build west from Duluth, Minnesota, to the tidewaters of the Pacific Ocean, all Smith would have to do would be to build or acquire trackage between his Vermont Central and Duluth. Smith all too soon

found himself in the company of Jay Cooke, one of the nation's most successful bankers—but not a railroad man.

Cooke was given the assignment of handling bond issues, stock sales, and finances in general. Almost immediately, Smith and Cooke disagreed over the high rate of interest that was being offered on Northern Pacific bonds. Later, Smith was offered bonds of the financially ailing St. Paul, Minneapolis & Manitoba Railroad (later to become part of the Great Northern system) at a very reasonable price. Smith felt it imperative that the Northern Pacific purchase the bonds and thus the control of this road. He reasoned that it would reduce competition and would secure the traffic to and from the rich Canadian provinces, as well as most of that from the northern tier of states. Cooke, however, refused to agree to Smith's porposal, so the Vermonter resigned the presidency of the Northern Pacific in 1870 and returned home to his Vermont Central.

Smith's return to St. Albans was most timely, as forces were at work to contain, if not destroy, the monopolistic position forged for the Vermont Central by the Smith family. Timothy Follett's Rutland & Burlington Railroad had reached Burlington on December 18, 1849, less than two weeks ahead of the Vermont Central, but by 1853 that road was in receivership and in 1863 it came under the control of Edwin A. Birchard and John B. Page, both of whom were trustees of the second mortgage bondholders. Birchard was

THIS ENGINE WAS built by Baldwin in 1851 as the "Oregon." It was rebuilt ten years later and subsequently renamed the "Bethel." (Gerry Fox Collection)

THE "JAMES M. FOSS" is seen headed south at the St. Albans trainshed shortly after being delivered in the fall of 1869. (Ed Steel Collection)

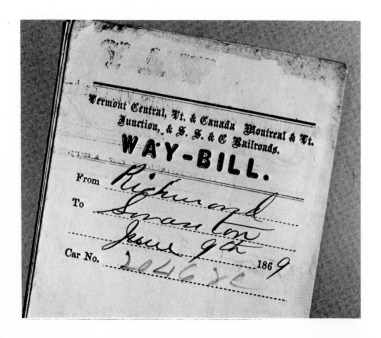

THIS 1869 WAYBILL covers a shipment from Richmond to Swanton in car VC 2046. (Jim Murphy Collection)

a Brandon, Vermont, businessman, while Page was a Rutland banker and president of the Howe Scale Company, the road's biggest shipper. Page improved the lot of the Rutland & Burlington considerably in a relatively short time, as he almost immediately asserted his influence in the daily operations of the road. He was a man who possessed many of the personal characteristics and entrepreneurial acumen and techniques of the Smiths.

One of the first actions of Birchard and Page was to lease the 23-mile Vermont Valley Railroad. This line operated between Brattleboro and the Rutland road's southern terminus at Bellows Falls. In 1868, the Rutland had a 258-foot car ferry built to operate between Burlington and Plattsburgh. The Lake Champlain Transportation Company built the vessel, which could steam across the lake at 19 knots—at least between the months of April and December. The "Oakes Ames" was soon transporting about 1,100 railroad cars per month in this manner—a rather significant figure.

Meanwhile, Page had found time to become elected governor of the state in 1867; the same year he reorganized his railroad, which included renaming it the "Rutland Railroad." Page successfully cultivated traffic arrangements with connecting roads from New York state, and soon had the Rutland on a relatively sound financial footing.

In 1870, he acquired control of the 16-mile Addison Railroad, which ran from Leicester Junction, Vermont, to Ticonderoga, New York. Page planned that this route, which bridged a very narrow bit of water at the southern tip of Lake Champlain, would provide a direct year-round rail route to eastern New York state. He further planned to extend the Addison Railroad northward along the western shore of Lake Champlain to Plattsburgh, where it would make connections to the north and west.

Smith immediately realized that if he didn't take appropriate steps without delay, Page would be in a position to provide stiff competition for the Vermont Central—more, perhaps, than it could handle. Thus, as one might imagine, J. Gregory Smith wasted little time in taking action. On March 1, 1870, he negotiated a 20-year lease of the 118-mile Ogdensburgh & Lake Champlain Railroad (formerly the Northern Railroad of New York). This line extended from Rouses Point on Lake Champlain to Ogdensburgh and access to the Great Lakes. With the railroad came the Ogdensburgh Transportation Company, which owned a fleet of eight steamers, ferries, and terminal facilities at Ogdensburgh at Prescott, Ontario, and at Chicago.

Ogdensburgh was an excellent inland port, and its large elevators were capable of storing one million bushels of grain. The steamers plied the waterways for eight months of the year transporting six to eight million bushels of grain each year. Much of this was transshipped to the railroad at Ogdensburgh, and for years this traffic represented a major source of revenue for the road.

The contract called for Smith to pay a total of $8.5 million over a period of 20 years. While the figure was high, Smith knew that his rival, John Page, would never dare to match it.

This railroad had been in the minds of the promoters since 1830 when it was first proposed as a major part of the projected line from Boston to Ogdensburgh. However, it was not until 1845 that sufficient interest in the idea had been aroused to make it possible to obtain a charter. The company

Continued on page 78

THE "GOVERNOR SMITH" at the left, the "Joseph Clark" in the foreground, and an unidentified 4-4-0 steam away in a pastoral setting in the early 1870s. (Wilbur Collection, University of Vermont)

ENGINE 211, THE "General Strong," was built by Taunton in 1851 for the Rutland & Burlington. She subsequently served the Rutland Division of the Central Vermont until being scrapped in 1891. (Lewis R. Brown, Inc., Collection)

THE RUTLAND & BURLINGTON'S "Chester" was built by Taunton in 1850, rebuilt by that road in 1868, and later served on that road when it became the Rutland Division of the Central Vermont. It is seen here with a single passenger coach at an unidentified country location. (Whitney Maxfield Collection)

THE NEW SWING-SPAN in the middle of Lake Champlain between West Alburgh and Rouses Point appears to be ready for service. (Louis Cameron Collection)

THE THREE PHOTOS on this page show different views of the new swing-span between West Alburgh and Rouses Point. The same individuals may be seen in varying poses in all three photos. The presence of the women and the child could be explained by these photos possibly marking a ceremony in which the new structure is being dedicated. (All three photos, Louis Cameron Collection)

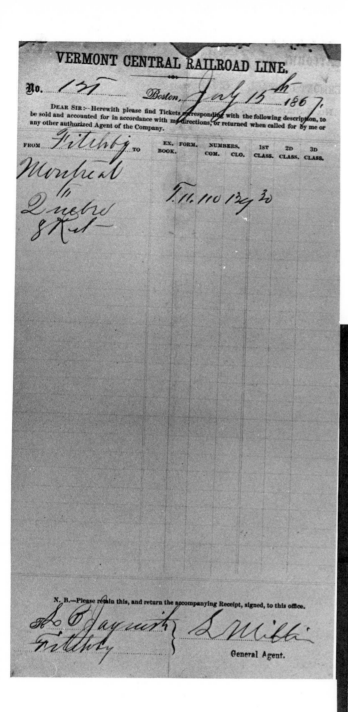

organized in the following year, and it was planned that the line could be built for about $1,750,000. The actual cost of the project, which was completed in the fall of 1850, however, was slightly in excess of $5,000,000.

The line was surveyed, and a contract was awarded to Sewall F. Belknap to build the 57-mile portion between Rouses Point and Malone. This was apparently the same Sewall F. Belknap who had failed while building the Vermont Central in 1849. The firm of Chamberlain, Worreall & Company was awarded the contract to build the 61-mile portion from Malone to Ogdensburgh. The work was started at each end of the line in March, 1848, and by the end of the year 14 miles of track had been laid between Rouses Point and Mooers. By late 1849 the line had reached Ellenburg, and in June of 1850 it was in Chateauguay. Malone was to become the headquarters of the road, and it was reached by rail on October 1. Simultaneously, similar progress had been made on the western portion, and by the end of October, 1850, the entire line was open for service.

THIS PAPER COVERS an 1867 shipment of tickets. (Chandler Cobb Collection)

PASSENGER TRAIN SERVICE during the winter of 1860-61 between New London, Connecticut, and Palmer, Massachusetts, on the New London, Willimantic, and Palmer Railroad is outlined in this notice. (Jim Murphy Collection)

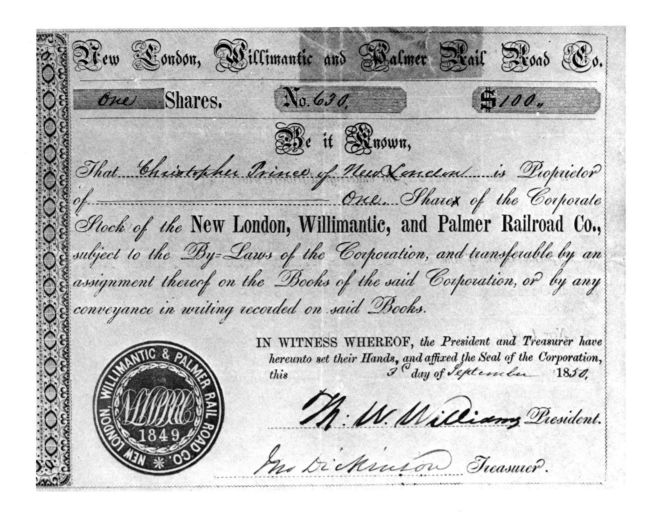

ONE CHRISTOPHER TRINER of New London bought one share of NLW&P stock in September, 1850, as evidenced by this stock certificate. (Jim Murphy Collection)

THIS ENGINE WAS built for the NLW&P by Taunton in 1849 and named the "Willimantic." In 1856 it was rebuilt and renamed the "T. W. Williams" in honor of the road's first president. (Albert C. Spaulding Collection)

The first train carried the directors and officials of the road, including T. P. Chandler, president; and Charles L. Schlater, superintendent. Engineer John Scharier was at the throttle of this first train.

With Page out-maneuvered on the north, Smith next turned his attention to the southern end of his railroad. On December 1, 1870, he leased a 21-mile segment of the Vermont & Massachusetts Railroad that ran between Brattleboro, Vermont, and Grouts Corners (Millers Falls), Massachusetts, where it connected with the recently completed New London Northern Railroad. The latter road operated right to Long Island Sound at the famous old whaling port of New London, Connecticut. On May 1, 1880, this trackage was sold to the New London Northern for $650,000.

This acquisition still left the 24-mile Vermont Valley Railroad between Bellows Falls and Brattleboro in enemy hands. But J. Gregory Smith knew just how he would take care of that. He approached John Page with an offer to lease the Rutland Railroad, including the leased Vermont Valley. But Page was a hard man to deal with, forcing Smith to raise his offer to $376,000 per year to lease the Rutland, while the fee for the Vermont Valley and the Addison roads was agreed upon separately. In addition, Smith agreed to pay $10,000 per year for the use of the lake steamer, "Oakes Ames," which the Rutland had been using as a car ferry between Burlington and Plattsburgh.

THE BEAUTIFUL "A. M. RAMSDELL" is seen shortly after she was delivered by the Manchester Company in 1866. She went through three New London Northern and Central Vermont renumberings before being scrapped in 1900. (Richard Sanborn Collection)

THIS BROADSIDE SHOWS some of the 1867 accommodations being offered by connecting roads. (Wilbur Collection, University of Vermont)

Smith was not pleased with the terms of these leases, as he felt the fees were far too high. Page, on the other hand, was quite satisfied. He knew that the income from the leases would be far more than his roads could otherwise earn in the course of a good year.

In succeeding years, Smith complained bitterly that Page had misrepresented the annual earnings of the Rutland, but such charges were never proven. In all likelihood, it was a case of someone getting the better of him in a business deal for once. And J. Gregory Smith was not a good loser.

Nonetheless, Smith went after the New London Northern, which ran between Millers Falls, Massachusetts, and Long Island Sound at New London, Connecticut. He wanted to be able to run trains from either Ogdensburgh or Canada through Vermont, Massachusetts, and Connecticut and—with a boat connection—be able to transport both passengers and freight right into New York City.

The 100-mile New London Northern had experienced a rather involved and confusing history. The road started in December, 1847, as the New London, Willimantic & Springfield Railroad Company. The intent was that this company would build northward from New London to the Massachusetts-Connecticut line. On April 10, 1848, the New London, Willimantic & Palmer Railroad Company was incorporated to build from the state border northward, but on January 17, 1849, the two roads merged as a matter of convenience. The latter corporate name was retained.

VERMONT CENTRAL NUMBER 41, the "Randolph," is at the scene of an accident near Rockingham, Vermont, on July 24, 1869. The "Down Mail" was derailed when it ran through a misthrown switch. (Donald A. Somerville Collection)

THIS BAGGAGE TAG was recently found in Georgia, Vermont, by William Brislin, III, some six or seven miles from any railroad tracks. (Jim Murphy Collection)

Thirty miles of track between New London and Willimantic, Connecticut, were completed and in operation by May 13, 1849. At Willimantic, connections were made with trains of the Hartford, Providence & Fishkill Railroad. Another 20-mile segment between Willimantic and Stafford went into operation on March 1, 1850. This was followed by the 15-mile section between Stafford, Connecticut, and Palmer, Massachusetts, that commenced operations on September 23, 1850. Early operations between New London and Palmer consisted of two round trips daily.

By 1856, the New London, Willimantic & Palmer was unable to pay the interest on its bonds, so the directors voted to sell that part of the line between Norwich and New London. No sale could be consummated, however, and on January 5, 1859, the road was placed in receivership. It was subsequently reorganized as the New London Northern, and on April 1, 1861, the new company took over operations from the trustees.

In the meantime, northward expansion on this line had continued from Palmer to Amherst, Massachusetts, 19.5 miles, between April 23, 1852, and May 5, 1853. Train service commenced on the latter date. This section was built under a charter granted to the Amherst & Belchertown Railroad Company, and it was built and operated by that company until January 1, 1858. Freight service was inaugurated on May 5, and passenger service commenced a few days later. On January 1, 1858, the trustees took control of the railroad until they sold it at auction to the bondholders some ten months later. A new company, the Amherst, Belchertown & Palmer Railroad, was formed, and it did moderately well for the next few years. On March 1, 1864, the New London Railroad Company purchased the road by exchanging three shares of Amherst, Belchertown & Palmer stock for two shares of New London Northern stock.

The final link in this great north-south route, the 14.5 miles between Amherst and Millers Falls, Massachusetts,

THE BEAUTIFUL FIRST "Governor Smith" is surrounded by a purposeful looking group of men shortly after being rebuilt in the company's St. Albans shops in 1866. Note the ornate stained glass windows in the cab. (Donald A. Somerville Collection)

was completed and operations started on October 8, 1866. This extension permitted a connection with the Vermont & Massachusetts Railroad at Millers Falls. The Vermont & Massachusetts road ran between Fitchburg & Greenfield, Massachusetts, with a branch line running northward from Millers Falls to Brattleboro.

The entire line between Millers Falls and New London was operated by the New London Northern Railroad Company until December 1, 1871, at which time it was leased by J. Gregory Smith, Worthington C. Smith, and Benjamin P. Cheney for 20 years at $155,000 per year. The contract, which was signed on November 21, 1871, specified that the Vermont Central would buy from the New London Northern "all the fuel, lumber, timber, new ties, oil, waste, stationery and shop stock furnished for use upon said railroad." This lease included a fleet of steamships that plied between New London and New York—a service that the New London Northern had inaugurated in June, 1868.

For a time, J. Gregory Smith contemplated building a new road that would give him an all-rail line into downtown New York and thereby compete directly with Vanderbilt's New York Central & Hudson River Railroad. This proposed road was to be known as the New York, Boston & Montreal Railway, but it never got beyond the armchair stage and died on paper in 1877.

Smith did, however, obtain the 115-mile Harlem Extension Railroad on December 1, 1873. This line ran from Rutland south to Chatham, New York, where it made a connection with the Boston & Albany and the Harlem Division of the New York Central & Hudson River Railroad. This gave Smith control of the vast majority of railroad mileage within Vermont's borders—and a great deal beyond them.

Due to marginal profits and increasing competition from Vanderbilt, however, the Harlem Extension lease was dropped on September 9, 1877. In the meantime, six passenger trains, three mixed trains, and several freight trains operated over the line daily.

For brief period of time, four other lines were in the Smith's railroad portfolio. The Whitehall & Plattsburgh, which ran 17.4 miles between Port Henry and Ticonderoga, New York, was leased by the Vermont Central on December 30, 1870. Then, the 23-mile Montreal & Plattsburgh, which operated between Plattsburgh, New York, and the international boundary, was leased on January 23, 1871. On the same day, the 20-mile Whitehall & Plattsburgh extension between Plattsburgh and Ausable, New York, was taken over by a lease agreement.

Finally, on December 1, 1871, the Ware River Railroad, a 16-mile branch of the New London Northern, which ran between Palmer and Gilbertville, Massachusetts, was brought into the fold. The latter road, which was leased the same day as its parent road, had been chartered in 1868 to build from Palmer to Winchendon, Massachusetts.

The end of 1871 thus saw the Vermont Central owning or controlling a total of 743 miles of trackage, a figure that remained stable for the next 14 months. Then, on March 1, 1873, the leases of the Montreal & Plattsburgh and the Whitehall & Plattsburgh were surrendered. Thirty days later, the lease of the Ware River Railroad was broken, and it was subsequently acquired by the Boston & Albany.

The matter of a narrow-gauge railroad in Vermont to serve the north-central part of the state was discussed at a meeting in Montpelier in March, 1872. This meeting was attended by citizens from Washington, Lamoille, Caledonia, and Orleans Counties. Funds were raised to conduct a survey from Montpelier to the Canadian border, with the idea that this road would eventually connect Rutland with

THIS JULY, 1869 photograph shows the Vermont Valley's Number 1 at the head end of a freight train. This engine was built by Rogers in 1851 as the "Putney," and then rebuilt in 1869. Less than two years later, the Vermont Central leased the Vermont Valley. (Edward Emery Collection)

Canada via Montpelier. Preliminary steps were taken to organize the company, but the entire scheme was soon abandoned.

With the entire Rutland system and the Ogdensburgh & Lake Champlain in the Vermont Central fold, many of Smith's fears of being circumvented by competitors had been allayed. However, he foresaw the possibility of a problem to the east. A new road—the Missisquoi Railroad Company—had been incorporated November 14, 1867, to build 27.4 miles from St. Albans eastward to Richford, Vermont, a small community situated on the international boundary exactly halfway between St. Albans and Newport. Smith's concern was that the expanding Connecticut & Passumpsic Rivers Railroad would build from Newport to Richford and then acquire the Missisquoi Railroad and an entrance into St. Albans. J. Gregory Smith viewed such a possibility as being tantamount to giving an enemy the keys to his castle.

The Missisquoi road left St. Albans at a point very near the Vermont Central's terminal facilities, climbed a steep grade eastward out of town, and then crossed rolling farmlands to the banks of the Missisquoi River about one and one-half miles east of Sheldon. Here the grade crossed the wide river on a trestle and then followed the river valley to Richford.

For part of the distance, the railroad was built on the grade of the St. Albans & Richford Plank Road Company, which had been in existence for many years. The plank road had fallen into the hands of directors Lawrence Brainerd and J. Gregory Smith because they had made good on outstanding debts of that company. The plank road company was then sold to the Missisquoi Railroad Company for $30,000. In turn, the Missisquoi Railroad was leased for twenty years to the Vermont Central effective November 28, 1870. The Vermont Central agreed to issue $500,000 of 20 year, seven percent bonds, and the contract stated that it was "For the best interest of the Missisquoi Railroad Company to make arrangements with the trustees and managers of the Vermont Central and Vermont & Canada Railroads to run and operate said railroad so that said

Vermont Central Railroad.

Notice to Enginemen, Conductor's, Brakemen, Station Agent's, &c.

On and after this date, the following Rules must be observed in taking Wood for Locomotives running on Vermont Central, Vermont & Canada, Montreal & Vt. Junction, and Sullivan Railroads.

1st. Station Agents, or the man in charge, will see that sufficient wood is prepared and thrown forward at the Shed so as to be taken on the Locomotives with the least possible delay. The men throwing out the wood, will be required to split any chunks of Wood that may be to large to enter the Furnace Door of the Engines.

2d. When commencing upon a Shed full of Wood, the man in charge will begin from one end, and not open more than two bents in front, and work upon them from front to rear, until the wood is all taken out, so that there shall not be more than two bents broken at a time.

3d. Engineers will be required to take the wood LARGE and SMALL, as thrown out, without selecting.

4th. The men in charge, will see that no Wood, Chips, Bark, or Rubbish, is left outside the Sheds, or near the track. They will watch the Wood and Shed closely after any train or Engine has passed, to prevent fires.

5th. Engineers, or Firemen must not throw from their Engines or Tenders, (except at Wood Sheds,) any Wood that may be too large to enter the Furnace door.

All employees in any way connected with the running of trains, must strictly observe the foregoing Rules, and report all violations thereof.

Per order,　　　　　G. MERRILL, GEN'L SUP'T.
J. G. SLAFTER, AGENT.
St. Albans, April 5th, 1870.

THIS VERMONT CENTRAL notice to company personnel regarding the handling of wood contains some extremely interesting regulations. (Jim McFarlane Collection)

THIS IS A builder's photo of the Vermont Central's Number 81, the ''Pacific,'' which was made at the Baldwin Locomotive Works in 1871. This engine was later sent to the Rutland Division, shortly after the Vermont Central leased the Rutland Railroad at the end of 1870. (Louis Cameron Collection)

THIS COMMUNICATION ON Northern Pacific Railroad stationery, a road which J. Gregory Smith had been deeply involved for a few years, covers a transaction between George Harris & Company and the Missisquoi Railroad Company. Harris was the contractor for the building of this line between St. Albans and Richford, Vermont. (Jim Murphy Collection)

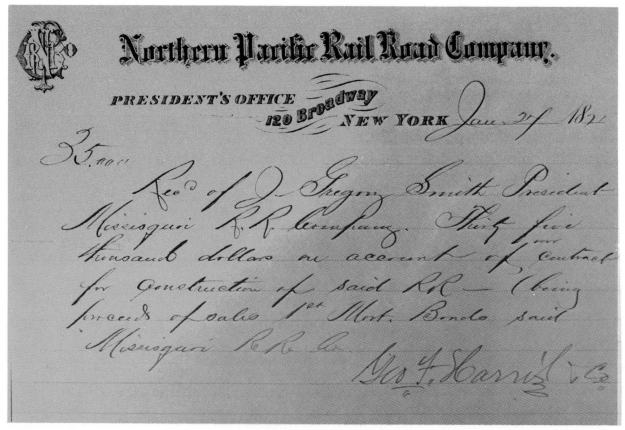

THE VERMONT VALLEY'S Number 3, the "Westminster," operated between Bellows Falls and Brattleboro. This line was leased by the Vermont Central on January 1, 1871. (Lewis R. Brown, Inc., Collection)

railroad may be run and operated in a prudent and economical manner, and that the payment of the mortgage bonds as it shall accrue, may be assured the holders thereof."

Meanwhile, construction had been started by contractor F. Harris & Company, and by the fall of 1870, nine miles of the line was graded and five miles of rail laid. The work progressed without serious difficulty, and the job was completed in December, 1872. Service was inaugurated that same day. The Smiths were thus able to rest a bit better at night, knowing that they had all but thwarted any future possibility of their stronghold being invaded by an enemy road. History has proven the point, as no other railroad was to enter St. Albans.

As previously recounted, the original line of the Vermont Central was run through Northfield amid bitter controversy. When president Charles Paine rejected the shorter survey through Williamstown in favor of his hometown, Montpelier was relegated to the status of a very short branch line terminus. Even worse, perhaps, was the fact that the busy granite producing city of Barre had no rail service at all.

However, in the mid-1860s a group of interested Montpelier and Barre businessmen formed the Montpelier & White River Railroad Company, and on November 8, 1867, they were granted a charter to build a railroad from Mont-

pelier to Barre. It was nearly four years, however, before the new road was organized. Finally, on August 23, 1871, the first stockholders' meeting was held, at which the road's first directors were elected. With this accomplished, the new directors then immediately adjourned to hold an election of corporate officers.

A 6.2-mile survey up the valley between Montpelier and Barre was approved and construction was eventually started. July 1, 1875, marked the date of the first revenue service between these two points, and the new line was leased by the Central Vermont Railroad Company that same day. Over the ensuing decades, great quantities of granite went out over this line to the main line at Montpelier Junction.

Later, this road was extended 8.4 miles from Barre south to Williamstown to serve the granite industry in that town—which Paine had snubbed decades earlier. In early March, 1887, the Central Vermont directors voted to build the extension, and the citizens of Williamstown pledged $30,000 in loans to the project. On September 19, 1887, the first sod was broken in Williamstown, with the town's oldest citizen—95-year old Enoch Howe—being given that honor. Appropriate remarks were made by Judge John Lynde and James R. Langdon of Montpelier. Langdon had now been active in railroad promotion in the area for some 50 years, and he was

Continued on page 90

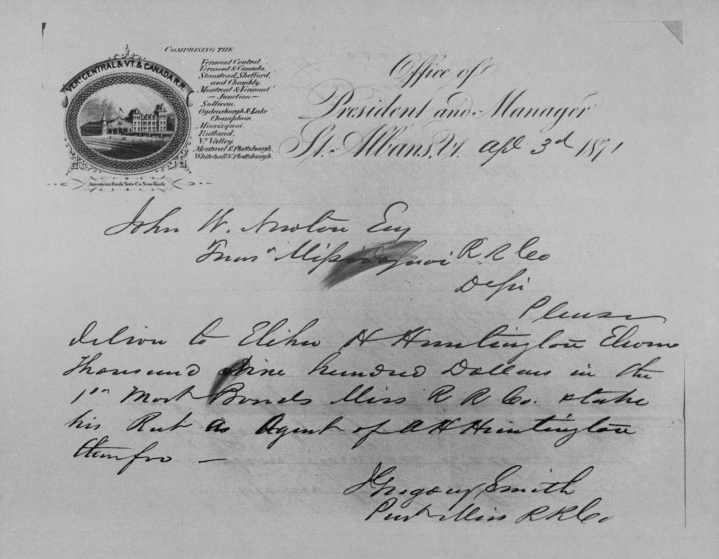

Estimate of the Cost of Buildings

4	Passenger Depots	@ $3000 2000	12,000.00
4	Freight	" 1500 1000	6,000.00
4	Combined	" 2500 2000	10,000.00
3	Woodsheds	" 600 400	1,800.00
3	Water Stations	1200	6,000.00
1	Engine House	1500	3,000.00
1	Turn Table	2000 $	3,000.00
	Total cost per cent added —		41,800.00

THIS LETTER AUTHORIZING a financial transaction involving the construction of the Missisquoi Railroad, was penned by J. Gregory Smith, president of both the Vermont Central and the Missisquoi Railroad, in 1871. (Jim Murphy Collection)

THIS PAPER IS a hand-written estimate of the cost of buildings for the Missisquoi Railroad prior to its construction. (Jim Murphy Collection)

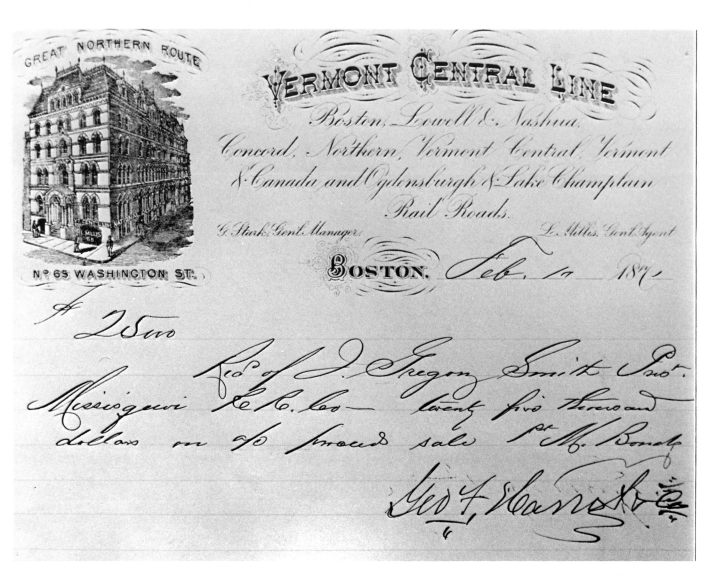

GEORGE F. HARRIS & Company, the contractor for the construction of the Missisquoi Railroad has used Vermont Central stationery for a receipt. (Jim Murphy Collection)

THIS WAYBILL COVERS the shipment of a turntable weighing 24,600 pounds which was installed at Richford, the end of the Missisquoi Railroad. (Jim Murphy Collection)

THE NEAT APPEARING Number 6 of the Vermont Valley served the Vermont Central after the VC leased the former road on January 1, 1871. (Lewis R. Brown, Inc., Collection)

THIS UNISSUED STOCK certificate of the Missisquoi Railroad Company was signed by its president, J. Gregory Smith. Of interest is the condition that has been penned in with handwriting similar to the printing on the form. (Jim Murphy Collection)

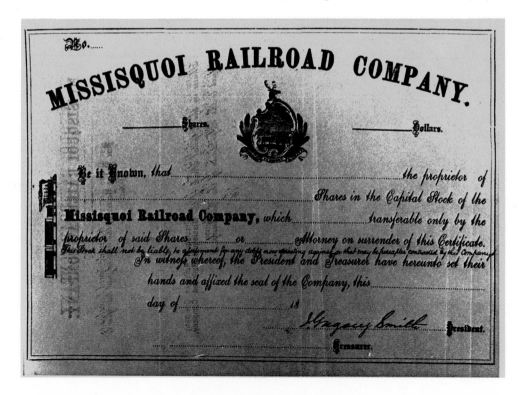

THIS ENGINE WAS built as the ''Swanton'' by Hinkley & Drury in 1852. It was rebuilt in 1870 and renamed ''Richford.'' Shortly thereafter, it was sent to the Rutland Division and again renamed. (William G. Rowley Collection)

THIS 1871 PIECE OF correspondence is included to show the ornate letterheads that were the order of the day. (Jim Murphy Collection)

held in much respect by the local citizens as he had been a proponent of the Williamstown Gulf route in the 1840s when Charles Paine was determined the main line should go through Northfield.

This line did not, however, pass through the famed Gulf, as that is located a few miles south of the village of Williamstown. Although there was talk of building the line through to a connection with the Central Vermont main line at Royalton, such an extension never advanced beyond the talking stage.

The Williamstown extension, as surveyed by Central Vermont civil engineers W. E. Babbitt and William Hale, was rather hastily constructed, with the trestlework being particularly light, as it was planned that these structures would be filled in soon after service was commenced. It turned out to be years before many of these critical improvements were made, however.

During the construction of the line, the embankments north of Williamstown started to slide onto the grade, and there had been a number of near accidents result. In late November, 1887, however, a young construction worker by the name of Broadway was buried under a huge slide on his first day on the job. It was nearly six minutes before his fellow workers could uncover him, and when they did, he was dead.

A large quantity of fir ties arrived from Quebec during April, 1888, and track laying commenced about the first of May. The construction train pulled by the "B. B. Smalley," reached Williamstown on June 16, and a large crowd assembled to witness the first train arrive in the village.

Just a week before this, the 15-year old son of R. Allen of Barre came near losing his life in a most unusual accident with the construction train. He was on his way to Barre Village with a load of milk, and he drove his rig onto an

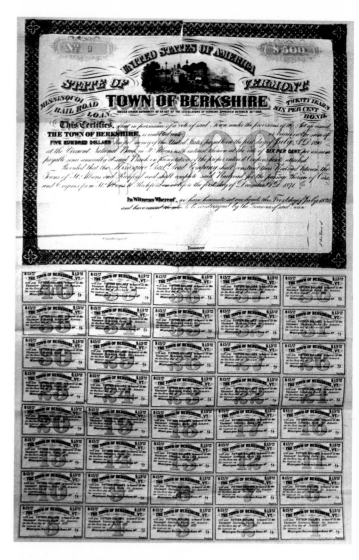

THIS $500 TWENTY-YEAR, six percent bond of the **Town of Berkshire** to the Missisquoi Railroad Company was never issued. It is still in pristine condition. (Dean Howarth Collection)

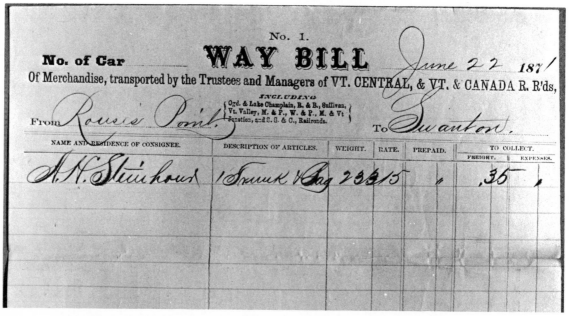

ACCORDING TO THIS 1871 waybill, A. H. Stinehour paid thirty-five cents to have one trunk and a bag transported from Rouses Point, New **York, to Swanton, Vermont, a distance of about eight miles.** (Jim Murphy Collection)

COMPRISING THE

Vermont Central
Vermont & Canada,
Stanstead, Shefford,
and Chambly,
Montreal & Vermont
—Junction—
Sullivan,
Ogdensburgh & Lake
Champlain,
Missisquoi,
Rutland,
V.t Valley,
Montreal & Plattsburgh,
Whitehall & Plattsburgh.

American Bank Note Co. New-York.

Steamboat and Railroad.

WAY-BILL OF MERCHANDISE

From NEW YORK, by

Steamer *Continental*

Hartford and New Haven, Conn. River and

Vermont Central Railroads,

to *Swanton Vt*

Forwarded *June 21* 1871.

448

THIS IS ANOTHER example of the ornate letter-heads used on stationery in the 1870s. The focal point of this one is a rendering of the St. Albans train shed and depot within an oval, as is the one illustrated on page 89. (Jim Murphy Collection)

THIS SHIPMENT WAS transported from New York to Swanton on the steamer ''Continental'' and over the Vermont Central. (Jim Murphy Collection)

Vermont Central Railroad. (Form No. 2.)

From *Richd* Station,

to *S. Merrill* St. Albans, *Dec 31* 18*72*

We understand we are to *Meet Number*

Eight 8 Train at

South Royalton

H. H. Woods Conductor. No.

Mark Rice Engineer. train

THIS ILLUSTRATION IS an early train order, signed by both the conductor and the engineer. Note the unusual wording of this order. (Jim Murphy Collection)

THE GLEAMING "E. F. PERKINS" poses outside the Northfield depot about 1870. This engine was built by Hinkley & Drury as the "Lamoille," rebuilt in 1862, and renamed the "E. F. Perkins" in 1869. She was scrapped in 1893. (Richard Sanborn Collection)

THE "N. L. DAVIS" is still "afloat," but the rest of her train is at least partially submerged in Lake Champlain, as the result of the trestle collapsing under the weight of the engine and train in 1871. This engine was being operated under the Vermont Central-Rutland lease agreement which went into effect on December 30, 1870, and has not been re-lettered. (Jim Shaughnessy Collection, from THE RUTLAND ROAD)

THE ORNATE COVERED trainshed, enclosed water tank, and covered platform in service in Essex Junction in the 1870s is clearly shown in this photo- graph. We are looking north, and the photographer is standing on the Main Street crossing. (Jim Shaughnessy Collection)

overpass just as the train was passing below. The horse became frightened and ran from one side of the bridge to the other, striking the railing on each side until at one point it gave away. The horse, wagon, milk, and boy went crashing down onto the moving train. Allen struck the engine boiler and was projected off into a ditch, miraculously suffering only scratches and bruises. The horse was not so fortunate. It fell between the engine and tender, and a newspaper account of the incident reported "the cars reduced the animal to mincemeat. The wagon was converted into tooth- picks and iron filings, and the vicinity of the accident flowed with fresh milk."

In July, 1888, grading was started at Williamstown for a 20 by 60-foot passenger and freight depot, an engine house, a water tank, and three sidings. The first northbound com- bination passenger-freight train arrived in Barre from Williamstown on July 16, consisting of two freight cars and a combine, with engineer Charles Briggs at the throttle. A newspaper account stated that there were "quite a number of passengers aboard."

One of the passengers was a very elderly man, who descended the rear steps of the combine and "picked his way carefully across the tracks, looked nervously about him as if he expected to be run over by a wild engine, and then gazed curiously at the iron trotter that had pulled him from his native hills in Williamstown to the granite-ribbed town of Barre. 'Is this your first trip on the cars,' he was asked? 'My first, by gosh,' he replied as he bit off a couple inches of

Mechanic's Delight. 'Seventy-five years I've lived in Williamstown and never did I see such goings on as these. I thought I would just come down once to see what kind of critters these cars are, but I swear I'm going back by team.' And the old gentlemen expectorated on a neighboring dog to express his emotion. 'Then you prefer the good old days of stagecoaches and quiet to railroad trains and noise?' he was asked. 'Well, I reckon!' he replied, and wandered his way up the street."

By late fall, the grading for the station at Williamstown was completed, the water tank was in operation, and the finishing touches were being put on the one-stall engine house. In December, C. R. Benedict made his last trip as a stage driver, and passengers and mail between Barre and Williamstown were to be henceforth handled by Central Vermont trains. During the early years of operations, the locomotives "Vermont" and "Williston" were normally assigned to this line.

Throughout much of its history, two mixed trains a day made round-trips over the line's 60-pound rails. One train left Williamstown for Barre at about 7:30 six mornings a week. At Barre this train would cut off its coach in front of the depot and spend much of the day switching the yard. The passengers for points beyond, meanwhile, would transfer to a connecting train that would take them to Montpelier Junction. Northbound freight would be picked up later by another train. Late in the afternoon, with the switching chores completed at Barre, the crew would pick up the coach

NUMBER 16, THE "Moosalamoo," is shown here as a Rutland Division engine in the early 1870s. She was built by Taunton in 1868 and scrapped in 1900. (Richard Sanborn Collection)

and return to Williamstown. There the engine would be turned by hand on a small wooden turntable, serviced, and made ready for morning.

In addition to this train, another mixed train would come into Williamstown near mid-day, turn its engine, and soon head back to Barre, Montpelier, and on to Montpelier Junction for a connection with a main line train.

At White River Junction, the 13.9-mile Woodstock Railway ran from its connection with the Central Vermont to Woodstock. This road was completed in 1875, and during the first years of operations it leased revenue equipment from the Central Vermont. In fact, the venerable 4-4-0 "Winooski" was used to power the Woodstock's construction trains.

The Central Vermont vigorously fought a Woodstock Railway crossing of its main line tracks in the yard at White River Junction, insisting instead that the new road's passenger trains must reach the union station by a series of complicated switching moves that required at least 15 minutes to complete. Three years of litigation ended in 1878 when the courts decided in favor of the Woodstock Railway. During the 58 years of the road's existence, a moderate amount of freight and passenger business was interchanged at White River Junction.

Another railroad that was to become directly associated with the Central Vermont was the Burlington & Lamoille Railroad Company, which was chartered on February 24, 1875. The road was conceived for the purpose of connecting the Rutland Railroad at Burlington with the Central

Vermont at Essex Junction and the newly built Portland & Ogdensburgh Railroad at Cambridge Junction. In addition to these connections, the promoters of this independent road foresaw considerable traffic in agricultural products along its 35-mile line.

This railroad was chartered in 1869, and three routes were subsequently surveyed for it by 70-year old William Hale of Essex Junction. After selecting the route for the new road, the directors engaged Daniel Linsley of Burlington to construct the entire line. He broke the first ground at Jericho on May 24, 1875, and the grading and trestle work continued through to the end of 1876. The two most impressive structures on the line were a two-level Howe truss bridge over the Winooski River near Burlington that was nearly 200 feet long and 90 feet high, and an even longer, but lower, pile trestle near Jericho. The work of laying the ties and rails commenced at Burlington on April 4, 1877, and the job was finished on June 30 when the connection was made with the tracks of the Vermont Division of the Portland & Ogdensburgh road. Regular service on the new road commenced on July 3, 1877.

The Burlington & Lamoille Railroad remained independent for a number of years, but it maintained a friendly working relationship with the Central Vermont over the years. It was reorganized as the Burlington & Lamoille Valley Railroad on May 1, 1889, and then leased to the Central Vermont on that date. The Central Vermont immediately abandoned the nine miles of trackage between

Burlington and Essex Junction, and operated both passenger and freight service over the remaining 26 miles until abandonment in 1938.

Despite the fact the section between Burlington and Essex Junction has been abandoned for over 90 years, one can still clearly see in wintertime short portions of the grade while travelling eastbound on Interstate I-89 just a few hundred yards west of the I-89 interchange.

The Central Vermont acquired its only narrow-gauge trackage on November 3, 1880, in the form of the three-foot gauge Brattleboro & Whitehall Railroad. This company had been incorporated on November 17, 1876, and organized on February 1, 1877. The company's charter granted it permission to build between the two towns in its name—Brattleboro, Vermont, and Whitehall, New York.

The directors of the road visited the two-foot gauge Billerica & Bedford Railroad in northeastern Massachusetts and came home most impressed with what they saw. However, after much discussion, it was decided that the road would be built to the more common three-foot gauge. The road never reached its objective, but 35.7 miles of track between Brattleboro and South Londonderry, Vermont, were put into operation on November 3, 1880. The little trains moved cautiously over the 36-pound rails.

The Brattleboro & Whitehall was first leased to the New London Northern Railroad when it was only partially built. The New London Northern completed the construction work as far as South Londonderry, and accepted in partial payment first mortgage bonds of the new road. The balance of the construction costs was held as an indebtedness against the narrow-gauge company. Upon completion of the road, it was turned over to the Central Vermont for operation in accordance with provisions in its lease with the New London Northern. The road was declared bankrupt in early 1905, and a new company—the West River Railroad—was formed. On a rainy July 30, 1905, new ties were put in, the rails moved apart, and the West River became a standard-gauge railroad.

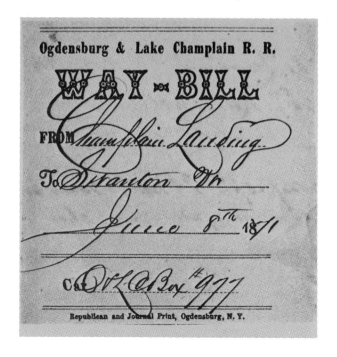

THE SHINING "B. P. CHENEY" stands in front of the Northfield station in the 1870s. It was built by the Essex Company in 1852 as the "Richmond" and was renamed and rebuilt in 1853 and rebuilt a second time shortly before this photograph was taken in 1869. It remained in service until being scrapped in 1897. (Whitney Maxfield Collection)

Chapter V

Expose and Reorganization 1873-1886

*T*HE VERMONT CENTRAL WAS, WITH ALL ITS OWNED AND CONTROLL-
ed lines, a very impressive railroad in 1873. In that year, its 793 miles of trackage qualified it as the largest railroad in New England and the seventh largest in the country. Competition on virtually all fronts had been successfully out-maneuvered, the physical plant was in relatively sound condition, and a time of prosperity would seemingly be all that would lie ahead. But everything was not as the Smiths would have liked it to be. The hoped for local and through traffic had not yet materialized to the degree anticipated and—while the area served by the railroad was great—it was virtually devoid of heavy industry.

A differential freight rate covering through traffic out of New York and Boston had been fought for long and hard, but it was not providing sufficient revenue to carry portions of the road. Further, the nation itself was unwittingly headed for a dramatic economic depression. All evidence seemed to be indicating that the Smiths and their Vermont Central colleagues had bitten off more than they could chew—and no one knew it any better than J. Gregory Smith.

As the railroad had grown through the 1860s, the finances of the organization had grown increasingly more confused and complex. It is virtually impossible to determine how much of this was circumstantial and how much was by design. Undoubtedly, there was more of the latter. Stockholders and bondholders alike had grown increasingly hostile with the uncertainty of their respective positions in the hierarchy of the road's financial mumbo-jumbo. Case after case had been introduced into the courts of the state, but precious little in the way of either clarification or satisfaction had come the way of the security holders. Their concerns centered primarily on the issue of whether the first and second mortgage bondholders of the Vermont Central and the stock holders of the Vermont & Canada were entitled to a preference in payment over the trust debts incurred by the receivers and managers, which had been made with the consent and approval of the road's security holders. After the issue had been heard three times by the Vermont Supreme Court, Judge Timothy Redfield finally ruled in favor of the trust debts.

In addition to the continuous court battles over internal matters, the Smiths were also constantly facing efforts of other major trunk lines to keep the Smith interests more or less confined to their home ground—Vermont. The New York Central & Hudson River, the Pennsylvania, the

Baltimore & Ohio, and the Erie roads were equally persistent and ruthless in waging rate wars that were costly to both sides.

The Smiths had formed a variety of related subsidiary companies over the years, the first of which was the St. Albans Foundry, which came into being in 1858. Within a few years, the operation covered nearly four acres and six buildings immediately adjacent to the Vermont Central depot. The firm was owned by J. Gregory Smith and Worthington C. Smith and was leased to Edward Curtis Smith, a son of J. Gregory and a nephew of Worthington C. Wheels and a variety of other castings for use on the railroad's rolling stock were manufactured, and the elder Smiths received a royalty as owners on each piece produced.

By the mid-1860s, however, operating and mechanical personnel alike reached the unfortunate conclusion that these wheels were of dangerously inferior quality. The wheels of 1867 and 1868 were breaking frequently and causing a great deal of trouble along the whole line. At one point, master mechanic Perkins refused to use the foundry's wheels under passenger equipment, and he subsequently bought some of better quality from firms in Troy, New York, and Springfield and Worcester, Massachusetts.

The St. Albans Foundry eventually agreed to manufacture wheels only of new Salisbury Iron, and an agreement was reached with the railroad to supply them at prices that were about $2.50 more per wheel than those charged for the inferior ones.

In 1868, the National Car Company was organized with capital stock authorized in the amount of $500,000. This corporation was owned and managed in precisely the same way as was the St. Albans Foundry. Prior to the organization of the National Car Company, a patent had been ob-

ESSEX JUNCTION IS A busy place, as three south-bound trains are simmering at the depot and a northbound train appears to be occupying the right-hand track in the trainshed. Main Street crosses the tracks in the foreground. (Gerry Fox Collection)

tained for an "adjustable axle," by which the wheels could be moved on the axle to fit either standard-gauge tracks or broad-gauge tracks such as those of the Grand Trunk Railway in Canada. A car equipped with such trucks could thus travel over both lines without a transshipment of merchandise. In order to get competitive through rates on freight between Chicago and points on the Vermont Central and other New England roads, it was necessary that the shipment be able to go through without breaking bulk.

The Smiths paid a reported $50,000 for the patent, found the Grand Trunk interested in developing the through route, and thus organized the National Car Company to build 200 cars equipped with these adjustable trucks for use in this service. These trucks at first were very successful, but as they became worn, they became costly and troublesome to maintain. Accidents began to happen, particularly on the Grand Trunk, and that road eventually decided to abandon the idea of the adjustable trucks entirely.

The Grand Trunk then bought 500 of these cars—the original 200 plus another 300 built subsequently—for $535,000, a rather high price for that time. Instead of trucks with adjustable axles, these cars were now equipped with two sets of trucks—one standard gauge and one broad gauge. At the interchange point between the Grand Trunk and the Vermont line, the cars were jacked up and the appropriate trucks put under them for the continuation of the trip.

THIS LOCOMOTIVE APPEARS to be posing among granite slabs at an unknown location. It was built by Taunton in 1869 and became the Rutland Division's "Shelburne" two years later. (Jim McFarlane Collection)

THIS 1874 PHOTOGRAPH SHOWS THE ORIGINAL Vermont Central depot on the right with the newly built Montpelier & Wells River grade in the background. The Vermont Mutual Fire Insurance Company building is in the center of what became known as Railroad Square and the Pavilion Hotel is on the left. (William Gove Collection)

THIS VERY EARLY photograph shows the St. Albans Foundry, which had close affiliations with the Vermont Central fortunes for a number of years. (Jim Murphy Collection)

THESE THREE VIEWS show the size and complexity of the St. Albans Rolling Mill in the 1870s. This mill was a very good customer of the railroad for many years. (Three photos, Ed Steel Collection)

The Vermont Iron and Car Company was a subsidiary of the National Car Company. President Reynolds of the Ottawa Railroad was preparing to extend his railroad into virgin timberlands on which large mills were being constructed. Reynolds wanted to ship his Canadian lumber into the United States, but he needed cars designed especially for this commodity. Freight cars at that time were generally 28 feet in length, but the lumber customers wanted cars constructed 33 feet in length, so they could ship two lengths of the 16-foot lumber in each car. This would, of course, represent a substantial savings to the lumbermen, as two normal length cars would otherwise be required. A minimum of 300 cars would initially be required to handle this new business, and the Vermont Iron and Car Company was organized for the purpose of manufacturing these special pieces of equipment. Soon after they were built and put into service, however, the lumber business fell upon hard times. These cars were not needed in large numbers in the lumber business because of the decline in the lumber market, but they quickly found their way into grain transportation.

The St. Albans Iron & Steel Works was incorporated in 1873 to manufacture rails, with the Smith family again holding all the key positions. Iron rails were produced until 1878, at which time the firm started manufacturing the more durable steel rails. The Vermont Central and other roads in the region were the firm's largest customers, although in later years nearly half of the company's production was shipped to the West.

Although expansion and diversification had characterized the corporate activities of the Vermont Central for years, by 1872 the Smiths had started falling behind in the lease and note payments, as well as on the interest payments on bonds. In November of that year, they commenced actions whereby they could buy some time on their obligations by reorganizing the Vermont Central as the Central Vermont Railroad Company. The new entity would take over the operations, the assets, and the liabilities of the existing corporation. The Smiths knew that if they could succeed in getting such a reorganization approved, it would be at least a few months before the new company would have to make good on the antecedent firm's obligations.

But before these arrangements could be completed, fate stepped in. The nation was struck by the Panic of 1873. Ironically, a major contributor to this economic chaos was the overexpansion of the railroads throughout the country. The Smiths were about to become, in a real sense, a victim of their own game. Within a matter of months, some 20 percent of the nation's railroads underwent foreclosure proceedings.

In the preceding quarter of a century, however, the Smiths had built a real dynasty. And in so doing, if they hadn't evaded the law countless scores of times, beneficence would dictate it safe to say they had avoided the law. There were examples of interlocking directorates, nepotism, retainers paid for which no services were rendered, bluffs, handouts, legislative amendments, patronage lists, multiple transfers, selective discounts, overcharges, excessive reimbursements, double leasings, and a myriad of transactions so extremely complicated that judges and legislators alike were aghast.

A VERMONT CENTRAL boxcar is spotted on a siding at the St. Albans Rolling Mill in the mid-1870s. (Ed Steel Collection)

THIS CLASSIC PHOTOGRAPH clearly shows several of the shop buildings and various pieces of rolling stock at St. Albans. We are looking in a northerly direction, with the large depot and train-shed just off the picture to the right. (Jim Murphy Collection)

In one way or another, the Smiths had seemed quite able to exert influence upon the legislative and judicial branches of the state government that invariably resulted in actions beneficial to their holdings and themselves. It was felt, at least by some, that J. Gregory Smith continued serving as the state's chief executive in St. Albans long after his term as governor in Montpelier had officially ended in 1864.

Past expansion and management techniques notwithstanding, the Smiths in 1873 continued their efforts for the reorganization of the Vermont Central. They viewed this cause as essential for their corporate survival in this troubled time. Although there was some bitter opposition from those who would be victimized by such a move, the Central Vermont Railroad Company was successfully incorporated on November 23, 1872, and formally organized on May 21, 1873.

The charter of the new organization stated: "Such bond-holders under the first or second mortgage of the Vermont Central Railroad, and such other persons as shall hereafter become stockholders, are hereby incorporated under the name of the Central Vermont Railroad Company, for the

THE ST. ALBANS FOUNDRY'S history was closely entwined with that of the Vermont Central. This advertisement indicates some of the products manufactured by this firm. (Ed Steel collection)

102

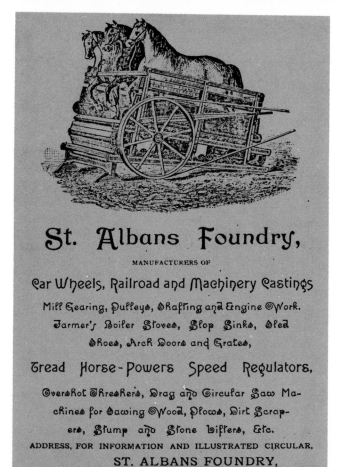

THE ST. ALBANS TRAINSHED and depot were only a few years old when this photograph was taken. In the distance one may see one of the early brick roundhouses. (Jim McFarlane Collection)

WE ARE LOOKING northward to the St. Albans shops and depot in 1874. Business must be good as there are only a few cars in the yard. (Jim Murphy Collection)

THESE TWO PHOTOS show a very attractive Central Vermont Railway Company stock certificate and an 1874 employees rulebook. (Upper photo, Glenn Davis Collection; lower photo, Jim Murphy Collection)

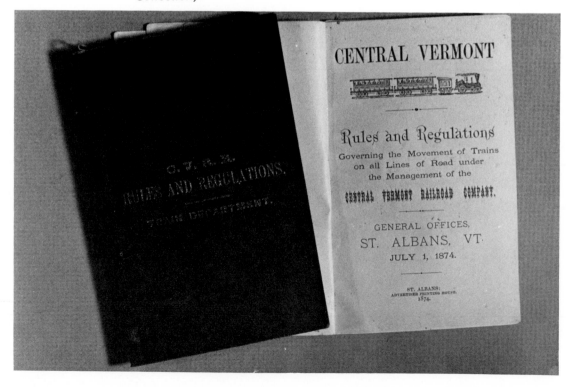

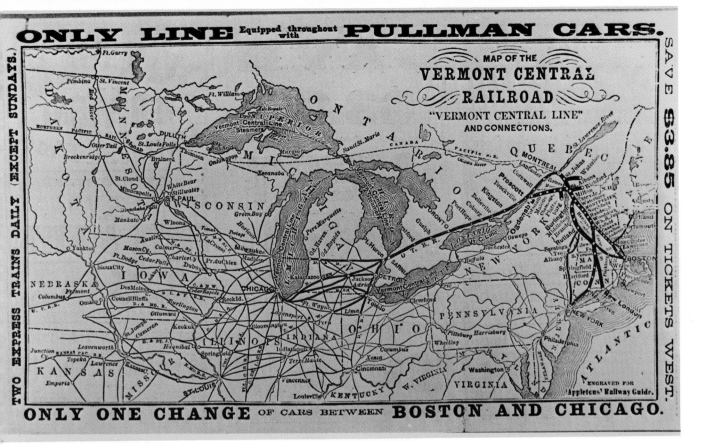

THIS MAP SHOWS Vermont Central passenger routes and major connections as they existed in 1873. The broadside promotes Central Vermont passenger service shortly after the company was reorganized in May, 1873. (Both photos, Jim McFarlane Collection)

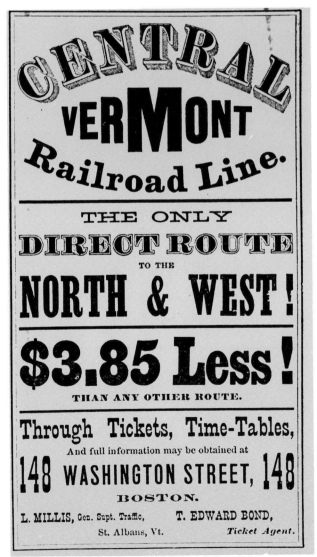

purpose of purchasing the Vermont Central and Vermont & Canada railroads, or either of said roads, and for the purpose of purchasing or retiring by exchange or otherwise, the stock and bonds of the Vermont Central and Vermont & Canada companies, and for the purpose of operating and maintaining such roads."

The new company's first board of directors was elected at this May 21, 1873, meeting; as might be expected, there were several familiar names: S. L. M. Barlow, George H. Brown, Benjamin P. Cheney, Joseph Clark, William B. Duncan, John Q. Hoyt, James R. Langdon, J. G. McCullough, John B. Page, Trenor W. Park, John S. Shultze, J. Gregory Smith, and Worthington C. Smith. The directors then met and elected the following officers of the newly reorganized company: J. Gregory Smith, president; Worthington C. Smith, vice-president; James R. Langdon, vice-president; George Nichols, secretary; and H. H. Lockwood, treasurer. In addition, an executive committee was comprised of J. Gregory Smith, S. L. M. Barlow, Trenor W. Park, and J. S. Schultze.

John W. Hobart was named general manager of the road at this time. Hobart was a highly respected man who had worked his way up through the ranks. He was born in Randolph, Vermont, and went to work on the Vermont Central at the age of 21 as a clerk at the time the road commenced operations through his home town in 1848. A year later he was named station agent at Montpelier, a position he held for ten years. In 1859, he was appointed to the position of general freight agent, an office he held until his appointment as general manager of the Central Vermont system.

105

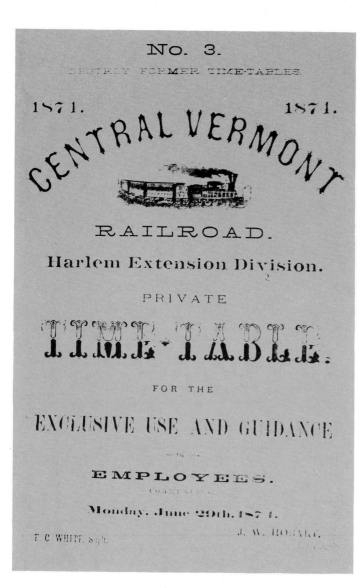

NO. 3.

DISTRICT FORMER TIME-TABLES.

1871.   1874.

CENTRAL VERMONT

RAILROAD.

Harlem Extension Division.

PRIVATE

TIME-TABLE.

FOR THE

EXCLUSIVE USE AND GUIDANCE

— OF —

EMPLOYEES.

COMMENCING

Monday, June 29th, 1874.

F. C. WHITE, Sup't.   J. W. HOBART,

DANGER SIGNALS.

DANGER SIGNALS MUST BE STRICTLY OBSERVED and when placed in a position to STOP TRAINS Train or Engine will pass such signal until signalled that ALL IS RIGHT; except, in case of accident to the signal, when an order to pass, from the man charge of the signal, will be observed.

A disregard of these instructions will be just cause for dismissal from the service of the Company.

MOOER'S JUNCTION.

ONE RED SIGNAL at top of the pole denotes the trains on PLATTSBURG & MONTREAL ROAD MUST STOP before coming to the crossing,—Central Vermont trains can pass.

Two RED SIGNALS denote that trains on Central Vermont Road MUST STOP,—Plattsburg and Montreal trains can pass. When NO SIGNAL is shown ALL TRAINS MUST STOP.

S. S. & C. JUNCTION.

AN ARM AT TOP OF A POLE.—When in a HORIZONTAL POSITION, trains on the MONTREAL & VERMONT JUNCTION Road have right to pass.

When in a PERPENDICULAR POSITION trains on S. S. & C. Road have right to pass.

THE SPECIAL INSTRUCTIONS contained in the 1874 employees timetable on this and the next page give us much information about operating procedures of the day. (All four photos, Jim Murphy Collection)

With the Central Vermont Railroad Company's reorganization completed, the officials of the old Vermont Central—J. Gregory Smith, Worthington C. Smith, Joseph Clark, Benjamin P. Cheney, and Lawrence Barnes— petitioned the Vermont Chancery Court on June 2, 1873, for the same powers and authority as had been granted them for the antecedent road. This was accomplished officially on July 1, 1873, and the Vermont Central property became part of the new Central Vermont Railroad, which operated it as receiver and manager for the next eleven years.

Among those on the long list of people who were irate over this bit of sleight of hand were the directors of the Vermont & Canada Railroad. Their report to the stockholders of that company in 1873 bluntly stated: "The charter of the Central Vermont Railroad Company, purporting to be granted for the benefit of the bondholders of the old Vermont Central Railroad, has been taken advantage of to

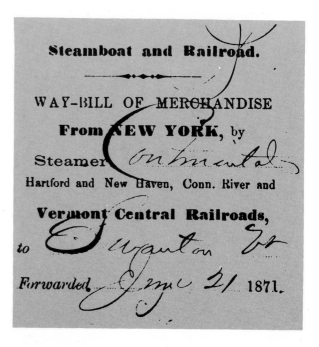

Steamboat and Railroad.

WAY-BILL OF MERCHANDISE

From NEW YORK, by

Steamer *Continental*

Hartford and New Haven, Conn. River and

Vermont Central Railroads,

to *Wyanton Vt*

Forwarded *June 21* 1871.

organize a sort of 'Credit Mobilier' in Vermont." They went on to state, "We cannot ourselves understand, much less satisfactorily explain to you, how this has come to pass."

Numerous earlier attempts by critics and victims alike to bring alleged misdeeds of the Vermont Central management to the courts had resulted in most cases in the discrediting of the accusations by judicial or legislative personnel sympathetic to the Smiths' cause. In at least one case, nothing more than a cautious and condescending reproof of those responsible for the actions resulted.

By 1875, however, the complaints had become numerous and loud enough to warrant increasing attention by the periodicals of the day. Smith and his associates were now being blamed publicly for the financial condition the Central Vermont found itself in. There were public charges of gross mismanagement and corruption.

42

SWANTON JUNCTION.

A DOUBLE SEMAPHORE SIGNAL ABOVE A FRAME.— The WEST ARM or a BLUE LIGHT in a PERPENDICULAR position, and the EAST ARM or a RED LIGHT in a HORIZONTAL position gives trains to or from WESTERN DIVISION right to pass

The WEST ARM or a RED LIGHT in a HORIZONTAL position and the EAST ARM or a BLUE LIGHT in a PERPENDICULAR position gives trains to or from the NORTHERN DIVISION right to pass.

Both ARMS or TWO RED LIGHTS in a HORIZONTAL position, ALL TRAINS MUST STOP.

———

ST. ALBANS.

Semaphore Signal at NORTH and SOUTH ENDS of YARD, and at WELDEN STREET CROSSING.

Arm in a PERPENDICULAR position, or GREEN LIGHT at top of pole, track is clear for trains to enter the yard.

Arm at an ANGLE OF 45 DEGREES, or a GREEN and RED LIGHT at top of pole, enter with *extreme caution*, prepared to stop train on short notice.

Arm in HORIZONTAL position or a RED LIGHT at top of pole, trains must not pass the signal until its position is changed.

Trains approaching St. Albans from the SOUTH, after having passed the first signal, must stop South of Welden Street crossing unless the signal at that point is set right for them to pass.

At PEARL STREET crossing a RED SIGNAL at top of pole gives trains on EASTERN DIVISION right to pass. When no signal is displayed, ALL OTHER TRAINS have right to pass.

43

WHITE RIVER JUNCTION.

CENTRAL & SOUTHERN DIVISIONS.—Semaphore signal at *North and South* ends of yard.

Arm in a PERPENDICULAR position, or GREEN LIGHT at top of pole,—track is clear for trains to enter the yard.

Arm at an ANGLE OF 45 DEGREES, or a GREEN AND RED LIGHT at top of pole,—enter with extreme caution, prepared to stop train on short notice.

Arm in HORIZONTAL position, or a RED LIGHT at top of pole,—trains must not pass the signal until its position is changed.

Trains approaching on CENTRAL DIVISION must not pass the " *Old Signal Post*" unless the signal is right for them.

Trains approaching on SOUTHERN DIVISION must not pass the SIGNAL POST unless the semaphore signal is right for them.

SIGNAL IN YARD.—ARM or two RED LIGHTS on top of pole.

When in a HORIZONTAL position trains from *Central Division* have right to pass.

When at an ANGLE OF 45 DEGREES trains from *Passumpsic Road* have right to pass.

When in a PERPENDICULAR position trains from *Central Division* and *Passumpsic Road must stop.*

PASSUMPSIC R. R. CROSSING.—This signal only governs the crossing of tracks at *right angles*, and Trainmen must exercise great care to prevent collision with trains standing upon or moving on the *same track with themselves.* The signal by day is a target placed horizontal, or across the signal pole.

If the target faces up and down the PASSUMPSIC R. R. TRACK, trains from *Southern Division*, and from Passumpsic Road MUST STOP.

Finally, on October 27, 1875, a brilliant and fearless young attorney from Brattleboro by the name of Charles N. Davenport brought the matter to a head. He appeared at the state capitol in Montpelier before the Masters in Chancery who were reviewing the accounts of the receivers of the Vermont Central, and it was said that his charges that day caused both people and buildings to shake!

Davenport, who was appearing as counsel for Colonel Rush C. Hawkins of New York and Austin Birchard of Newfane, Vermont, made charges against the management of the Central Vermont Railroad that were both sweeping and specific. He commenced by stating that Smith had drawn from the trust for his services an amount of $65,706.52. He explained how money had been taken from trust funds of the Vermont Central and Vermont & Canada and had found its way into the pockets of the Smiths and

NOT ALL COVERED BRIDGES in New England were of the "through" type, as can be witnessed by this photograph of the Georgia High Bridge a few miles south of St. Albans. The exposed span on the left gives us an idea of the manner in which the bridge is constructed. It appears as though staging has been erected and the Bridge & Building men are working on the bridge. The more conventional type of roadway covered bridge may also be seen over the Lamoille River to the right. (Jim Murphy Collection)

THIS LOCOMOTIVE WAS built by Baldwin in 1849 as a unique 4-2-2. She soon proved to be totally ineffective in terms of tractive effort and was rebuilt into a more conventional 4-4-0 at St. Albans in 1863. She was renamed the "Joseph Clark" at that time, and sold to the Southeastern Railway in 1877. (Donald A. Somerville Collection)

No. 4.

DESTROY ALL FORMER TIME TABLES.

CENTRAL VERMONT RAILROAD.

NORTHERN, EASTERN & WESTERN DIVISIONS.

PRIVATE

TIME-TABLE

—FOR THE—

EXCLUSIVE USE AND GUIDANCE

—OF—

EMPLOYEES,

COMMENCING

Monday, May 14th, 1877.

THIS 1877 EMPLOYEES TIMETABLE, four pages of which are shown on this and the next page, contains additional information about train operations at various key points on the line. (Jim Murphy Collection)

Joseph Clark in the form of both profits and royalties. He further charged that "up to 1867 or 1868" J. Gregory Smith had ordered master mechanic E. F. Perkins to use wheels made by the St. Albans Foundry owned by Smith on the road's passenger equipment, although Perkins had protested he would not be responsible for the lives of the passengers if the inferior wheels were used.

Davenport continued with explanations of the activities of the Vermont Central's lobbyists in the legislative halls of the capitol. He charged that free passes had long been issued to newspapermen, state and federal officers, and judges. The fearless Davenport even went so far as to state that the Masters in Chancery whom he was at that moment addressing were recipients of the Vermont Central's gratuities.

53

DANGER SIGNALS.

DANGER SIGNALS MUST BE STRICTLY OBSERVED, and when placed in a position to STOP TRAINS, no Train or Engine will pass such signal until signaled that ALL IS RIGHT; except, in case of accident to the signal, when an order to pass, from the man in charge of the signal, will be observed.

A disregard of these instructions will be just cause for dismissal from the service of the Company.

WEST FARNHAM.

Junction with South Eastern and M. P. & B. Railroads. Two red balls in day and two red lights at night.

When no signal is shown, S. S. & C. trains have right to track.

When one red ball or one red light is shown South Eastern trains have right to track.

When two red balls or two red lights are shown M. P. & B. trains have right to track.

S. S. & C. JUNCTION.

AN ARM AT TOP OF A POLE.—When in a HORIZONTAL POSITION, trains on the MONTREAL and VERMONT JUNCTION ROAD have right to pass.

WHILE IN A PERPENDICULAR POSITION, trains on S. S. & C. Road have right to pass.

55

ESSEX JUNCTION.

CENTRAL & RUTLAND DIVISIONS.—One Signal South of Passenger Depot and one near Freight House.

A Red Signal at top of pole South of Passenger Depot, permits Burlington and Lamoille trains to pass to and from Depot, and Central Vermont trains will be very particular to keep clear of that portion of main line, between Depot and Burlington and Lamoille Switch, when such signals are displayed.

Signal near Freight House on Burlington main line : an arm in *Horizontal* position by day, or *Red Light* by night, permits the Burlington and Lamoille trains to use main line between the North and South Y Switches, and Central Vermont trains will keep clear of that portion of the main line, when such signals are displayed.

When no signals are displayed at either point, Central Vermont trains ONLY have right of track.

WHITE RIVER JUNCTION.

CENTRAL & SOUTHERN DIVISIONS.—Semaphore signal at *North and South* ends of yard.

Arm in a PERPENDICULAR position, or GREEN LIGHT at top of pole,—track is clear for trains to enter the yard.

Arm at an ANGLE OF 45 DEGREES, or a GREEN AND RED LIGHT at top of pole,—enter with extreme caution, prepared to stop train on short notice.

Arm in HORIZONTAL position, or a RED LIGHT at top of pole,—trains must not pass the signal until its position is changed.

Davenport continued his charges all that day and through the following morning. He alleged that on May 1, 1867, by order of Chancellor Pierpont, the Vermont & Canada stock was increased to $2,500,000, with only the second mortgage trustees receiving notification of the order. Further, Davenport said that on May 17, 1871, the stock of this road was further increased $500,000, again without proper notice. A total of 327 of these shares, he pointed out, were issued to W. C. Smith, in violation of a Supreme Court decision. The young attorney then went on to detail various unique features of numerous trust and equipment loans and manipulations.

Davenport exposed a donation of $1,000 to the "Vermont Central Library" at St. Albans and questioned the morality of the Smiths for being benevolent with that which was not their own. "This property has been managed too much on

the theory that it is all the private property of John Gregory Smith, Worthington C. Smith, and Joseph Clark, too much on the theory that it is merely a carcass to be fed upon. Upon that theory, if they own it, of course, they may give away its property. They have a right if they please, if that is the theory, to take $500,000 of these security holders' money and put it into a hospital and a church and call it the Vermont Central Hospital and the Vermont Central Church. They have just as much right legally to take $500,000 of this trust to found an asylum for broken-down railroad men, like those who have managed the Erie, the Boston & Lowell, and the Eastern roads. They are going to need the hospital by and by, gentlemen, and it would be just as legitimate an appropriation of that trust for them to set aside $500,000 to found an asylum where they can be taken care of in the future as to take $1,000 out to aid a library."

57

BELLOWS FALLS.

Three balls in day, or red, white, or green lights by night.

One ball or *red* light allows Rutland Division trains to pass. Two balls or *one green* light allows Cheshire trains to pass. Three balls or *one white* light allows Vermont Valley trains to pass. When no signal is shown, trains on Southern Division have right to pass.

RUTLAND.

JUNCTION WITH HARLEM EXTENSION and RUTLAND & WASHINGTON Railroads. Arm at top of pole.

When in a HORIZONTAL position, trains on the *Rutland Division* have right to pass.

When in a PERPENDICULAR position, trains on the *Rutland Division must stop,*—trains on the other roads having right to pass.

BURLINGTON.

Arm or Red Light on top of pole, on South Tower of Passenger Depot.

When the arm of the Signal stands East and West, or a *Red Light* is displayed by night, trains of the Burlington and Lamoille Railroad have the right to use the track between the Passenger Depot and the *switch*, south of the Draw Bridge, Central Vermont trains being held.

Central Vermont trains must pass over that portion of the track, at all times very carefully, and see that the signal is right before entering the yard.

THIS SHARP PHOTOGRAPH shows the Malone, New York, yard, roundhouse, and engine facilities in the 1870s during the period in which the Central Vermont leased this line from the Ogdensburgh & Lake Champlain Railroad. (Jim Bowler Collection)

By the time Davenport was finished with his remarks on October 28, there was little else to be said—unless, of course, you were a Smith. A 16-page booklet entitled "THE VERMONT CENTRAL RING: How The Road Was Plundered By Its Managers' Bribery and Corruption," summarized Davenport's charges. It immediately became a best seller all around New England.

Just before Davenport's charges became public, both the Rutland and the Ogdensburgh roads proposed the termination of their leases to the financially troubled Central Vermont Railroad. Rental payments had fallen in arrears and the Rutland wasted no time in asking that its property be returned by the Central Vermont. The Smiths, however, dared not return these properties as they were deeply concerned as to what might eventually be done with them by their competition.

Accordingly, a new plan was hammered out, and in February, 1875, both parties signed the new agreement. Basically, it stipulated that the gross earnings of the Central Vermont, the Rutland, and the Addison railroads were to be lumped together and 36¼ percent of this total would be credited to the Rutland and the Addison roads' accounts. Then, the Central Vermont would keep 27.2 percent of this amount to cover operating expenses of those roads.

Annual reports from the period show that the Central Vermont ended up paying a monthly rental of about $21,000 into the coffers of the other roads. This figure represented and annual decrease of about $124,000 per year from the original agreement reached in 1870. The terms of the new agreement undoubtedly caused the Smiths to breathe a bit easier, although the directors of the Vermont & Canada continued to doggedly fight the parent road.

THE SOUTHBOUND BURLINGTON-RUTLAND afternoon passenger train pauses at the brick depot at Brandon in 1875. The engineer oils around the "N. L. Davis" while he awaits the conductor's highball. (Jim Shaughnessy Collection, from THE RUTLAND ROAD)

THIS PRINT WAS MADE from a colored post card in the author's collection. Although a good amount of artist's license has been used, this rendering nevertheless gives the viewer an accurate "feel" for the terrain traversed by the line through the Green Mountains of Vermont.

Sharon, from C.V.R.R.
Greetings from the Green Mountain State

THE CENTRAL VERMONT-RUTLAND union station on the waterfront at Burlington was a most ornate and impressive building. It served the Queen City from 1861 until 1916 with one major rebuilding.

Three commercial enterprises have been located very close to the depot. Note the sign for the "Studebaker Wagon" on the building in the rear. (Gerry Fox Collection)

They had never succeeded in getting a single dollar of rent due them from the Central Vermont, but it was not through a lack of effort. The Vermont & Canada was claiming $1,000,000 in unpaid rent for the parent road. However, despite their vigorous protests, Judge Royce approved the new agreement between the Central Vermont and the Rutland and Addison roads; he refused to allow any appeals to his decision. The Vermont & Canada directors continued to try, but the system was just too much for them to buck successfully.

Legal battles notwithstanding, in the mid-1870s the Central Vermont was offering impressive service. It advertised Pullman Palace sleeping cars and Pullman drawing-room and parlor cars on all express trains travelling over the line. One could comfortably travel on a sleeping car between St. Albans and New York City without changing cars. The schedule called for a 6 p.m. departure from St. Albans and a 6:30 a.m. arrival in New York the following morning. Smoking cars were also available on all through trains. Full meals were served at dining halls and restaurants at various locations en route, with provisions made in the schedules for these stops.

All passenger equipment by this time had Miller platforms and Westinghouse air brake systems. Operation of trains on Sunday was still frowned on by many, although the Central Vermont did so with bible racks located at each end of the passenger cars. By this time, all trains were handled by train orders and telegraph.

The Central Vermont was very active in promoting excursions and vacation travel to resorts and to other attractions throughout the northeast. In 1876, special rates and arrangements were offered to patrons who wished to visit the nation's great Centennial Celebration in Philadelphia. A vast number of publications were issued for decades by the general passenger office, all of which publicized both the railroad's service as well as the wonderful things one could visit while using this service. These publications came in all shapes and sizes, with some actually in the form of relatively large bound volumes.

The 1876 biennial report of the receivers and managers of the Central Vermont Railroad covered operations on the Vermont Central, the Vermont & Canada, the Rutland, the Vermont Valley, the Addison, and the Missisquoi Railroads. It claimed 87 passenger depots, 57 freight houses, 9 engine houses, 6 repair shops, 52 water stations, 32 dwellings, 68 wood sheds, and 11 turntables. The road owned 106 pieces of passenger equipment and 2,229 freight cars. As in past years, hardly a fortnight passed without someone being seriously injured or killed on or about the railroad property.

A bridge carpenter fell to his death while working on a bridge at Waterbury, and a young man was killed while jumping from a moving train near West Alburgh in order to avoid paying his fare. On the Rutland Division, a drunken passenger fell to his death between Burlington and Shelburne while passing from one car to another on a passenger train. At Sheldon a passenger stuck his arms and

THE "LAMOILLE" AND the "Mansfield" were unique engines built for the Burlington and Lamoille Railroad. The engines were built with a single frame for both the engine and "tender." Swiveling lead and trailing trucks permitted them to negotiate curves. (Gerry Fox Collection)

head out a coach window and was promptly dismembered by posts that projected from a wood car standing on a siding. In another incident, a rail broke under a passing passenger train on the Harlem Extension Railroad, precipitating a sleeping car over an embankment. The car promptly caught on fire and two trapped passengers were killed.

In September of 1876, the Central Vermont officials permitted their lease of the Sullivan County Railroad to lapse when it came up for renewal. At the same time, the lease of the connecting Vermont Valley was also dropped. At this far-removed point in time, it is impossible to understand why such actions were taken. Despite the financial woes with which the Central Vermont was beset at the time, it was singularly uncharacteristic of the Smiths to put themselves at the mercy of outside interests without so much as putting up a fight. It would have seemed that the annual rental fee of $25,000 was reasonable enough to pay for such a strategic piece of rail line.

Such, however, was the case; and it was now necessary to bridge this 49-mile gap in the rail line in southeastern

Vermont by obtaining running rights over the Connecticut River Railroad, which later became part of the Boston & Maine.

Shortly thereafter, the creditors of the Ogdensburgh & Lake Champlain Railroad successfully arranged for an independent receiver to take over the management of their road. The Smiths, however, came up with the necessary amount of cash and were able to bring that road back into the Central Vermont fold.

By now, another new railroad coming from the east had entered the picture. This was to be called the Portland & Ogdensburgh Railroad, and it was planned to operate between the port cities comprising its name. The Smiths were concerned, but fortunately for them the new company experienced the almost universal financing problems that had plagued railroad construction efforts in the United States since the 1830s. Progress was slow, although rails did enter Vermont at Lunenburg in 1876. By July, 1877, the new road had pushed across the state from St. Johnsbury, through Morrisville, to Swanton.

Continued on page 123

114

THE "MANSFIELD" AND her crew pose on a trestle shortly after entering service on the Burlington & Lamoille Railroad. This road became part of the Central Vermont in 1889. (Gerry Fox Collection)

THIS BURLINGTON-BOUND TRAIN has just departed the Cambridge Junction station, which is just off the picture to the right. The grade and covered bridge in the background is that of the Portland & Ogdensburgh (later the St. Johnsbury & Lake Champlain Railroad). (Gerry Fox Collection)

A TWO-CAR BURLINGTON & Lamoille passenger train stops for the photographer on what appears to be newly constructed trackwork in the 1870s. (Gerry Fox Collection)

THIS ENGINE WAS built in 1849 by Taunton for the Rutland & Burlington Railroad. It was rebuilt at Rutland in 1866 and sold to D. C. Linsley in 1875 for construction of the Burlington and Lamoille Railroad. The B&L renamed the engine the ''William Hale.'' Ground was broken for the construction of this road on May 24, 1875, and construction was completed June 30, 1877. The engine is shown in front of the Cambridge station. (Gerry Fox Collection)

B&L NUMBER 3 simmers at Cambridge Junction, her tender piled high with a sufficient wood supply for the return trip to Burlington. (Gerry Fox Collection)

THE B&L'S "WILLIAM HALE" in this late 1870s photograph somewhat belies her 1849 construction date. She was used in the construction of the road between 1875 and 1877. (Whitney Maxfield Collection)

THE "BRADLEY BARLOW" is a unique engine. It was designed by J. M. Foss, the Central Vermont's superintendent of motive power, but it was never built. This sketch is the only evidence of this phantom locomotive. (St. Albans Historical Society Collection)

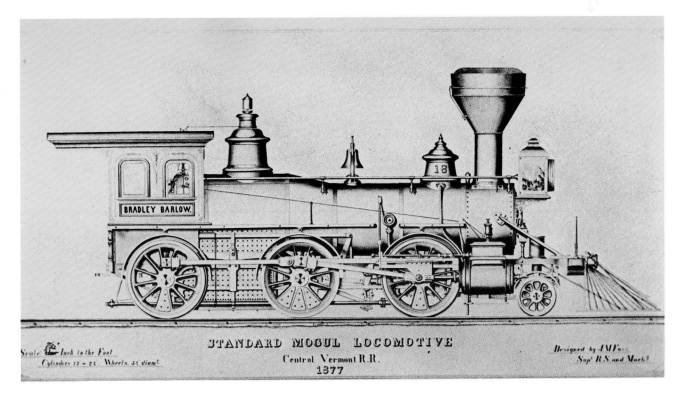

ST. A

THIS 1877 ENGRAVING of St. Albans clearly shows the railroad facilities and the surrounding town. The present-day Italy Yard, which was built in the mid-1890s, is located where the train is depicted just north of Elm Street near the top of the illustration. (St. Albans Historical Society Collection)

THIS IS THE NORTH end of White River Junction yard. The Connecticut & Passumpsic Railroad heads north in the background through the double-tracked covered bridge. (Jim McFarlane Collection)

THIS CIRCULAR ENTHUSIASTICALLY promotes the Central Vermont's "Butter Train," which by this time had been in operation for nearly twenty years. (Jim McFarlane Collection)

Central Vt. Railroad.

SPECIAL BUTTER TRAIN!

As Shippers of Butter and Cheese do not all seem to fully understand in regard to the continuance of the Special Butter Train, we beg leave to call the attention of the public to the fact that we shall continue to run the Special Butter Train to Boston and Boston Points during the Fall, Winter and Spring, upon the same plan as the Special Butter Train of Refrigerator Cars which has been running during the Summer.

The Special Butter train will leave Stations on the O. & L. C. R. R., on Train No. 15, leaving Ogdensburg at 12 o'clock,

MONDAY P. M., of EACH WEEK,

(passing Stations on the O. & L. C. R. R., on Tuesday,) and will leave Stations on the Vermont Central Railroad on train No. 5, and Stations on the Rutland Railroad, on train No. 9.

On Tuesday of each week.

The Conductor of this Train will run through to Boston, and such special care and attention will be given shipments by this train as to ensure

GOOD TIME,

And Delivery at Destination, in good order and condition.

It will however be necessary for shippers by this train to assume the ORDINARY risk, including RISK OF WEATHER, the same as heretofore, and the same as by other trains. As this is a special train and run especially to accommodate the Butter, Cheese and Egg traffic, all shipments of Butter, Cheese and Eggs each week, will be taken by this train, which will be greatly to the advantage of shippers, in consideration of the special care and attention given to shipments so forwarded. Agents will please call the attention of shippers to this, so that Butter, Cheese and Eggs will each week go by this train and not be forwarded by any other train.

Butter, Cheese and Eggs, forwarded by other trains than the Special Butter Train will be charged extra as per Circular No. 97, dated Feb. 13th, 1875.

Other articles of perishable property will be sent in this train when so ordered.

BUTTER CARS WILL BE RUN TO THE BOSTON AND LOWELL DEPOT IN BOSTON, from O. & L. C. R. R., and Northern and Central Divisions, and to FITCHBURG DEPOT, from Rutland Division.

AGENTS must be careful to pack butter, cheese &c., closely in the cars so as to prevent the packages from tipping over.

The attention of Agents is especially called to the rules in the General Freight Tariff, in regard to marking.

L. MILLIS,
Gen'l Sup't Traffic.

St. Albans, Vt., Nov. 10th, 1876.

Burlington & Lamoille R. R.

Time Table No. 2,—to take effect Monday, July 2, 1877,

	Trains Moving East.				STATIONS.		Trains Moving West.			
	No. 4.	No. 2.	No. 1.					No. 5.	No. 6.	No. 7.
	Freight.	Freight.	Pass.	Miles.		Miles.	Pass.	Freight.	Freight.
	P. M.	A. M.	P. M.				A. M.	A. M.	P. M.
READ DOWN.			L 4.15		Burlington.	9.1	8.52			READ UP.
	4.50	11.05	4.45	9.1	Essex Junction.	3.2	8.22	10.50	4.35	
	5.05	11.20	4.55	3.2	Essex Center.	3.8	8.12	10.30	4.15	
	5.20	11.35	5.07	3.8	Jericho.	2.	8.00	10.10	3.55	
	5.30	11.45	5.13	2.	Gravel Pit.	2.	7.50	10.00	3.45	
			5.20	2.	Underhill.	4.3	7.45			
			5.35	4.3	North Underhill.	6.5	7.30			
			5.55	6.5	Cambridge.	2.7	7.10			
			6.03	2.7	Jeffersonville.	1.	7.03			
			6.06	1.	P. & O. Junction.		L 7.			

Trains Nos. 1 and 5, will have "RIGHT OF WAY," and all other Trains or Engines will keep at least 15 minutes out of the way until these trains arrive or are heard from.

In case of orders by telegraph directing movement of Trains, both conductor and engineer will sign dispatch stating their understanding of order, and they will not leave the station until they get "O. K."

D. C. LINSLEY, Gen'l Manager.

REGULAR SERVICE ON the Burlington & Lamoille Railroad commenced on June 30, 1877. This employees timetable is the first to cover the entire line. (Gerry Fox Collection)

THIS ENGINE WAS BUILT in 1853 by Amoskeag for the Rutland & Burlington as the "Timothy Follett." It was rebuilt in 1866 and was renamed the "Colonel Merrill" in 1875. It was operated by the Central Vermont during its lease of the Rutland road. (Jim McFarlane Collection)

THE FREIGHT CHARGES shown on this 1876 freight waybill are interesting, as is the variety of articles listed. (William G. Rowley Collection)

A WASHOUT CAUSED this wreck at Northfield Farms, Massachusetts, on August 6, 1878. (Lewis R. Brown, Inc., Colleciton)

THE JUNCTION HOUSE was built at White River Junction in 1879. It is seen here shortly after completion. The hotel was located near the busy railroad depot, and it served rail passengers for many years. (Jim McFarlane Collection)

MARKS AND NUMBERS.	ARTICLES.	WEIGHT OR MEASURE.
Hibbard Spencer & Co. N♭ 1548 Chicago Ill	2 Cases Forks 21 Bdls Rakes	860 lb 525 1385 lb 70 9695-0

Rate 70

STAFFORD & HOLDEN, a large tool manufacturing firm in Barre, Vermont, shipped out 2 cases of forks and 21 bundles of rakes over the CV on May 6, 1878. (Whitney Maxfield Collection)

The Swanton terminus was some twelve miles from Rouses Point, and the Vermont Division of the Portland & Ogdensburgh had about run out of money. Receivers took over and two years later the firm's bondholders took charge. In January, 1880, the road was reorganized as the St. Johnsbury & Lake Champlain Railroad Company and was operated as such for many decades. J. Gregory Smith watched this new road very carefully to see how it would affect traffic going over his line, but is was not until 1883 that he became seriously concerned.

At that time, the Lamoille Valley Extension Railroad Company, which had been organized in August, 1880, commenced building track from Swanton, around Maquam Bay, toward the New York state line. This 12-mile piece of road was opened for service on December 31, 1883, and it was leased by the Ogdensburgh & Lake Champlain Railroad until July, 1884. In order to throttle this competition, Smith made his move. He simply bought controlling interest in the Ogdensburgh & Lake Champlain and immediately suspended operations on the Lamoille Valley Extension on account of it being "a parallel line."

Bondholders of the Lamoille Valley Extension Railroad brought suit against the Ogdensburgh company, and the lease was declared valid. The matter was settled by exchanging Ogdensburgh bonds which were guaranteed by the Central Vermont for Lamoille Valley Extension bonds. Subsequently, the Ogdensburgh bonds were taken up by the Central Vermont under the guarantee, and the Central Vermont also purchased all the capital stock of the Lamoille Valley Extension Railroad from the Ogdensburgh company. Operation of the Lamoille Valley trackage was never resumed.

In the mid-1870s, considerable interest had been aroused on the matter of extending the Stanstead, Shefford & Chambly Railroad another 23 miles from Waterloo to Magog. The latter community was situated at the northern end of

RATES OF FARE FROM BOSTON.

January 1st, 1879. Subject to changes.

Children under 5 years of age, Free. Between 5 and 12, Half Price.

*Acton	P.Q.	$11.00	Norwood	N.Y.	$11.75
Alburgh Springs	Vt.	9.00	Ogdensburg	N.Y.	12.00
Barre	Vt.	7.30	Orwell	Vt.	7.05
Bethel	Vt.	5.80	*Ottawa	P.Q.	13.50
Braintree	Vt.	6.30	Plainfield	Vt.	7.50
Brandon	Vt.	6.50	Plattsburgh	N.Y.	9.25
Burlington	Vt.	8.00	Proctorsville	Vt.	4.55
Champlain	N.Y.	9.40	*Quebec	P.Q.	13.00
Charlestown	N.H.	3.80	Randolph	Vt.	6.05
Claremont	N.H.	4.15	Richford	Vt.	9.60
Cuttingsville	Vt.	3.85	Richmond	Vt.	7.45
Chateaugay	N.Y.	10.80	Rouse's Point	N.Y.	9.25
Chester	Vt.	4.10	Royalton	Vt.	5.60
Des Rivieres	P.Q.	9.65	Roxbury	Vt.	6.60
East Berkshire	Vt.	9.40	Rutland	Vt.	5.75
Ellenburgh	N.Y.	10.40	Salisbury	Vt.	6.80
Enosburgh Falls	Vt.	9.20	Saratoga Springs	N.Y.	6.70
Essex Jc. (via W.R. Jc.)	Vt.	7.75	Sheldon Springs	Vt.	8.85
Gassett's	Vt.	4.25	Shoreham	Vt.	6.95
Georgia	Vt.	8.20	South Royalton	Vt.	5.50
Granby	P.Q.	10.60	Springfield	Vt.	3.90
Highgate Springs	Vt.	9.00	Stanbridge	P.Q.	9.50
Jonesville	Vt.	7.40	St. Albans	Vt.	8.50
Leicester Jc.	Vt.	6.70	*St. Hilaire	P.Q.	11.00
Ludlow	Vt.	4.70	St. Armands	P.Q.	9.25
Malone	N.Y.	11.00	*St. Hyacinthe	P.Q.	11.00
Marshfield	Vt.	7.80	*St. Johns	P.Q.	10.00
Middlebury	Vt.	7.10	Ticonderoga	N.Y.	7.30
Middlesex	Vt.	7.10	Vergennes	Vt.	7.50
Milton	Vt.	8.10	Waterbury	Vt.	7.25
*Montreal	P.Q.	11.00	Waterloo	P.Q.	11.10
Montpelier	Vt.	7.00	*West Farnham	P.Q.	10.00
New Haven	Vt.	7.30	West Hartford	Vt.	5.10
Northfield	Vt.	6.75	White River Jc.	Vt.	4.75
No. Ferrisburg	Vt.	7.75	Windsor	Vt.	4.50

* Second-Class Tickets also sold to these points.

RAILROAD CONNECTIONS.

At *Lowell* with Salem & Lowell Railroad.
" *Nashua* with Worcester & Nashua Railroad.
" *Manchester* with Man. & Law.; also, Con. & Ports., Man. & No. Weare Railroads.
At *Concord* with Bos., Con. & Mont.; also, Con. & Clar. Railroads.
" *White River Jc.* with So. Div. C. V., Pass., Woodstock Railroads.
" *Montpelier* with Montpelier & Wells River Railroad.
" *Essex Jc.* with Rutland Div. Central Vermont Railroad.
" *St. Albans* with North., West., and Eastern Divs. C. V. Railroad.
" *Rouse's Point* with Ogdensburg & Lake Champlain, and D. and H. C. Co. Railroads.
At *St. Johns* with Grand Trunk Railway.
" *St. Lambert* " " " for Quebec.
" *Montreal* " " " for Ottawa and the West; also, Steamers for Ottawa, Quebec, and river points.
At *Fitchburg* with Cheshire and B. C. F. & N. B. Railroads.
" *Winchendon* with Boston, Barre & Gardner Railroad.
" *Bellows Falls* with Southern and Rutland Divs. C. V. Railroad.
" *Rutland* with Bennington & Rutland; also, Delaware and Hudson Canal Co. Railroads.
At *Leicester Jc.* with Addison Div. C. V. Railroad for Ticonderoga.

STAGE CONNECTIONS.

Central Division, Central Vermont Railroad.

At **W. Hartford**, for Pomfret, North Pomfret, S. Pomfret; **S. Royalton**, for Tunbridge, Chelsea, E. Barnard, N. Tunbridge, S. Tunbridge; **Royalton**, for E. Bethel, N. & E. Randolph, E. Brookfield; **Bethel**, for Barnard, Gaysville, Stockbridge, Rochester, W. Rochester; **Randolph**, for Randolph Centre, Braintree, Brookfield; **Roxbury**, for E. Warren, Warren; **Montpelier**, for Worcester, Calais, Wolcott; **Barre**, for S. Barre, Williamstown, Washington; **Middlesex**, for Moretown, Waitsfield, N. Fayston; **Waterbury**, for Waterbury Centre, Stowe, Mt. Mansfield, Hyde Park, Craftsbury, Morrisville; **Jonesville**, for W. Bolton, Underhill Centre, Pleasant Valley; **Richmond**, for Huntington, Huntington Centre, S. Hinesburg, Starksboro; **Essex**, for Jericho, Jericho Centre, N. Underhill, Underhill, Mt. Mansfield, Cambridge, Belvidere; **Georgia**, for Fairfax, Fletcher, Westford, Cambridge, Buck Hollow, Waterville; **St. Albans**, for Highgate Falls & Centre, E. Highgate, Swanton Centre, Bakersfield, Franklin, Fairfield.

Northern Division, Central Vermont Railroad.

At **St. Armands**, for Frelighsburgh, Phillipsburg, St. Armands Cen., La Grange & Abbott's Corners; **Stanbridge**, for Allen's Corner, Bedford, Stanbridge, N. Stanbridge, Riceburg, Mystic, Pearceton, Stanbury, Dunham, E. Dunham; **Des Rivieres**, for Malmaison, St. Charles, St. Sebastian, Pike Riv., Venice, Henryville; **W. Farnham**, for Canrobert, St. Cesaire; **Granby**, for Abbottsford, Mawcook, Roxton Pond, S. Roxton, Milton, St. Pie; **Alburgh Springs**, (Western Div.) for Alburgh Centre, La Grange, Aird, Henryville, Clarenceville, Nutt's Corners, Isle La Motte, N. Hero.

Southern Division, Central Vermont Railroad.

At **Brattleboro**, for Guilford, Guilford Centre, Green River, Halifax, W. Halifax, Jacksonville, Whitingham, W. Brattleboro, Marlboro, W. Marlboro, Wilmington, Chesterfield, W. Drummerston, Williamsville, E. & W. Dover, Dover, Fayetteville; **Bellows Falls**, for Townshend, Saxton's River, Athens, Cambridgeport, Grafton, Houghtonville, Langdon, N. H., Alstead, N. H., South Acworth, N.H., Lampster, N.H.; **Charlestown**, for Acworth, N.H.; **Springfield**, for Acworth, N. H.; **Claremont**, for Ascutneyville, Weathersfield; **Windsor**, for West Windsor, Plainfield, Brownsville, Felchville, Reading, South Reading, Ludlow.

Rutland Division, Central Vermont Railroad.

At **Chester**, for Simonsville, Andover, Weston, Windham, Londonderry; **Gassett's**, for North Springfield and Springfield; **Proctorsville**, for Upper Falls; **Ludlow**, for Tyson Furnace, Plymouth, Bridgewater; **Cuttingsville**, for Shrewsbury, North Shrewsbury; **Rutland**, for Mendon, Sherburne; **Brandon**, for Forest Dale, Sudbury, Orwell, Chipman's Point; **Shoreham**, (Addison Div.) for Shoreham and Richville; **Leicester Junction**, for Leicester; **Salisbury**, for Salisbury, Lake Dunmore; **Middlebury**, for E. Middlebury, Ripton, Hancock, Granville, Weybridge; **Vergennes**, for Addison, Panton, West Addison, Chimney Point; **No. Ferrisburg**, for Monkton, Monkton Ridge; **New Haven**, for Bristol, Lincoln, New Haven Mills, Starksboro; **Burlington**, for Hinesburg and St. George.

DINING ROOMS AT

WHITE RIVER JUNCTION,	**BELLOWS FALLS,**
ST. ALBANS,	**RUTLAND,**

Where first-class meals are furnished at reasonable prices. Train Conductors announce the time each train will stop, so that none need be hurried, and no passenger left.

THESE TWO ILLUSTRATIONS are from a January 1, 1879, timetable. They give a great amount of information on stage connections and rail fares. (Jim Murphy Collection)

---

the 30-mile long Lake Memphremagog. Capital was secured, and construction was easy through the rolling farmlands of the Eastern Townships of Quebec. The line went into operation in April, 1878, with the Central Vermont's lease of this new line becoming effective on April 29, 1878.

In 1885, the ambitious Waterloo & Magog extended itself another 22 miles from Magog to Sherbrooke, and this addition immediately became part of the Central Vermont lease. The intended Grand Trunk Railway connection near Sherbrooke never amounted to much traffic-wise, nor did local business live up to expectations. Thus, within three years—on May 24, 1888—the Central Vermont surrendered its lease on the 45 miles of trackage between Waterloo and Sherbrooke. This line was eventually sold to the young Canadian Pacific Railway, and parts of it were incorporated into that company's main line from Montreal to the Maritimes.

On the opposite end of the line, the New London Northern built a short 1.6-mile spur from the main line into the village of Fitchville, Connecticut, in 1880, principally to serve a cotton sheet manufacturing firm. This new trackage was immediately added to the existing lease of that road by the Central Vermont.

The advent of the use of coal on Central Vermont locomotives occurred by 1877 or 1878. However, its use at this time remained rather negligible for a few years. The road's biennial report of 1878 revealed that $541,450 had been spent for wood, while only $7,787 had been spent for coal. This two-year period saw receipts total $4,076,700 from all sources, while operating expenses came to $2,615,560.

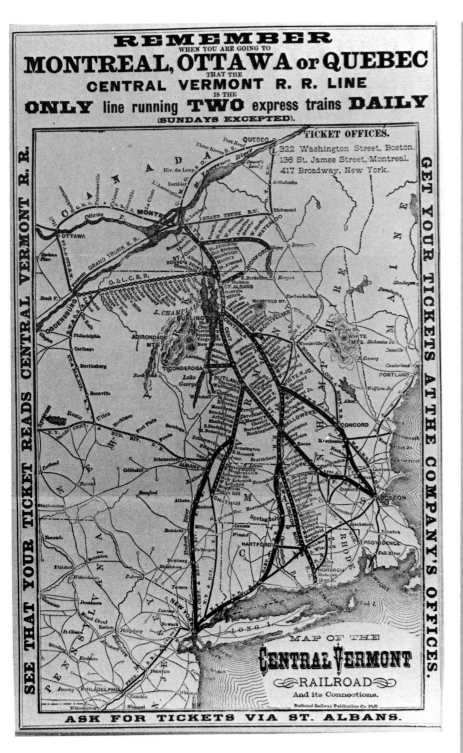

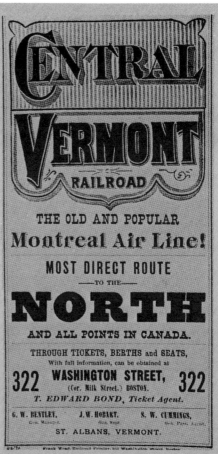

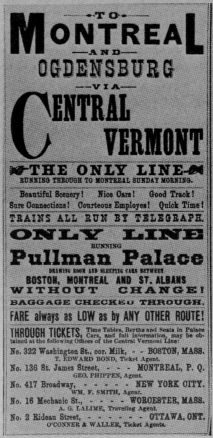

THIS MAP IS from the same 1879 timetable as were the illustrations on the preceding page. It graphically shows many of the major rail lines operating in the area served by the Central Vermont. (Jim Murphy Collection)

THESE ARE THE covers of the January 1, 1879, passenger timetable. The CV's promotional material at this time was obviously directed to the long-distance traveller. (Jim Murphy Collection)

THESE TWO BROADSIDES were used to promote different excursions over the Central Vermont.
(Wilbur Collection, University of Vermont)

A total of 27 deaths and serious injuries occurred during the period, including an accident in which a freight brakeman "was knocked from a train by a water spout and considerably bruised." Engineers were receiving an average of $2.84 per day, conductors between $40 and $76.50 per month, brakemen about $1.25 per day, firemen about $1.50, and laborers about $1 a day. The pay for station agents varied from $10 to $90 per month, while clerks received $8.33 to $75 per month.

In September, 1880, the citizens of Montpelier received a new, larger station they felt was befitting their stature as the capital of the state. It was built of brick on the same site as the original facility. An account of the day stated: "The interior is well and conveniently finished for the Capital depot; a very wide central hall—wide enough for the town representatives of several of the smaller counties of the State to walk through abreast—gentlemen and ladies' waiting rooms upon the left, baggage room, telegraph and express offices upon the right. The whole building, warmed by steam, has all the modern conveniences."

Although the Central Vermont was generally good about providing accommodations and service for local patrons, the residents of Samsonville, a small settlement a mile or so west of East Berkshire, felt that they had long been neglected. They met in late May or early June, 1882, to discuss the situation. They agreed to petition the railroad for suitable recognition, and such a document with 25 signatures was forwarded to president J. Gregory Smith on June 8. The petition said, in part: "We do not expect or ask for a large outlay at this place, but we do ask for a stopping place here and think it justly over due. You gentlemen will notice that this is the only village, be it ever so small, between St.

Continued on page 131

ENGINE 66, "DES RIVIERES," was built at St. Albans in 1870. It served the road for the next 35 years, being renumbered "9" in 1900. It is steaming lustily here in front of an unidentified woodshed. (Richard Sanborn Collection)

THE TRAIN SCHEDULES of the Southern Division as well as those of various connecting branch roads are shown in the October, 1880 timetable. (Jim McFarlane Collection)

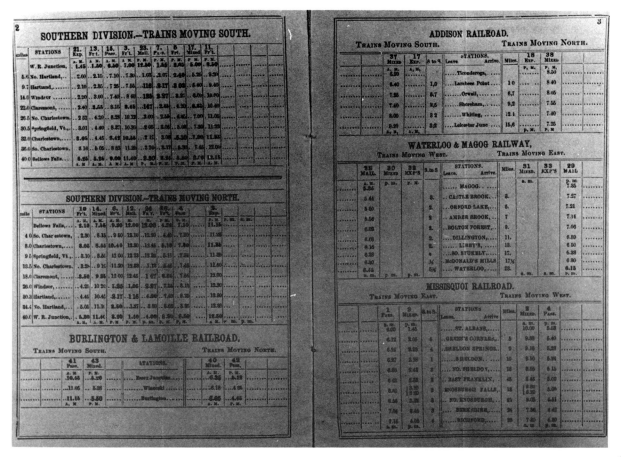

THE THREE-FOOT GAUGE Brattleboro & White-hall Railroad was opened on November 3, 1880. This line was almost immediately leased by the Central Vermont. Here Number 3, the ''J. L. Martin,'' a little 2-4-0, heads a passenger train at South Londonderry, Vermont soon after the line opened. This engine was later rebuilt to a 4-4-0, and was scrapped in 1901. (Lewis R. Brown, Inc., Collection)

THE NEWLY BUILT Brattleboro and Whitehall never extended beyond South Londonderry. This photograph was taken at about the time the line was completed to that point. (Lewis R. Brown, Inc., Collection)

THE BRATTLEBORO & WHITEHALL'S "London-derry," was built by Danforth & Cooke in 1879. This builder's photo was taken shortly before she went to work on the narrow-gauge line. (Whitney Maxfield Collection)

THIS IS THE SECOND CV depot in Montpelier, which was rebuilt from the old one in 1880 because the city fathers desired a "better" building in which to receive arriving legislators. (William Gove Collection)

BURLINGTON & LAMOILLE RAILROAD.

Time Table No. 29. To take effect Monday, March 13th, 1882.

Trains Going South and West, Read Downward.

1 C.V. Pass. A.M.	23 C.V. Pass. A.M.	27 C.V. Freg't A.M.	2 B&L Freg't 51 A.M.	7 C.V. Mail A.M.	17 C.V. Mixed P.M.	4 B.&L. Pass. 41 (P.M.)	13 C.V. Pass. P.M.	6 B&L Mail 43 P.M.	19 C.V. Pass. P.M.	25 C.V. Pass. P.M.	15 C.V. Freg't P.M.	21 C.V. Pass. P.M.	Miles	STATIONS
			11.45	9.40		6.30								**Cambridge Junc.**
			11.55	9-43		6.33							1	Jeffersonville,
			12.18 / 12.28	9.50		6.42							4	Cambridge,
			1.15	10.08		7.03							11	North Underhill,
			1.40 / 1.50	10.18		7.18							15	Underhill,
			—			—							16	Dixon's,
			2.14 / 2.34	10.29		7.33							19	Jericho,
			2.50	10.42		7.48							23	Essex Center,
			3.10 / 3.40	10.55 / 11.00		**8.00**							26	Essex Junction,
			4.08	11.15		8.15							31	Winooski,
			4.25	11.25		8.25							34	Burlington.

Leave. — Arrive. — STATIONS.

Trains Going North and East, Read Upward.

Miles	STATIONS	2 C.V. Night Exp. A.M.	18 C.V. Freg't A.M.	1 B&L Mail 40 A.M.	4 C.V. N.Y. Exp. A.M.	26 C.V. Pass. A.M.	16 C.V. Pass. A.M.	28 C.V. Pass. A.M.	10 C.V. Mixed A.M.	3 C.V. Freg't P.M.	B&L Pass. 50 P.M.	5 B&L Freg't 42 P.M.	12 C.V. Exp. Mail P.M.	14 C.V. Pass. P.M.	22 C.V. Pass. P.M.
34	**Cambridge Junc.**			9.10							6.09	10.35			
33	Jeffersonville,			9.07							6.06	10.25 / 10.10			
30	Cambridge,			8.58							6.00	9.50 / 9.43			
23	North Underhill,			8.38							5.44	8.52			
19	Underhill,			8.28							5.36	8.28 / 8.11			
18	Dixon's,			—							—	—			
15	Jericho,			8.18							5.26	7.47			
11	Essex Center,			8.08							5.18	7.23			
8	Essex Junction,			8.00							5.10 / 5.00	7.05 / 6.35			
3	Winooski,			7.45							4.45	6.08			
	Burlington.			7.35							4.35	5.50			

☞ Meeting places are designated by full-faced figures. Passenger Trains will meet at these places unless otherwise ordered. Mixed or Freight Trains will be subordinate to, and will keep at least 5 minutes off the time of Passenger Trains, and in no case be run between Stations faster than twenty miles per hour without special permission of General Manager.

In case of order by telegraph directing movement of Trains, both the Conductor and Engineer will sign their understanding of order, and they will not leave the Station until they get O. K.

☞ Engineers will not pass Lime Kilns or Decked Bridges near that point faster than twenty miles per hour.

Numbers 1 and 3 trains will not stop at Winooski excepting when flagged, and then only for passengers going beyond Essex Junction. Numbers 4 and 6 trains will stop at Winooski only to leave passengers coming from beyond Essex Junction.

Between Burlington and Essex Junction, Train-men will be governed by rules and regulations of Central Vermont, and will be subject to orders of Train Despatcher of that road.

Conductors of all Trains and Engineers of engines running without trains will report to C. V. Telegraph Operator immediately upon their arrival at Burlington and Essex Junction, and before leaving either of these Stations for the other, both Conductor and Engineer will be particular to inform themselves in relation to Trains of Central Vermont.

Numbers 1, 3, 4 and 6 Trains will not Stop at Essex Center and Jeffersonville, excepting when flagged or to leave passengers.

G. L. LINSLEY, Gen'l Manager

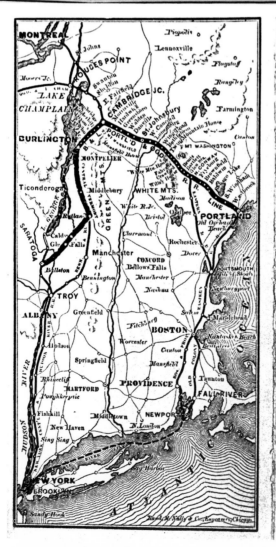

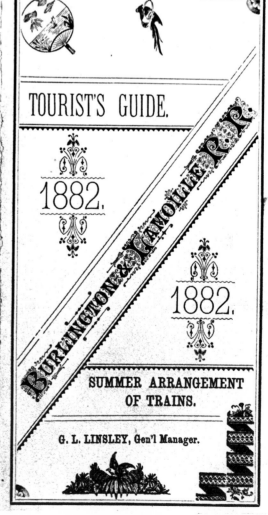

TOURIST'S GUIDE.

1882.

BURLINGTON & LAMOILLE R.R.

1882.

SUMMER ARRANGEMENT OF TRAINS.

G. L. LINSLEY, Gen'l Manager.

Albans and Richford that the road has passed without noticing, and there are many stations that will be of minor importance when compared with this, both to the road and to citizens interested." Unfortunately, information has not been found that would indicate what action was taken to this poignant request.

Since the mid-1850s, the Central Vermont and its predecessors had been partners with the Grand Trunk Railway and the Michigan Central Railroad in the operation of the National Despatch Line, a fast freight service between New England and the Midwest. The revenues from this integrated service were pro-rated among the three carriers on a mileage basis. The Central Vermont's predecessor, the Vermont Central, had fallen behind in its payments to the other participants within a few years of the inauguration of this service. The Grand Trunk permitted these debts to accumulate for a while, but in 1863, it demanded settlement.

As the Vermont Central did not have adequate cash to spare, an agreement was reached whereby that road provided the Grand Trunk with an appropriate amount of Vermont Central stocks and bonds to cover the obligation. By 1876, the Vermont Central securities had become increasingly attractive to the Grand Trunk officers.

The Grand Trunk's eastern terminus—the port city of Portland, Maine—had not lived up to expectations in terms of traffic figures, so its officials were at this time casting their eyes elsewhere for traffic. The heart of New England which could be easily reached via the Vermont Central was thus a prime objective to consider. However, all plans for expansion into New England were subsequently halted by the Grand Trunk's preoccupation with the formation of a great new rival, the Canadian Pacific Railway.

For about 30 years, costly litigation had been going on between the Smiths and minority elements in both the Vermont Central and the Vermont & Canada. All levels of the state's court system had been inundated with these proceedings—session after session, year after year. Finally, in 1882, the Supreme Court declared that there was nothing left to be said on the matter, and the presiding judge ruled that any further complaints and testimony would be unwarranted.

CONDENSED TIME-TABLE.

TRAINS GOING EAST.

STATIONS.	MAIL.	WHITE Mountain EXPRESS.	BOAT.
New York.........	6.30 p. m.	....	....
Albany...........	11.10 "	....	....
Troy.............	11.25 "	....	....
Saratoga	....	....	....
Rutland..........	2.20 a. m.	....	....
Caldwell.........	....	....	9.50 a. m.
Baldwin..........	....	....	12.50 p. m.
Fort Ticonderoga..	....	....	1.30 "
Burlington.......	4.50 } "a. 10.00 } " l.	2.15 p. m.	5.40 "
Essex Junction...	10.20 "	2.35 "	....
Cambridge Junction	11.37 "	3.50 "	....
St. Johnsbury.....	2.40 } a. 2.50 } l.	6.30 } a. 6.40 } l.	....
Whitefield........	3.50 p. m.	7.45 "	....
Wing Road........	3.57 "	8.00 "	....
Bethlehem Junction.	4.07 "	8.10 "	....
Profile House......	6.00 "	8.50 "	....
Fabyan's..........	4.30 "	8.40 "	....
Crawford's........	4.45 "	9.00 "	....
North Conway.....	5.55 "	....	....
Portland.........	8.30 "	....	....
Old Orchard.......	9.00 "	....	....

Mail train leaving Burlington at 10.00 o'clock, a. m., has Passenger car through to Portland without change, connecting at Burlington with Night Express train leaving New York at 6.30 p. m.; Albany 11.10; Troy 11 25 p. m.; Rutland 2 20 a. m., with Wagner Palace Sleeping Car through from New York to Burlington without change.

Passengers leaving Caldwell at 9.50 a. m. by Lake George Steamers, connecting at Fort Ticonderoga with Champlain Transportation Co's elegant Steamer Vermont, arrive at Burlington at 5.40 p. m. Remaining in Burlington over night and taking the 10 00 o'clock a. m. train from Burlington, arrive at the White Mountains at 4.30 p. m., and at Portland at 8.30 p. m.; thus enjoying the beautiful scenery of Lake George and Champlain, and passing through the White Mountains by daylight.

CONDENSED TIME-TABLE.

TRAINS GOING WEST.

STATIONS.	MAIL.	SARATOGA EXPRESS.	BOAT.
Old Orchard Beach .	7.45 a. m.	....	....
Portland.........	8.25 "	....	....
North Conway.	10.53 "	....	....
Crawford's.........	12.20 p. m.	7.20 a. m.	....
Fabyan's..........	1.00 "	7.40 "	....
Profile House.......	11.00 a. m.	7.25 "	....
Bethlehem Junction.	1.24 p. m.	8.04 "	....
Wing Road	1.36 "	8.20 "	....
Whitefield.........	1.45 "	8.30 "	....
St. Johnsbury.....	3.10 } a. 3.25 } l.	9.35 "	....
Cambridge Junction	6.08 "	12.33 p. m.	....
Essex Junction......	7.18 "	1.30 "	....
Burlington	7.43 "	1.50 "	8.40 a. m.
Rutland...........	....	6.40 "	....
Fort Ticonderoga...	....	....	12.20 p. m.
Caldwell...........	....	....	4.15 "
Saratoga..........	....	....	5.55 "
Troy.............	....	....	7.30 "
Albany...........	....	....	7.45 "
New York.........	....	....	6.00 a. m.

Train leaving Portland at 8.25 a. m. has passenger car through to Burlington without change. Passengers by this train can remain in Burlington over night, take the Champlain Transportation Company's

STEAMER "VERMONT,"

leaving Burlington at 8.40 a. m.; Fort Ticonderoga 12.00 m.; Caldwell 4.15 p. m.; and arrive at Saratoga at 5.55 p. m.

This is the Favorite Route for Pleasure Travel
—— BETWEEN ——
Saratoga and the White Mountains.

For Through Tickets and rates of fare enquire of any of the Ticket Agents on the line.

With this decision ringing in their ears, the directors of the Central Vermont incorporated the Consolidated Railroad Company of Vermont on April 23, 1883. This organization was to be the legal instrument to meld the dissident Vermont Central-Vermont & Canada elements. The firm's first board of directors was composed of J. Gregory Smith, Joseph Hickson, James R. Langdon, Edward C. Smith, B. P. Cheney, E. H. Baker, and W. H. H. Bingham. The directors immediately voted J. Gregory Smith as president, as was to be expected. Hickson was an official of the Grand Trunk Railway, and he represented his road's vested interests in the Central Vermont properties. This was the first instance of a non-New Englander appearing on the board of directors of a Smith-controlled railroad.

The Consolidated Railroad Company bought both the Vermont Central and the Vermont & Canada at forced sale, and the new company issued $750,000 of preferred stock to retire the first and second mortgage bonds. Five percent, 30-year bonds totaling $7,000,000 were exchanged for the various classes of claims and securities. These bonds were secured by a mortgage on both roads and were exchanged as follows: $3,000,000 of Vermont & Canada stock for $1,000,000 of new bonds; and $4,357,000 of floating debt and Central Vermont claims for a like amount of new bonds.

The new company operated the railroads from May 10, 1883, until June 30, 1884. On the latter date, the Consolidated Railroad Company of Vermont leased the railroads to the Central Vermont Railroad Company for 99 years, and the corporate existence of the Consolidated Railroad Company was terminated. In this complicated legal

THE B&W'S LITTLE three-foot gauge 2-4-0 was later rebuilt to a 4-4-0. She is at the dual-gauge tracked Brattleboro roundhouse prior to her rebuilding. In 1900 she became the CV's Number 1, and was scrapped a year later. (Jim McFarlane Collection)

THIS ENGINE, WHICH was rebuilt and renamed the "F. H. Prescott" in 1870 by the New London Northern was built in 1852 by Souther as the "Vermont." In the interim, she was renamed "Ware" and was used on the Ware River Railroad in Massachusetts, a short feeder line of the New London Northern. (Jim McFarlane Collection)

A SOUTHBOUND STANDARD-GAUGE passenger train pauses at the Brattleboro depot. Note the dual-gauge trackage connecting the two main line tracks. (Jim McFarlane Collection)

THIS IS THE AFTERMATH of a spectacular accident that occurred at East Granville, Vermont, on May 23, 1883. Details of this accident are covered elsewhere on this page. (Wilbur Collection, University of Vermont)

THE SEVEN PHOTOGRAPHS on these two pages illustrate a multiple fatality accident that occurred on November 5, 1883, near North Enosburgh, Vermont on the Missisquoi Railroad. Engineer Thomas Flood realized that the switch to a lightly laid spur to a gravel bank on the edge of the Missisquoi River was set for the siding. Before he could stop his passenger train, it had run the length of the siding and reportedly traveled over twenty feet in the air before dropping into nearly twenty feet of water. Twenty-four year old Fred Hauver, the fireman, was killed instantly, as he was crushed in the engine cab. Engineer Flood, age 36, leaped from the cab at the last instant, but he was so badly injured he died the following day. The engine and tender, as well as two butter cars went into the Missisquoi River. Evidence indicated that the person responsible for throwing the switch had hidden himself at the scene to watch the results of his misdeed. Later in the day he was tracked to Richford, about 8 miles away, and apprehended. He was identified as Edmund Ellis, a brakeman on the Southeastern Railway, who reportedly had had a minor quarrel with the Missisquoi Railroad a short time earlier. There were no injuries among the rest of the crew or passengers,

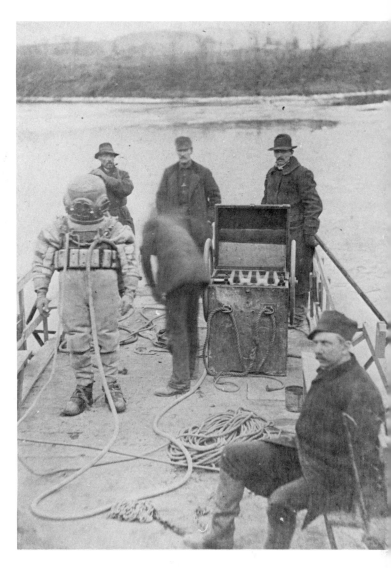

except for minor bruises suffered by a passenger and Superintendent T. Deal who happened to be riding the train.

The photo at the upper left shows the location of the accident, with the main line curving to the left and the gravel spur to the right. To the right is a view showing more of the siding, with the wreck train in evidence. The photo at center left shows the passenger car at the rear of the train, with the work train's engine in the foreground. At the bottom of page 134 is the locomotive after it has been pulled back to the river bank. A raft that was built to aid in this work is in the water to the right. The three photos on this page show different views of the recovery operation, under the direction of Wreck Gang Foreman Kemp. Of particular interest, is the diver that was used in this long-ago salvage operation. (Four photos on page 134, Jim McFarlane Collection; photo at upper left of page 135, Ed Steel Collection; other two, Jim McFarlane Collection)

THE BEAUTIFUL NUMBER 83, "Joseph Hickson," was built by the Rhode Island Locomotive Works in December, 1883. This engine, which was named after a director of the company, became Number 100 in 1900 and was scrapped in 1923. (Donald A. Somerville Collection)

THIS ENGINE WAS built in 1865 by McKay & Aldus as the "St. Johns." It was rebuilt and renamed the "T. M. Deal" in 1881 in honor of the road's superintendent. (Richard Sanborn Collection)

maneuver, the Central Vermont Railroad Company became both the owner and operator of the various companies that constituted its sphere of influence. And J. Gregory Smith seemingly had pulled off another financial and legal trans- action unique in the country's railroad annals.

While the legal maneuvering was taking place, daily operations were continuing as usual. The Central Vermont was unique in that the number of steam locomotives built in its own shops was inordinately high for a road of its size. Company records show that between 1859 and 1884, a total of 54 locomotives were completed and put into service. Nine of these were 2-6-0's, one was an 0-6-0, and the remainder were 4-4-0's. Eight were built at the Northfield Shops and the other 46 were constructed at St. Albans.

A spectacular accident occurred at East Granville, Vermont, on May 23, 1883. The northbound express ran into an open switch, and the engine, baggage and mail car, and two freight cars standing on an adjacent siding were badly damaged. The derailed locomotive struck the freight cars, which in turn were driven into the front of the station. Mrs. Lucy Spaulding, who was engaged as a housekeeper at the depot boarding house was thrown into the side of the building. Miraculously, she was not killed, although she did sustain serious injuries. Engineer Thomas Buck was also seriously hurt in the crash, but the remainder of the crew and passengers received nothing more than scratches and bruises.

During the first week of January, 1884, an unusual

THE "NORTH STAR" was built at the company's St. Albans shops in 1872, rebuilt a few years later, and scrapped in 1898 after a relatively short life. (Donald A. Somerville Collection)

THE "COLCHESTER" IS seen adjacent to a large woodshed at St. Albans. This engine was built in 1865 at the Vermont Central's Northfield shops, and scrapped in 1895. (William G. Rowley Collection)

THE "E. A. CHITTENDEN," Number 6, was built at St. Albans in 1880. It went through two renumberings subsequently, and was scrapped in 1902. Judging from the amount of smoke in the air, the large roundhouse must be full of live engines. (Jim Murphy Collection)

THE "SHELBURNE" WAS built for the Rutland Railroad in 1869, went through at least three renumberings, and was on the Central Vermont roster long after 1900. Note the large woodshed in the background. (Richard Sanborn Collection)

incident took place at Montpelier. The locomotive "Vermont" was sitting in front of the Montpelier station during the wee hours of the morning, awaiting its 3:25 a.m. departure for Montpelier Junction and a connection with the "Night Express." During a brief absence by the watchman, someone boarded the engine and succeeded in releasing the brakes and opening the throttle. The unattended engine chugged along to the junction, where it rounded the north leg of the wye and went onto the main line. The watchman returned to his charge only to see it disappearing down the moonlit track.

Arrangements were promptly made to sidetrack the run-

away at Waterbury and to keep the main line open until the train was stopped. The engineer was located and he followed with a team. Fortunately, the engine ran out of steam about four miles up the line near Middlesex, and the engineer was able to board the engine and return the train to Montpelier. A Mr. Smiley of Burlington was the only passenger on the train, and he reportedly had dozed off for much of the trip and was quite unaware that he was the sole person on the train as it moved through the night.

The Central Vermont, during the period it functioned as the Consolidated Railroad of Vermont, acquired two new passenger locomotives from the Rhode Island Locomotive

THIS FIREMAN'S SIDE view of the "E. A. Chitten-den" clearly shows the extremely flimsy looking pilot or cow-catcher that seemed to be in vogue during the 1880s. (Richard Sanborn Collection)

THE "A. ARNOLD" was an 1869 Manchester product. It was rebuilt in 1885 and subsequently sold in 1900. (Richard Sanborn Collection)

THE "JAMES M. FOSS" has just come out of the St. Albans paint shop in this photo which was taken in the mid-1880s. This distinctive and ornate letter-ing style was in use for only a few years, as the cost of applying it possibly could no longer be justified. (Jim Murphy Collection)

THE "J. M. HAVEN" was built in the Rutland shops in 1870 and was scrapped 30 years later. The lettering on the tender denotes that this engine was assigned to the CV's Rutland Division. Here we see the engine equipped with a snowplow pilot near the passenger depot in Rutland. (Richard Sanborn Collection)

THIS UNUSUALLY SHARP photograph shows the New London Northern's "Yantic" at a location that has been tentatively identified as Brattleboro. This engine was built in 1882, and it appears that this photograph was taken not long afterward. (Jim McFarlane Collection)

THE NEW LONDON Northern's "Charles Osgood" was built in 1872 by Manchester and served its working years on the Brattleboro-New London line. (Richard Sanborn Collection)

THIS STOCK CERTIFICATE indicates that J. Gregory Smith owned 938 shares of $100 par value stock in the Vermont & Canada, by this time absorbed into the Central Vermont Railroad. (Jim Murphy Collection)

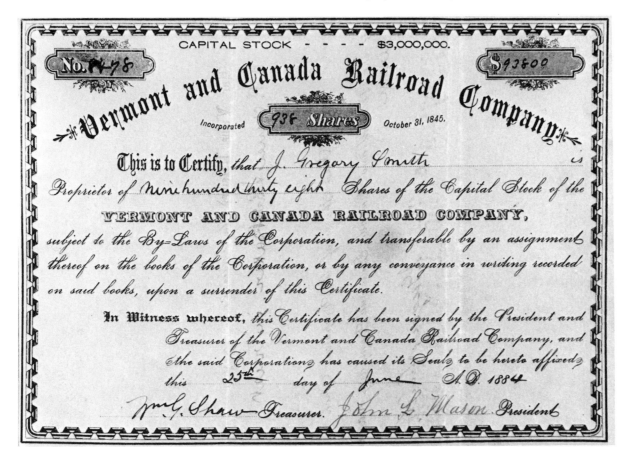

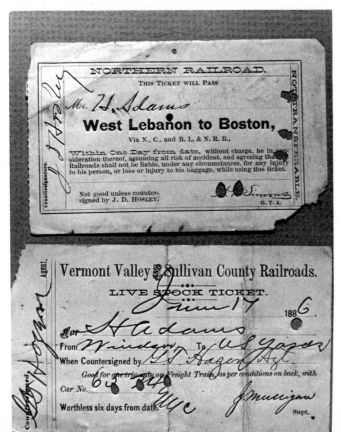

THIS PANORAMIC VIEW of St. Albans shows the city in 1885. The depot, roundhouse, and other facilities are located just to the right of center. The large dark building in the background to the left of center is the rolling mill. (Jim Murphy Collection)

ONE H. ADAMS was the recipient of passes permitting free transportation over the Northern Railroad of New Hampshire and the Vermont Valley and Sullivan County Railroads. Possibly Mr. Adams was a drover, an attendant who traveled with livestock while in transit from one point to another. (Jim Murphy Collection)

THESE THREE WAYBILLS cover different shipments from Chester, Vermont, on the CV's Rutland Division. (Jim Murphy Collection)

Works and promptly named them for two directors of the Consolidated Railroad—Joseph Hickson and E. H. Baker.

In January, 1884, the road started running a fruit car between Boston and St. Albans on a weekly basis. The car was heated and the fruit arrived in good condition. In mid-May a refrigerated car for butter transport to Boston went into service. This car featured the latest in refrigeration equipment and techniques.

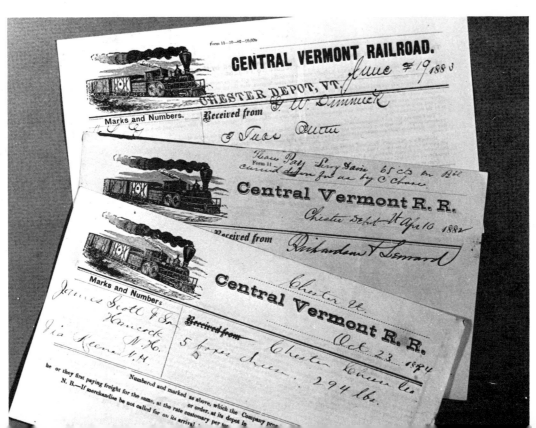

143

THE "GOVERNOR SMITH" occupies the Lake Street crossing in St. Albans in this classic Chandler photograph from the late 1880s. As soon as the conductor gives the highball, the southbound "Governor Smith" and the "Boston Fast Express" will soon be on its way. (Chandler photograph, Whitney Maxfield Collection)

THIS PHOTOGRAPH OF the second "Governor Smith" was taken at St. Albans in 1885. This engine was the last 4-4-0 on the Central Vermont, being scrapped in the late 1830s. (Richard Sanborn Collection)

THE ANNUAL DOG RIVER Valley Fair at Northfield was the social highlight of the year for miles around. The Central Vermont ran special trains for years carrying people to and from the fairgrounds. (Jim McFarlane Collection)

THIS CLOSE-UP OF the photo above shows the exquisite paint jobs that were applied to locomotives in this era. The reason for the young person occupying the fireman's seat is not known. (Richard Sanborn Collection)

146

THE 4-4-0 "GILES MERRILL" was built at the Northfield shops in 1865 and scrapped in 1893. (Richard Sanborn Collection)

THE SECOND "GOVERNOR SMITH" is about to be turned—just as soon as the photographer has completed his work. The wall of the turntable pit is made of granite blocks. (Albert C. Spaulding Collection)

THE "A. C. BEAN" had an unusually short working life. It was built at the St. Albans shops in 1882 and was scrapped in 1904. (Richard Sanborn Collection)

THIS LOCOMOTIVE, WHICH was assigned to the CV's B&L Division, is on the drawbridge at the south end of the Burlington yard. This engine was an 1877 Mason product. A more modern lift span was installed at this point in later years by the Rutland Railroad. This latter structure still exists, although it has not been operated for many years. (Gerry Fox Collection)

THIS NEW LONDON NORTHERN public timetable details that line's connections with the New York & New England Railroad and the steamers. (Both, Jim McFarlane Collection)

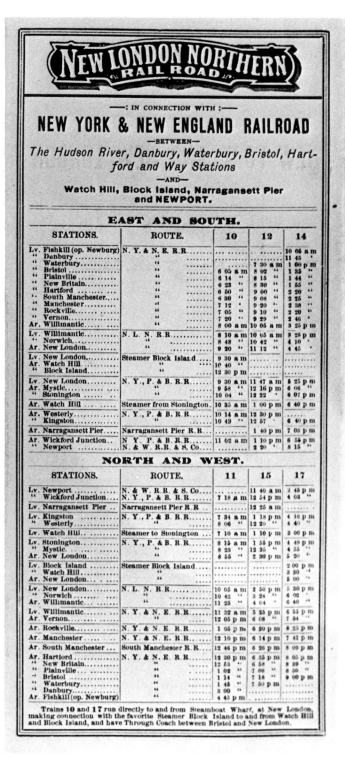

NEW LONDON NORTHERN RAIL ROAD

—: IN CONNECTION WITH :—

NEW YORK & NEW ENGLAND RAILROAD

—BETWEEN—

The Hudson River, Danbury, Waterbury, Bristol, Hartford and Way Stations

—AND—

Watch Hill, Block Island, Narragansett Pier and NEWPORT.

EAST AND SOUTH.

STATIONS.	ROUTE.	10	12	14
Lv. Fishkill (op. Newburg)	N. Y. & N. E. R.R.	......	......	10 05 a m
" Danbury	"	......	......	11 45
" Waterbury	"	......	7 30 a m	1 00 p m
" Bristol	"	6 05 a m	8 02	1 35 "
" Plainville	"	6 14 "	8 15 "	1 44 "
" New Britain	"	6 23 "	8 30 "	1 55 "
" Hartford	"	6 50 "	9 00 "	2 20 "
" South Manchester	"	6 30 "	9 08 "	2 25 "
" Manchester	"	7 12 "	9 20 "	2 38 "
" Rockville	"	7 05 "	9 10 "	2 20 "
" Vernon	"	7 20 "	9 29 "	2 46 "
Ar. Willimantic	"	8 00 a m	10 05 a m	3 25 p m
Lv. Willimantic	N. L. N. R.R.	8 10 a m	10 05 a m	3 25 p m
" Norwich	"	8 48 "	10 42 "	4 10 "
Ar. New London	"	9 20 "	11 12 "	4 45 "
Lv. New London	Steamer Block Island	9 30 a m	......	......
Ar. Watch Hill	"	10 40 "	......	......
" Block Island	"	12 30 p m	......	......
Lv. New London	N. Y., P. & B. R.R.	9 30 a m	11 47 a m	5 25 p m
Ar. Mystic	"	9 58 "	12 16 p m	6 06 "
" Stonington	"	10 04 "	12 22 "	6 07 p m
Ar. Watch Hill	Steamer from Stonington	10 35 a m	1 00 p m	6 40 p m
Ar. Westerly	N. Y., P. & B. R.R.	10 14 a m	12 30 p m	......
" Kingston	"	10 49 "	12 57 "	6 40 p m
Ar. Narragansett Pier	Narragansett Pier R.R.	......	1 40 p m	7 03 p m
Ar. Wickford Junction	N. Y. P. & B. R.R.	11 02 a m	1 10 p m	6 54 p m
" Newport	N. & W. R.R. & S. Co.	......	2 20 "	8 15 "

NORTH AND WEST.

STATIONS.	ROUTE.	11	15	17
Lv. Newport	N. & W. R.R. & S. Co.	......	11 40 a m	2 45 p m
" Wickford Junction	N. Y., P. & B. R.R.	7 18 a m	12 54 p m	4 03 "
Lv. Narragansett Pier	Narragansett Pier R.R.	......	12 25 a m	
Lv. Kingston	N. Y., P. & B. R.R.	7 34 a m	1 18 p m	4 16 p m
" Westerly	"	8 06 "	12 20 "	4 40 "
Lv. Watch Hill	Steamer to Stonington	7 10 a m	1 10 p m	3 00 p m
Lv. Stonington	N. Y., P. & B. R.R.	8 15 a m	1 55 p m	4 49 p m
" Mystic	"	8 23 "	12 35 "	4 55 "
Ar. New London	"	8 55 "	2 30 p m	5 20 "
Lv. Block Island	Steamer Block Island	......	......	2 00 p m
" Watch Hill	"	......	......	3 30 "
Ar. New London	"	......	......	5 00 "
Lv. New London	N. L. N. R.R.	10 05 a m	2 50 p m	5 30 p m
" Norwich	"	10 42 "	3 24 "	6 02 "
Ar. Willimantic	"	11 25 "	4 04 "	6 40 "
Lv. Willimantic	N. Y. & N. E. R.R.	11 32 a m	5 25 p m	6 55 p m
Ar. Vernon	"	12 05 p m	6 08 "	7 34 "
Ar. Rockville	N. Y. & N. E. R.R.	1 05 p m	6 20 p m	8 25 p m
Ar. Manchester	N. Y. & N. E. R.R.	12 10 p m	6 14 p m	7 41 p m
Ar. South Manchester	South Manchester R.R.	12 46 p m	6 26 p m	8 09 p m
Ar. Hartford	N. Y. & N. E. R.R.	12 30 p m	6 35 p m	8 05 p m
" New Britain	"	12 53 "	6 58 "	8 20 "
" Plainville	"	1 02 "	7 08 "	8 30 "
" Bristol	"	1 14 "	7 18 "	9 00 p m
" Waterbury	"	1 45 "	7 50 p m	
" Danbury	"	3 00 "		
Ar. Fishkill (op. Newburg)	"	4 45 p m	......	......

Trains 10 and 17 run directly to and from Steamboat Wharf, at New London, making connection with the favorite Steamer Block Island to and from Watch Hill and Block Island, and have Through Coach between Bristol and New London.

THIS NLN PUBLIC TIMETABLE page shows additional steamship and rail connections that may be made by NLN patrons. (Jim McFarlane Collection)·

NEW LONDON NORTHERN RAIL ROAD

—: IN CONNECTION WITH :—

N. Y., P. & B. R. R. & NEW LONDON STEAMBOAT CO.

—FROM—

Newport and Narragansett Pier, Block Island and Watch Hill

—TO—

Saratoga and Lake George, Albany and all Points WEST

NORTH AND WEST.

STATIONS.	ROUTE.	9	15	17
Lv. Newport............	Newport & W'kf'd R.R. and Steamboat Co.	......	11 40	2 45
" Wickford Junction....	N. Y., P. & B. R. R......	......	12 54	4 03
Lv. Narragansett Pier.....	Narragansett Pier R.R.	......	12 25	......
Lv. Kingston............	N. Y., P. & B. R. R......	......	1 18	4 16
" Westerly..............	"	......	12 29	4 40
Lv. Watch Hill	Steamer to Stonington.	......	11 30	3 00
Lv. Stonington........	N. Y., P. & B. R. R..	5 50	1 55	4 49
" Mystic..............	"	6 03	12 35	4 55
Ar. New London........	"	6 50	1 40	5 20
Lv. Block Island........	Steamer Block Island.	......	......	2 00
" Watch Hill..........	"	......	......	3 30
Ar. New London........	"	......	......	5 00
Lv. New London........	New London Nor. R.R.	7 55	2 50	5 30
" Norwich...........	"	8 25	3 24	6 02
" Willimantic........	"	9 05	4 04	6 45
" Stafford...........	"	9 52	4 48	7 23
Ar. Palmer...........	"	10 30	5 24	8 00
Lv. Palmer...........	Boston & Albany R.R.	11 04	5 30	9 07
Ar. Springfield.......	"	11 30	5 55	9 40
" Westfield........	"	11 53	6 28	10 24
" Pittsfield........	"	1 23	8 12	12 08
" Albany...........	"	2 50	9 45	1 40
Lv. Albany...........	D. & H. C. Co..	3 05	12 05	6 50
Ar. Saratoga.........	"	4 25	1 25	8 07
" Fort Edward......	"	7 10	......	8 45
" Caldwell..........	"	8 10	......	9 35
Lv. Albany...........	N. Y. C. & H. R. R. R..	3 00	10 00	2 15
Ar. Utica............	"	5 45	12 30	5 15
" Syracuse..........	"	7 15	2 05	7 00
" Rochester........	"	9 45	4 15	9 50
" Batavia..........	"	11 05	5 20	11 10
" Buffalo...........	"	12 15	6 15	12 15
(Central Time.)				
Lv. Buffalo...........	Mich. Cent. R.R..	11 35	5 45	11 35
Ar. Niagara Falls.....	"	12 15	6 30	12 25
" Detroit...........	"	8 05	1 05	8 45
" Chicago..........	"	6 40	9 30	8 05
(Central Time.)				
Lv. Buffalo...........	L. S. & M. S. R'y.	11 40	5 40	11 55
Ar. Erie.............	"	2 21	8 03	2 55
" Cleveland........	"	5 20	10 50	6 15
Ar. St. Louis........	C. C. C. & I. R'y.	7 30	7 30	6 00
Ar. Toledo..........	L. S. & M. S. R'y.	9 35	2 10	10 45
" Chicago..........	"	6 50	9 30	8 00

Train No. 9 has First Class Coaches New London to Palmer, where it connects with Fast Express which has Drawing Room Cars to Syracuse, and Sleeping Cars Syracuse to Chicago.

Train No. 15 has Drawing Room Cars, Wickford Landing and Narragansett Pier to New London, and First Class Coaches New London to Palmer, and connects at Palmer with Fast Western Express which has Sleeping Cars to Buffalo and St. Louis.

Train No. 17 connects at Steamboat Wharf New London with the Steamer Block Island from Watch Hill and Block Island, and has First Class Coaches New London to Palmer. Passengers by this train take Sleeping Cars for the West at Springfield.

NEW LONDON NORTHERN RAIL ROAD

—: IN CONNECTION WITH :—

NEW YORK & NEW ENGLAND RAILROAD

—BETWEEN—

The Hudson River, Danbury, Waterbury, Bristol, Hartford and Way Stations

—AND—

Watch Hill, Block Island, Narragansett Pier and NEWPORT.

EAST AND SOUTH.

STATIONS.	ROUTE.	10	12	14
Lv. Fishkill (op. Newburg)	N. Y. & N. E. R.R.	......	......	10 05 a m
" Danbury	"	......	......	11 45 "
" Waterbury	"	......	7 30 a m	1 00 p m
" Bristol	"	6 05 a m	8 02 "	1 55 "
" Plainville	"	6 14 "	8 15 "	1 44 "
" New Britain	"	6 23 "	8 30 "	1 55 "
" Hartford	"	6 50 "	9 00 "	2 20 "
" South Manchester..	"	6 58 "	9 08 "	2 25 "
" Manchester	"	7 12 "	9 20 "	2 38 "
" Rockville	"	6 55 "	9 10 "	2 25 "
" Vernon	"	7 20 "	9 29 "	2 46 "
Ar. Willimantic.......	"	8 00 a m	10 05 a m	3 25 p m
Lv. Willimantic.......	N. L. N. R.R.	8 10 a m	10 05 a m	3 25 p m
" Norwich	"	8 48 "	10 42 "	4 10 "
Ar. New London......	"	9 20 "	11 12 "	4 45 "
Lv. New London......	Steamer Block Island.	9 30 a m	......	......
Ar. Watch Hill	"	10 42 "	......	......
" Block Island.......	"	12 30 p m	......	......
Lv. New London......	N. Y., P. & B. R.R.	9 30 a m	11 47 a m	5 25 p m
Ar. Mystic...........	"	9 58 "	12 16 p m	6 08 "
" Stonington........	"	10 04 "	12 22 "	6 07 p m
Ar. Watch Hill	Steamer from Stonington.	10 35 a m	1 00 p m	6 40 p m
Ar. Westerly	N. Y., P. & B. R.R.	10 34 a m	12 30 "	......
" Kingston	"	10 49 "	12 57 "	6 49 p m
Ar. Narragansett Pier	Narragansett Pier R.R.	......	1 40 p m	7 03 p m
Ar. Wickford Junction.	N. Y., P. & B. R.R.	11 02 a m	1 10 p m	6 54 p m
" Newport	N. & W. R.R. & S. Co.	......	2 20 "	8 15 "

NORTH AND WEST.

STATIONS.	ROUTE.	11	15	17
Lv. Newport	N. & W. R.R. & S. Co...	......	11 40 a m	7 45 p m
" Wickford Junction	N. Y., P. & B. R.R...	7 18 a m	12 54 p m	4 03 "
Lv. Narragansett Pier	Narragansett Pier R.R..	......	12 25 a m	......
Lv. Kingston	N. Y., P. & B. R.R...	7 34 a m	1 18 p m	4 16 p m
" Westerly	"	8 06 "	12 29 "	4 40 "
Lv. Watch Hill	Steamer to Stonington ...	7 10 a m	1 10 p m	3 00 p m
Lv. Stonington.......	N. Y., P. & B. R.R...	8 15 a m	1 55 p m	4 49 p m
" Mystic...........	"	8 23 "	12 35 "	4 55 "
Ar. New London......	"	8 55 "	2 30 p m	5 20 "
Lv. Block Island	Steamer Block Island....	......	......	2 00 p m
" Watch Hill	"	......	......	3 30 "
Ar. New London......	"	......	......	5 00 "
Lv. New London......	N. L. N. R.R.	10 05 a m	2 50 p m	5 30 p m
" Norwich	"	10 42 "	3 24 "	6 02 "
Ar. Willimantic......	"	11 25 "	4 04 "	6 45 "
Lv. Willimantic......	N. Y. & N. E. R.R.	11 32 a m	5 25 p m	6 55 p m
Ar. Vernon	"	12 05 p m	6 08 "	7 34 "
Ar. Rockville	N. Y. & N. E. R.R.	1 05 p m	6 29 p m	8 35 p m
Ar. Manchester	N. Y. & N. E. R.R.	12 19 p m	6 14 p m	7 41 p m
Ar. South Manchester	South Manchester R.R.	12 46 p m	6 26 p m	8 29 p m
Ar. Hartford	N. Y. & N. E. R.R	12 30 p m	6 35 p m	8 05 p m
" New Britain	"	12 55 "	6 58 "	8 39 "
" Plainville	"	1 02 "	7 08 "	8 50 "
" Bristol	"	1 14 "	7 18 "	9 00 p m
" Waterbury	"	1 45 "	7 55 p m	......
" Danbury	"	3 00 "	......	......
Ar. Fishkill (op. Newburg)	"	4 45 p m	......	......

Trains 10 and 17 run directly to and from Steamboat Wharf, at New London, making connection with the favorite Steamer Block Island to and from Watch Hill and Block Island, and have Through Coach between Bristol and New London.

150

THE CENTRAL VERMONT, its leased lines, and their connections are clearly depicted on this 1885 map. (Jim McFarlane Collection)

THIS ENGINE WAS built by Taunton in 1849, rebuilt in the Rutland shops in 1865, and scrapped in 1887. Despite the rebuilding, a number of mechanical features give away the engine's true age. Note the unusual "engineer" posing in the cab window. (Richard Sanborn Collection)

THE WRECK OF THE "Brattleboro" at Thamesville, Connecticut, in the 1880s very nearly demolished factory buildings on either side. The truckless tender rests on the adjacent track. The engine was rebuilt, became Number 152 in 1892, and served the CV well into the twentieth century. (Lewis R. Brown, Inc., Collection)

THIS SPECTACULAR WRECK occurred in front of the Ludlow, Vermont, depot in 1885. The north-bound 4-4-0 "Lake Dunmore" handling Train 6 was stopped at the station when a runaway freight train headed by the "H. E. Chamberlin" struck it head on. It appears as though the Rutland Division wreck train crew will have its hands full for the next several hours. (Robert Adams Collection, courtesy Jim Shaughnessy, from THE RUTLAND ROAD)

THIS ACCIDENT TOOK place near Amherst, Massachusetts, in 1884. The main line will be blocked for some time from the appearance of things. (Lewis R. Brown, Inc., Collection)

THE "N. L. DAVIS" simmers outside the Rutland shops in her shining new paint job during the period that the CV leased the Rutland road. She was built for the Rutland & Burlington by the Taunton Works in 1868, rebuilt in 1891, and scrapped in 1900. (Robert Adams Collection, courtesy Jim Shaughnessy, from THE RUTLAND ROAD)

THE "LAWRENCE BARNES" poses for her picture with a tender filled with neatly stacked firewood. She was an 1870 Taunton product, which was scrapped in 1899. (Ed Steel Collection)

THE "ETHAN ALLEN" was built by Hinkley for the Rutland & Burlington in 1854. It is shown here lettered for the Rutland Division of the Central Vermont circa 1880. (Jim Shaughnessy Collection, from THE RUTLAND ROAD)

THE "WINOOSKI" WAS built by Hinkley and Drury in 1848, rebuilt in 1857, and scrapped in 1888. Note the absence of a pilot (cow-catcher) of any kind. (Richard Sanborn Collection)

THIS ENGINE WAS built in 1848 as the "Lamoille." She was rebuilt in 1862, renamed the "E. F. Perkins" in 1869, and scrapped in 1893. This rather poor quality print shows her in the St. Albans yard prior to 1880. (Ed Emery Collection)

THE "I. B. FUTVOYE" was originally built by Souther in 1852 as the "Iron Horse." It was rebuilt by the CV in 1866 and renamed "Governor Smith." Early in 1884, it was sold to the SS&C, but she was returned four months later. Upon her return to the CV, she was renamed the "I. B. Futvoye." The engine was scrapped in 1895. (Richard Sanborn Collection)

THE "WATERLOO" WAS built at St. Albans in 1870 and served the CV until she was sold in 1900. Judging from the headgear on the men, it must have been an extremely warm day. (Richard Sanborn Collection)

THIS LOCOMOTIVE WAS named for S. W. Cummings, the road's general passenger agent for many years. She was scrapped in 1921. (Richard Sanborn Collection)

THE "GOVERNOR PAGE" was built by Taunton in 1868, and subsequently went through three renamings and renumberings. With her tender piled high with firewood, she is lettered here for the CV's Rutland Division. (Richard Sanborn Collection)

THE "FAIRFAX" was a product of the St. Albans shops. She was renumbered as "8" in 1900 and was sold almost immediately thereafter. (Richard Sanborn Collection)

THE ṪAUNTON COMPANY built the "Chester" in 1850. She was rebuilt in 1868 and scrapped in 1892. In this photograph, the "Chester" is seen at Brattle-boro in 1888. (Richard Sanborn Collectin)

THE "HARTFORD" WAS built in the Vermont Central's Northfield shops in 1865 and scrapped thirty years later. Note the variety in the shape of the three domes. (Richard Sanborn Collection)

THE "GENERAL SHERMAN" was built by Manchester in 1866, renamed "R. Camp" in 1871, rebuilt in 1887, and scrapped in 1899. The location of this photo has not been verified. (Richard Sanborn Collection)

THE "STOWE" WAS built by the St. Albans shops in 1872. She is being turned on the platform turntable at St. Albans about 1880. (Donald A. Somerville Collection)

THE OGDENSBURGH & Lake Champlain had the Essex Company build the "Genesee" in May, 1851. Prior to the CV surrendering its lease of the O&LC in 1877, the "Genesee" was photographed with her tender lettered for the O&LC Division of the Central Vermont. The photographer succeeded in rounding up a very interesting group of men to pose for this picture. (Jim Shaughnessy Collection, from THE RUTLAND ROAD)

THIS BUILDER'S PHOTO of CV Number 89 was taken in 1887. This engine was renumbered 318 in 1900 and scrapped in 1928.(Chandler B. Cobb Collection)

THIS BEAUTIFUL PHOTOGRAPH was taken just north of Brattleboro shortly after the line curved over the trestle—the Brattleboro & Whitehall—was completed in 1880. The road on the left has now become busy Route 5. Note the admonition to travelers on the road to "Walk Your Horse" through the long covered bridge. (Dan Foley Collection)

THE THREE-FOOT GAUGE "Brattleboro" is being wooded up somewhere along the line between Brattleboro and South Londonderry, Vermont. This engine was scrapped in 1906, shortly after this line was standard-gauged. (Richard Sanborn Collection)

NUMBER 191 HAS stopped on the trestle at West Dummerston, just north of Brattleboro, on the narrow-gauge line to South Londonderry. The trestle and grade look quite new, which would place the date of this photograph in the early 1880s. (Lewis R. Brown, Inc., Collection)

THE TEAM TRACK in the old freight yard at Brattleboro appears very busy. The large brick passenger depot is located at the end of the string of boxcars on the left. (Lewis R. Brown, Inc., Collection)

THIS DERAILMENT UPENDED an empty flatcar and stood it nearly on end at the Vernon Street ice house siding in Brattleboro. There was considerable property damage, but no serious injuries. (Albert C. Spaulding Collection)

THIS PHOTOGRAPH SHOWS the wreckage of the Brattleboro ice house siding accident from the opposite direction from the photograph above. (Lewis R. Brown, Inc., Collection)

TWO PEOPLE WERE KILLED in this 1886 bridge collapse on the narrow-gauge Brattleboro & Whitehall Railroad just north of Brattleboro. Virtually the entire train was wrecked. The covered bridge to the left has been damaged by the accident. These bridges may be seen in much better condition on page 162. (Lewis R. Brown, Inc., Collection)

THIS VIEW OF THE wreckage of the bridge collapse was taken from the west side of the bridge. The engineer and one passenger were killed at this spot which was located about two miles north of Brattleboro and known as "Three Bridges Crossing." The third bridge was the Central Vermont's which is located just to the left of the highway bridge. (Rich Yates Collection)

THE "C. H. BAKER" was built by Rhode Island in 1883, became Number 101, in 1900, and was scrapped in 1922. In this picture, she is on the Brattleboro turntable. (Richard Sanborn Collection)

THE CV'S SECOND 39 was built at St. Albans in 1874, and retained her original number until she was scrapped in 1918. (Richard Sanborn Collection)

THIS ENGINE WAS built by Hinkley in 1854 for the Rutland & Burlington as their "Lake Dunmore." She became the CV's Rutland Division Number 215 during the period of the CV's lease of the Rutland Railroad, and she is so lettered in this photograph which was taken on the bank of the Connecticut River at Bellows Falls in the late 1880s, a few years before she was scrapped. (Robert Adams Collection, courtesy Jim Shaughnessy, from THE RUTLAND ROAD)

THE LIME KILNS just south of Fonda Junction (north of St. Albans) were a good source of revenue for the Central Vermont for many years. (Jim Murphy Collection)

THE FRANKLIN COUNTY Cooperative Creamery at St. Albans was one of the largest creameries in the country before the turn of the century. Many thousands of carloads of milk and butter were shipped from this building over the years to the metropolitan markets. (Jim Murphy Collection)

THE LARGE E. W. BAILEY mill in Montpelier received large shipments of grain from the Midwest and milled it for sale to area farmers. (William Gove Collection)

SEVERAL MEMBERS OF the St. Albans round-house crew pose with 2-6-0 ''George Nichols'' in the background. The company shop built the engine in 1878; and she was renumbered 300 in 1900 and scrapped twelve years later. (St. Albans Historical Society Collection)

THE ROUNDHOUSE GANG at Brattleboro were also amenable to posing for the photographer in the 1880s. (Jim Murphy Collection)

THIS ENGINE WAS built by Manchester for the New London Northern in 1866. After undergoing three renumberings, she was scrapped in 1900. She is heading a southbound passenger train at Palmer, Massachusetts, in the 1880s. (Jim McFarlane Collection)

A NEW LONDON NORTHERN local freight is switching at Norwich, Connecticut, prior to 1890. (Jim McFarlane Collection)

THIS PHOTOGRAPH SHOWS a rare close-up of an 1880s CV caboose. The crew members look as though they are thoroughly enjoying the break from their labors. (Jim McFarlane Collection)

THIS SOUTHBOUND PASSENGER train is traveling south of Palmer, Massachusetts, on the New London Northern. (Jim Murphy Collection)

THE "W. J. RUST" is seen at the Malone trainshed in the 1880s. She was built by Amoskeag for the Northern Railroad of New York, rebuilt by that road's successor, the Ogdensburgh & Lake Champlain at their Malone shop, and she was eventually scrapped in 1892. (Jim Shaughnessy Collection, from THE RUTLAND ROAD)

THE NEW LONDON Northern's "W. W. Billings" is at the head end of a passenger train in front of the large granite depot at Palmer, Massachusetts. (Jim Shaughnessy Collection)

ENGINE NUMBER 8 of the New London Northern is taking water at South Windham, Connecticut, circa 1870. (Jim Shaughnessy Collection)

THE NLN'S "HENRY P. HAVEN" has pulled up to the South Windsor water tank in the 1880s. (Lewis R. Brown, Inc., Collection)

NEW LONDON NORTHERN'S "Benjamin Stark," has stopped so that the passengers may have twenty minutes for a quick lunch before resuming their journey. This engine was built in 1872 and scrapped in 1899. (Albert C. Spaulding Collection)

THE UNNAMED SECOND Number 88 of the Central Vermont was built by Baldwin in 1887. Interesting is the fact that a very unusual style of number has just been painted on her cab panel. This photograph is believed to have been taken at Northfield. (Jim McFarlane Collection)

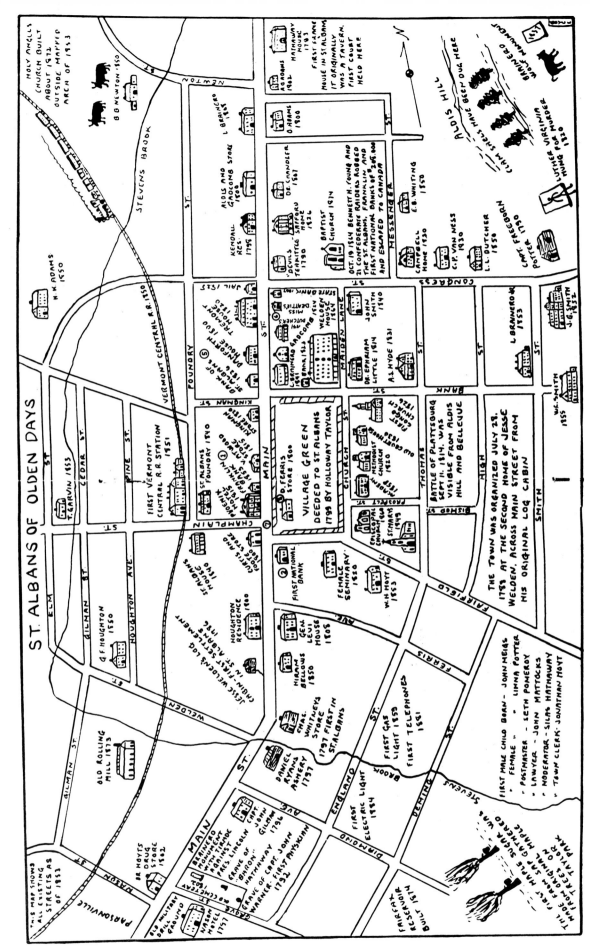

THIS SIMPLE DRAWING of St. Albans contains a
great deal of historical information. (Armand Premo
Collection)

STEAM LOCOMOTIVE ROSTER
1845-1900

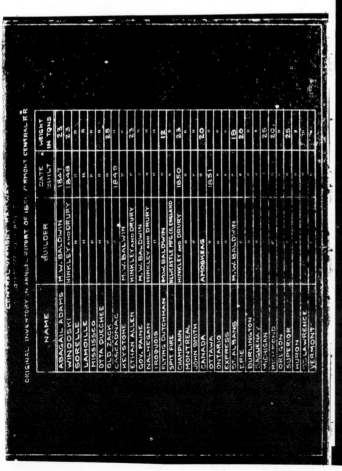

CENTRAL VERMONT RAILWAY
ORIGINAL INVENTORY IN ANNUAL REPORT OF 1851, VERMONT CENTRAL RR

NAME	BUILDER	DATE BUILT	WEIGHT IN TONS
ABAGAIL ADAMS	M.W. BALDWIN	1847	23
WINOOSKI	HINKLEY AND DRURY	1848	23
SORELLE	"	"	
LAMOILLE	"	"	
MISSISCO	"	"	
OTTA QUECHEE	"	"	25
OLD ZACK	"	1849	
CASCADNAC	"	"	
KEYSTONE	M.W. BALWIN	"	
ETHAN ALLEN	HINKLEY AND DRURY	"	23
GOV. PAINE	M.W. BALDWIN	"	
NALHEGAN	HINKLEY AND DRURY	"	
IROQUOIS	R.W. BALDWIN	"	12
FLYING DUTCHMAN	NEWCASTLE MFG.CO, ENGLAND	"	
SPIT FIRE	HINKLEY AND DRURY	"	23
CHAMPLAIN	"	1850	
MONTREAL	"	"	
JOHN SMITH	"	"	
CANADA	AMOSKEAG	"	20
OTTAWA	"	1851	
ONTARIO	"	"	
EXPRESS	"	"	
ST ALBANS	M.W. BALDWIN	"	18
ERIE	"	"	20
BURLINGTON	"	"	
MICHIGAN	"	"	25
RICHMOND	"	"	20
OREGON	"	"	
SUPERIOR	"	"	25
HURON	"	"	
ST LAWRENCE	M.W. BALDWIN	"	
VERMONT	"	"	

CENTRAL VERMONT RAILWAY INC.
LOCOMOTIVE LIST AND DATA, 1855 to 1873 INCL.

CENTRAL VERMONT RAILWAY INC.
LOCOMOTIVE LIST AND DATA 1852 to 1873 INCL.

NAME AS OF / **WEIGHTS** / **BOILER** etc. (two-part table)

ENG N°	JULY 1852	JULY 1853	MARCH 1869	JULY 1870	MARCH 1871	JULY 1873	BUILDER	DATE BUILT	DATE RE-BUILT	REMARKS
32	ESSEX	ESSEX	B.P.CHENEY	B.P.CHENEY	B.P.CHENEY	B.P.CHENEY	ESSEX C°	1852		
33		ESSEX	ESSEX	ESSEX	ESSEX	ESSEX	ESSEX C°	1852		
34	THE STRANGER	THE STRANGER	THE STRANGER	THE STRANGER	THE STRANGER	THE STRANGER				
35	SWANTON	SWANTON						1852		
36	ROYALTON	ROYALTON	RICHFORD	RICHFORD	ROYALTON	ROYALTON	TAUNTON			
37	ETHAN ALLEN	ETHAN ALLEN	ROYALTON	ROYALTON	ETHAN ALLEN	FOREST CITY				RENAMED 1873
38	MICHIGAN	MICHIGAN	MICHIGAN	MICHIGAN	MICHIGAN	CASCADNAC	BALDWIN	1851		
39	KEYSTONE	KEYSTONE	JOHN CROMBIE	JOHN CROMBIE	JOHN CROMBIE	JOHN CROMBIE	JOHN CROMBIE	1849		
40	IRON HORSE	IRON HORSE	GOV. SMITH	GOV. SMITH	GOV. SMITH	GOV. SMITH	SOUTHER	1852		
41			RANDOLPH	RANDOLPH	RANDOLPH	RANDOLPH	BOSTON	1856		AT ONE TIME CALLED "WHISTLER"
42			BOLTON	A.B.FOSTER	A.B.FOSTER	A.B.FOSTER	TAUNTON	1860		
43			BOLTON	BOLTON	BOLTON	BOLTON		1845		
44			WILLISTON	WILLISTON	WILLISTON	WILLISTON				
45			L.BRAINERD	L.BRAINERD	L.BRAINERD	L.BRAINERD	NORTHFIELD			
46			HARTLAND	HARTLAND	HARTLAND	HARTLAND				
47			HARTFORD	HARTFORD	HARTFORD	HARTFORD				
48			SHARON	SHARON	SHARON	SHARON	P.M.& G.'s			
49			COLCHESTER	COLCHESTER	COLCHESTER	COLCHESTER	NORTHFIELD			RENAMED 1873
50			ALBURGH	ALBURGH	ALBURGH	ALBURGH				
51			H.H.LOCKLIN	H.H.LOCKLIN	H.H.LOCKLIN	H.H.LOCKLIN	ST.ALBANS			
52			G.MERRILL	G.MERRILL	G.MERRILL	G.MERRILL	NORTHFIELD			
53			BERLIN	BERLIN	BERLIN	BERLIN	NORTHFIELD			
54			ST.JOHNS	ST.JOHNS	ST.JOHNS	ST.JOHNS				
55			MANSFIELD	MANSFIELD	MANSFIELD	MANSFIELD				
56			GEN'L GRANT	GEN'L GRANT	GEN'L GRANT	GEN'L GRANT	MANCHESTER			
57			GEN'L STANNARD	GEN'L STANNARD	GEN'L STANNARD	GEN'L STANNARD				
58			GEN'L SHERIDAN	GEN'L SHERIDAN	GEN'L SHERIDAN	GEN'L SHERIDAN	R.CAMP			
59			R.F.TAYLOR	R.F.TAYLOR	R.F.TAYLOR	R.F.TAYLOR	ST.ALBANS			
60			HIGHGATE	HIGHGATE	HIGHGATE	HIGHGATE				
61			RICHMOND	RICHMOND	RICHMOND	GEO.M.RICE	WM.MASON			SOLD TO O.&L.C. "JOHN SCHRIER"
62					STOWE	STOWE	WM.MASON	1872		SOLD TO O.&L.C. "W.A.SHORT"
63					BRAINTREE	BRAINTREE	WM.MASON	1872		SOLD TO O.& L.C. "CHATEAUGAY"

LOCOMOTIVE LIST AND DATA 1852 to 1873 INCL. (continued)

ENG N°	MARCH 1869	JULY 1870	MARCH 1871	JULY 1873	BUILDER	DATE BUILT	TYPE	REMARKS
65	FAIRFAX	FAIRFAX	FAIRFAX	FAIRFAX	WM.MASON	12-7-68	4-4-0	SOLD TO O.& L.C. "ST. REGIS"
66		DES RIVIERES	DES RIVIERES	DES RIVIERES	ST.ALBANS	1872		
67		WATERLOO	WATERLOO	WATERLOO	FAIRFAX	4-14-70		
68		J.W.HOBART	J.W.HOBART	J.W.HOBART	MANCHESTER	3-12-70		
69		A.ARNOLD	A.ARNOLD	A.ARNOLD	A.ARNOLD	8-6-64		
70		ST.ARMAND	ST.ARMAND	ST.ARMAND	ST.ALBANS	8-9-70		SOLD TO RUTLAND DIV. J.BURDETT N° 26
71		H.W.C.SMITH	W.C.SMITH	W.C.SMITH	TAUNTON	6-12-64		
72			SWANTON	SWANTON	ST.ALBANS	1873		
73			J.D.HATCH	J.D.HATCH	SWANTON	6-21-70		
74			ATLANTIC	ATLANTIC		11-16-70		
75		ATLANTIC				1-70		
76		WOODSTOCK	WOODSTOCK	WOODSTOCK	WOODSTOCK	1871		
77			ST.ALEXANDER	ST.ALEXANDER	ST.ALEXANDER			
78			EDWARD BLAKE	EDWARD BLAKE	EDWARD BLAKE			
79			LANSING MILLIS	LANSING MILLIS				
80			OTIS DRURY	OTIS DRURY				
81			J.H.PINKERTON	J.H.PINKERTON				
82		PACIFIC	PACIFIC	PACIFIC	BALDWIN	6-20-71	2-6-0	SOLD TO RUT GOV. 3⅛/14 "AMERICA N° 38"
83			GEO.L.STONE	GEO.L.STONE	ST.ALBANS	1871		
84			NORTH STAR	NORTH STAR		1872		CHANGED TO N°16 IN 1874
85			GEO.G.HUNT	GEO.G.HUNT		1873		
86			T.G.ELLIOTT	ARCTIC		1872	4-4-0	NO FURTHER RECORD CAN BE FOUND

KINGS N° 2 ST. ALBANS AND N° C.SMITH WERE ORIGINALLY BUILT FOR THE UNION PACIFIC R.R. BUT WERE SOLD TO THE CENTRAL VERMONT INSTEAD.
* NEW "ST. ALBANS" BUILT IN 1872. FOR DIMENSIONS SEE NEXT LIST.
WITHOUT DOUBT THE WHEEL ARRANGEMENT OF THE EARLIEST ENGINES AS BUILT DIFFERED FROM THAT GIVEN,
* NEW "PACIFIC" BUILT IN 1873 WITH SAME NUMBER. FOR DIMENSIONS SEE NEXT LIST.
COSTS AS BUILT: 1-J.CLARK*8411°°, 2-ST.ALBANS*14512°°, 5-D.D.RANLETT*10400°°, 18-W.H.H.BINGHAM*1122°°,
ENGINES WITH INSIDE CYLINDERS IN 1870
34 STRANGER
36 ROYALTON

ENGINES BUILT AT NORTHFIELD AND ST. ALBANS WERE AT RAILWAY COMPANY'S SHOPS.

WHICH IS THAT AS RE-BUILT, AS NO DEFINITE RECORD IS AVAILABLE EXCEPT AS TO THE N°1 GOV.PAINE.
40-GOV.SMITH*16000°°, 47-HARTFORD*15000°°, 58-R.CAMP*20002°°, A.ARNOLD*13500°° 2, J.H.FOSS*11254°°

WHEELS ON PASSENGER ... 'GOVERNOR PAINE' ... 'BALDWIN ENGINE' WITH 78-INCH DRIVERS BUILT FOR ... THE LOCOMOTIVES WERE EITHER RE-CONSTRUCTED, AS WAS THE GOV.PAINE, OR SCRAPPED.

CENTRAL VERMONT RAILWAY INC.
LOCOMOTIVE LIST AND DATA 1876 to 1885 INCL.

CENTRAL VERMONT RAILWAY INC.
LOCOMOTIVE LIST AND DATA 1876 to 1885 INCL.

ENG Nº	NAME AS OF JAN. 1, 1876	JAN. 1, 1879	MAY 1, 1881	JUNE 1, 1885	BUILDER	DATE BUILT	DATE RE-BUILT	TYPE	CYL'S	DRI-VERS	GRATE				REMARKS

NOTE:
ENGINE Nº 24 "PACIFIC" WAS SOLD TO THE RUTLAND DIV. IN AUG. 1886 AND NAMED CHAS. CLEMENT Nº 17.
COAL BURNERS IN 1862 WERE Nºs 2, 17 AND 78.
... 2,3,5,18,19,23,24,25,26,29,30,38,39,41,42,43,48,63,64,65 AND JUNE 1,1885 ...
ENGINES WITH WESTINGHOUSE AIR BRAKES JAN., 1876 : 8,15,16,20,25,26,32,40,42,44,47,51,60,71
JUNE 1, 1885: 3,8,15,16,19,20,24,25,26,27,29,30,32,36,40, ...

THE FOLLOWING ENGINES HAD DUTIES PAID AND WERE ASSIGNED PERMANENTLY TO CANADIAN SERVICE
ON THE "STANSTEAD, SHEFFORD AND CHAMBLY" AND "WATERLOO AND MAGOG" ON APRIL 1, 1884.

13 - ENOSBURGH (VALUE 2800.00)	40 - I.B. FUTVOYE (VALUE 2500.00)
14 - OTTA QUEECHEE (" 1600.00)	45 - L. BRAINERD (" 3000.00)
15 - EXPRESS	46 - HARTLAND (" 2300.00)

CENTRAL VERMONT RAILWAY INC. — LOCOMOTIVE LIST AND DATA 1888 TO 1900 INCL.

ENG No	NAME OR NUMBER AS OF JUNE 1,1888	AUG.1,1890	FEB.1894	NEW No AS OF JAN.1,1900	BUILDER	BUILDERS NUMBER	DATE BUILT	DATE REBUILT	TYPE	TRACTIVE POWER	CYLS	DRIVERS	GRATE	BOILER PRESS AS OF 1890	REMARKS
1	J.CLARK	J.CLARK	No.1	306	St.Albans		1880		2-6-0		18½x24	57	35x66	130	
2	B.P.CHENEY	ST.ALBANS	No.2	33	"		1872	10-1873	4-4-0		16x24	63	35x66	130	
3	J.Q.HOYT	J.Q.HOYT	No.3	37	"		10-1873						35x66	135	
4	GEO.G.HUNT	GEO.G.HUNT	No.4	35	"		1872		2-6-0		19x24	57	35x78	130	
5	D.D.RANLETT	D.D.RANLETT	No.5	311	"		1880				19x24		35x68		
6	E.A.CHITTENDEN	E.A.CHITTENDEN	No.6	307	"		1878		4-4-0		17x24	57	35½x66	125	
7	GEO.NICHOLS	GEO.NICHOLS	No.7	300	Hinkley & Drury		1849	10-10-42			15x20	60	35x59		DEMOLISHED IN 1893
8	E.F.PERKINS	No.8			Baldwin		1850	10-15-81	4-4-0		16x24	57	35x59½	130	JULY.1890
9	MILTON	(SEE COUNTY LINE BELOW)									16x24	57	35x40	125	
10	ST.ALEXANDER	ST.ALEXANDER	No.10	10	P.Drury		1848	12-3-83	0-4-0		14x24	42	36x47		DEMOLISHED 12-3-1888. ORIG A=5 L.#3 IN SERVICE ON CVRY 12-2-42
11	WOODSTOCK	WOODSTOCK	No.11	11	Baldwin		1873	4-22-40	2-6-0		14x18	42	36x58½	125	1 ON CVRY 12-4-42 DEMOL.1899
12	WINOOSKI		No.12	4			1850		4-4-0		10x16		34x41		OUT OF SERVICE 1890
13	ENOSBURGH	ENOSBURGH	No.13	42	Sch'dy	5627	1871	6-18-90			15x24	63	35x57½	130	ORIG A=5 L. 6 IN SERVICE ON CVRY 12-10-42
14	No.14	No.14	No.14	313	Sch Dy	828	1871		2-6-0		16x24	57	35x47	165	ROAD No.92 WHEN BUILT
15	EXPRESS	EXPRESS	No.15	315	Baldwin	8661	1881	4-13-84	4-4-0		19x26	60	34x71		DEMOLISHED BEFORE 5-24-95
16	M.G.ELLIOTT	M.G.ELLIOTT	No.16	43	St.Albans		1873				15x20	68	35x68	140	SENT TO N.L.N.RR OCT.1894
17	No.17	No.17	No.17	314	Baldwin	8660	1887				19x24	57	34x71		ROAD No.94 WHEN BUILT
18	W.H.BINGHAM	W.H.BINGHAM	No.18	308	Baldwin		1881		4-4-0		17½x24	68	35½x71½	140	
19	VERMONT	J.W.HOBART	J.W.HOBART	54			1884				15x20	68	34x71		W.H.BINGHAM
20	VERMONT	VERMONT	No.20	49	Baldwin	3515	1851	9-21-86	0-4-0		15x24	50	35x50	135	ON N.L.M.RR 3-1-90 DEMOLISHED JAN.1891
21	OTIS DRURY	OTIS DRURY	No.21	36	Sch'dy		1891		4-4-0		16x24	57	35x59½	125	ORIG A=5 L. 2 IN SERVICE ON CVRY NOV.1892
22	LAMOILLE	No.22	No.22	44	St.Albans		1890		6-VL		14x24	54	34x71	140	DEMOLISHED OCT.1892
23	No.24	No.23	No.23	315	Baldwin	8662	1887		2-6-0		14x24	57	34x71		DEMOLISHED OCT.1895
24	No.24	No.24	No.24	46	St.Albans	8312	1874		0-4-0		16x24	50	34x53	135	ROAD No.95 WHEN BUILT
25	J.R.LANGDON	No.25						12-26-47	4-4-0		19x24	68	34x71		CHANGED TO No.25 IN NOV.1892
26	No.26	No.26					1871				16x22	60	35x55	130	SOLD TO N.L.N.RR NOV.1840 (No.175)
27	MIDDLESEX	MIDDLESEX	No.27	24	Baldwin		1871				15x24	57	35x55	125	RENUMBERED NOV.1892. TO REPLACE J.R.LANGDON
28	EDWARD BLAKE	EDWARD BLAKE	No.28		St.Albans		1883				16x24	54	35x60	130	DEMOLISHED 1897
29	GOV.SMITH	GOV.SMITH	GOV.SMITH	53	St.Albans		1891		2-6-0		17x24	63	35x71¼	140	
30	No.24	No.30					1871		0-4-0		17x24	68		140	
—	GEORGIA? 31	GEORGIA? 31			Hinkley		1892		4-4-0		15x22	66	35x72	40	

CENTRAL VERMONT RAILWAY INC. — LOCOMOTIVE LIST AND DATA 1888 TO 1900 INCL.

ENG No	NAME OR NUMBER AS OF JUNE 1,1888	AUG.1,1890	FEB.1894	NEW No AS OF JAN.1,1900	BUILDER	BUILDERS NUMBER	DATE BUILT	DATE REBUILT	TYPE	TRACTIVE POWER	CYLS	DRIVERS	GRATE	BOILER PRESS AS OF 1890	REMARKS
31	B.P.CHENEY	B.P.CHENEY	No.31	51	Sch'dy	3593	1892		4-4-0		17x24	63	34x72	125	ORIG A=5 L. No.12 ON CVRY JAN.'93
32	B.P.CHENEY	B.P.CHENEY	No.32		Essex Co		1852		"		16x24	66	38x41		DEMOLISHED 1897
33	ESSEX	ESSEX	ESSEX	52	St.Albans		1872		"		15x24	60	35x72		CHANGED FROM No.88 AS BUILT
34	J.M.FOSS	J.M.FOSS	No.34	34	"		1874		"		16x24	57	35x60	130	
35	STRANGER	RICHFORD	No.35	14	"		1872		"		16x24	60		130	
36	RICHFORD	NORTH STAR	No.36				1887		2-6-0			57			DEMOLISHED 1898
37	NORTH STAR	No.37	No.37	316	Baldwin	8667	1887		4-4-0		19x26	57	34x71	140	CHANGED FROM No.93 AS BUILT
38	L.MILLIS	L.MILLIS	No.38	15	St.Albans		1871		"		16x24	60	34x71	130	IN SERVICE ON N.L.N.RR JULY-NOV 1890
39	JOHN CROMBIE	JOHN CROMBIE	No.39	39	"		1874		"		15x20	54	35x59	125	DEMOLISHED 1895
40	L.B.FUTVOYE	L.B.FUTVOYE	No.40	41	"		1866		2-6-0		15x24	60	35x59		IN SERVICE ON N.L.N.RR FEB.1893
41	J.H.PINKERTON	J.H.PINKERTON	No.41		"		1873		4-4-0		16x24	63	35x59	130	DEMOLISHED 1897
42	No.42	No.42	No.42	44	St.Albans		1864	1-9-69	"		16x24	60	35x56	125	
43	G.MERRILL	G.MERRILL	No.43	312	Northfield		3-65		2-6-0		19x24	68		130	JUNE 1897
44	B.B.SMALLEY	B.B.SMALLEY	No.44		Northfield		8-66		4-4-0		15x24	63	35x56	125	
45	JACOB EDWARDS	JACOB EDWARDS	No.45	40	St.Albans		1872		"		16x24	57	35x47	130	DEMOLISHED 1897
46	WILLISTON	WILLISTON	No.46	41	"		1887	2-8-65	"		15x24	68	34x56	130	DEMOLISHED MAY 1899
47	L.BRAINERD	L.BRAINERD	No.47	24	T.M.DEAL		1864	6-15-65	"		15x24	57	35x47	125	1891
56	HARTLAND	HARTLAND	No.56		T.M.DEAL		1871	12-25-81	Z			63	35x59½		Nov.27, 1895
57	HARTFORD	HARTFORD	No.57		"		1-14-66		"			60	34x56	125	HARTFORD
48	A.C.BEAN	A.C.BEAN	No.48	38	Dunkirk		1882		4-4-0		16x24	63		130	A.C.BEAN
49	COLCHESTER	COLCHESTER	No.49	44	St.Albans		4-19-65	4-11-87	"		15x24		35x59	125	DEMOLISHED 1895
50	ALBURGH	ALBURGH	No.50		Northfield		12-28-64		"		16x24	54			FEB.1892
51	M.W.LOCKLIN	M.W.LOCKLIN	No.51	26	St.Albans		4-11-66	4-1-87	2-6-0		15x24	68	35x60	130	DEMOLISHED 1895
52	G.MERRILL	G.MERRILL	No.52		Northfield		11-68		4-4-0		15x24	68	35x56	125	JUNE 1897
53	B.B.SMALLEY	B.B.SMALLEY	No.53				8-66		"			63	35x59		
54	T.M.DEAL	T.M.DEAL	No.54				1872		"		16x24	60	34x55	120	
55	J.H.KIMBALL	J.H.KIMBALL	No.55	12	St.Albans		1887		"		16x24	57	34x55	135	
61	HIGHGATE	HIGHGATE	No.61	47	St.Albans		1872		"		15x24	57	35x56	130	HIGHGATE
62	GEO.M.RICE	GEO.M.RICE	No.62	13	Baldwin	8123	1887		"		16x24	68			GEO.M.RICE
63	No.63	No.63	No.63				1877		0-4-0			57			BRAINTREE
64	BRAINTREE	BRAINTREE	No.64				4-4-70		"			63		130	FAIRFAX
65	FAIRFAX	FAIRFAX	No.65	8			1871		"		17x24	66	35x72	140	
66	DES RIVIERES	DES RIVIERES	No.66	9	Hinkley		1892		"		15x22	66	34x72	40	DES RIVIERES

CENTRAL VERMONT RAILWAY, INC.
LOCOMOTIVE LIST AND DATA 1888 to 1900 INCL.

CENTRAL VERMONT RAILWAY INC.
NEW LONDON NORTHERN R.R. LOCOMOTIVE LIST

ENG No	ORIGINAL LIST	JAN 1, 1891	1892	3-31-1892	1900 (C.V.Ry)	BUILDER	BUILDERS NUMBER	DATE BUILT	TYPE	COST	CYL'S	DRIVERS	GRATE	STEAM PRESS 1901	BOILER TUBES DIA	No	HEAT SURF F.BOX	TUBES LENGTH	ENGINE WT TRUCK	DRIVERS	TOTAL	TENDER AND TRUCK	CAP'Y ENG AND TENDER GALS	REMARKS
	NEW LONDON																							
1	W.H.BARNES	151			304	TAUNTON		1849	4-4-0		14x18	60				130		10.0			36000			SOLD 1875
2	STAFFORD	151			304	HINKLEY		1874	2-6-0		18x24	57	125				10.0	11.0			84000		1600	INSIDE CONNECTED
3	BRATTLEBORO	152			301	C.V.Ry		1849	2-6-0		14x18	54	130					11.0			39608		1500	EXPLODED AT "NEW LONDON PARADE"
	WILLIMANTIC					TAUNTON		1849	4-4-0		15x20	54				146		11.0						RENAMED T.S.WILLIAMS BEFORE 1872
3	3	153			200	BALDWIN	10242	1884	4-6-0	8850"	19x24		140			155	192	24	12'-3"	25000	73600	98600	44800	3000	ORIG "O•L.C No 220 TRANSFERRED 1890
4	CHICOPEE	154			201	TAUNTON		1884	4-4-0	8850"	15x20					12	140	14½	11.0			44800		1600	ORIG "O•L.C No 222 TRANSFERRED 1890
5	MONSON	155			202	BALDWIN	10236	1883	4-6-0	8850"	19x24		140			155	192	24	12'-3"	25000	73600	98600	44000	3000	ORIG "O•L.C No 250 TRANSFERRED 1890
5		155			202	HINKLEY	10229	1851	4-4-0	8850"	16x20		140			125	2	24	12'-3"					1600	WRECKED
6	THAMES	THAMES				MANCHESTER		1867	4-4-0		15x22					126	2"		11'3"			50000		1800	WRECKED
7	MONTAGUE	MONTAGUE	176		6	HINKLEY		1879				63				126	2¼		11'3"			58010		1800	SCRAPPED 1901
8	CANADA	BLOCK ISLAND	161		27	MANCHESTER		1863								144	2"		10'3"			62000		1800	RENAMED
9	WARE	F.H.PRESCOTT						1867								130						64000		1600	SEE NOTE
10	A.M.RAMSDELL	A.M.RAMSDELL	162		28	SOUTHER		1854	4-4-0		15x20	56										40000			SCRAPPED 1899 OR 1900 OUTSIDE CONNECTED
11	BELCHERTOWN	BELCHERTOWN	162		28	MANCHESTER		1867			16x24	63										64000			SCRAPPED BEFORE RECEIPT OF MONTVILLE
12	MONTVILLE	MONTVILLE	160		305	ST.ALBANS		1852	2-6-0		18x24	57										84000			FROM ST.ALBANS OLD No 11 D.D.RANLETT
13	PALMER	PALMER	159		303	RHODE ISLAND	1205	1882	2-6-0	14000"	18x24	56		130		130	10.04					36000			PURCHASED 2ND HAND FROM SHORE LINE R.R.
14	NORWICH	NORWICH	163		29	MANCHESTER		1867	4-4-0		16x24	63										91000			
15	B.P.HAVEN	B.P.HAVEN	164		30			1870			15x20					144	2"		11'3"			60000		1900	SCRAPPED 1900
16	W.W.BILLINGS	W.W.BILLINGS	165		31			1872			16x24			130								66000		1600	
17	J.W.DOJ	166		23			1873				63													1800	
18	ROBERT COIT	167					1873	0-4-0	10960"				57											WHEELS CHANGED AT RUTLAND
19	CHAS.OSGOOD	168		22			1873																	SCRAPPED DEC.1895
20	BENJ.STARK	170					1874	0-4-0	5500"	15x22	69										64000			SOLD AS SCRAP ON WHEELS 1899
21	C.F.SPAULDING	169					1882	2-6-0	14000"	15x22	50										60000			
22	KONOMAC	172					1874	4-4-0		16x24	56		130								49000			
23	YANTIC	158		302	RHODE ISLAND	1206	1882	2-6-0	14000"	15x22	51										62000			
24	NAMEAUG	174		48	BALDWIN	8311	1881	0-4-0		16x24	50		135								64000			
25	STAFFORD	157		310	ST.ALBANS		1881	2-6-0		16x24	51		130								83000			FROM ST.ALBANS
26	AMHERST	156		309			1880			19x24											86000		1600	

ENG 153 WAS REC'D ON O•L.C ON 12-9-1889 AND MADE ONLY 19473 MILES ON O•L.C AND FULL DVS. BEFORE BEING TRANSFERRED TO THE M.L.N R#
154 " " " 12-9-1889 " 17470..
155 " " " 12-7-1889 " 9,400

THE "CHAMPION" BUILT AND RAN ON THE AMHERST, BELCHERTOWN AND PALMER R.R.

THE M.L.N. RR IS MADE UP OF THE NEW LONDON, WILLIMANTIC+PALMER BUILT FROM NEW LONDON TO PALMER IN 1849 AND 1850; THE AMHERST, BELCHERTOWN+PALMER, WHICH WAS A REORGANIZATION OF THE AMHERST, BELCHERTOWN BUILT IN 1853 FROM PALMER TO AMHERST AND THE VERMONT+MASSACHUSETTS EXTENDING FROM MILLERS FALLS TO BRATTLEBORO. THE LINE BETWEEN AMHERST AND MILLERS FALLS WAS BUILT IN 1866. THE M.L.N. WAS LEASED ON 11-21-1871 TO J.G.SMITH, W.C.SMITH AND B.P.CHENEY FOR 20 YEARS BUT THE LEASE WAS ASSIGNED TO THE C.V.RR ON 6-25-1873. ON 12-1-1899 THE ROAD WAS LEASED FOR 99 YEARS TO THE CONSOLIDATED RAILROAD OF VERMONT AND ON 4-20-1899 THAT COMPANY ASSIGNED THE LEASE TO THE CENT.VT.RY.

*BETWEEN DEC.1890 AND JUNE 1891 ITEM ENGINES WERE RENUMBERED AS SHOWN IN PARENTHESES, THEN ALL ENGINES WERE GIVEN NUMBERS OF THE 151 TO 176 SERIES BETWEEN AUG.1841 AND APR.1892.

BRATTLEBORO AND WHITEHALL R.R.

ENG No	ORIGINAL LIST	JAN 1, 1891	1891	1892	BUILDER	BUILDERS NUMBER	DATE BUILT	TYPE	COST	CYL'S	GRATE	DRIVERS	STEAM PRESS 1901	BOILER TUBES DIA	No	ENGINE WEIGHTS	TENDER	CAP'Y TANK GALS	REMARKS
1	BRATTLEBORO	191		2	DANFORTH		1879	2-6-0	4260"	12x16	36		125			40000	31000	71000	
2	LONDONDERRY	192		3															
3	J.L.MARTIN	193		1	BALDWIN		1880	4-4-0	6600"	10x16	42					33000	35000	68000	SCRAPPED 1901, REPLACED BY No 4 REBUILT

ON APRIL 15, 1893 C.V.RR ENGS No's 27, 42, 314 AND 317 WERE IN SERVICE ON THE M.L.N

9 "WARE" WAS AN OLD INSIDE CONNECTED ENGINE PURCHASED FROM SOME OTHER RAILROAD.
9 F.H.PRESCOTT ORIGINALLY BUILT AND PURCHASED FROM LOWELL MACH. WKS. (SOUTHER) IN 1854 AND APPARENTLY RENAMED F.H.PRESCOTT UPON ABSORPTION BY THE M.L.N.R.R.
OLD "PALMER" AND AN OLD "AMHERST" WEIGHTS 18 TONS WERE SCRAPPED ABOUT JAN 1, 1891 ALL ENGINES WERE COAL BURNERS IN 1891 EXCEPT No 9 F.H.PRESCOTT.

ON 12-2-1847 M.L.N. ENGINES WERE EQUIPPED WITH BRAKES AS FOLLOWS:
WITH DRIVER AND TRAIN AIR BRAKES No's 153,154,155,158,159,160,161
WITH TRAIN BRAKES ONLY No's 161,162,163,164,165,166,167,171,175,176
WITHOUT EITHER DRIVER OR TRAIN BRAKES No's 151,156,157,172

* BELCHERTOWN. THIS WAS APPARENTLY THE ORIGINAL "AMHERST" OF THE N.L.W+P AND ACQUIRED BY THE AMHER.J. AND BELCHERTOWN. IT LATER WAS SOLD TO THE WATERTOWN AND ROME.

BRATTLEBORO AND WHITEHALL R.R.

THE B+W.R.R BUILT ORIGINALLY AS THE WEST RIVER R.R WAS OPENED FOR OPERATION ON NOV.3,1880. MEANWHILE ON 5-10-1880 THE PROPERTY WAS LEASED TO THE M.L.N.R.R FOR A PERIOD OF 99 YEARS. THEN ON 12-1-1899 THE M.L.N.R.R. LEASED ITS PROPERTY TOGETHER WITH THAT OF THE C.V.R.R. TO THE CONS.R.R OF VT. FOR 99 YEARS. THE B+W.R.R. WAS ORIGINALLY BUILT WITH A GAUGE OF THREE FEET BUT IN THE FALL OF 1904 THE TRACK WAS CHANGED TO STANDARD GAUGE. AS A RESULT OF FLOOD DAMAGE EXPERIENCED IN NOV.1927 THE LINE WAS NOT RECONSTRUCTED BY THE C.V.RY HOWEVER WITH THE HELP OF A LOAN FROM THE STATE OF VERMONT IT WAS AGAIN PUT INTO OPERATION BY OTHER PARTIES BUT IN EARLY 1936 PERMISSION WAS GIVEN BY THE I.C.C. FOR ITS ABANDONMENT.

AFTER BEING RECONSTRUCTED IN 1929 THE B+W PURCHASED ONE NEW STEAM LOCOMOTIVE AND OBTAINED OTHER EQUIPMENT FROM THE C.V.RY AS FOLLOWS:

NEW LOCOMOTIVE N°1 BUILT BY AMER LOCO CO N°6?6198 IN 1930, 2-8-0 TYPE, 14"DIA DRIVERS, 18x24 CYLS, 180 LBS. PRESSURE, 71000 LBS TRAC POWER, WT.ON TRUCK: 15000LBS; DRIVERS: 105000LBS.TOTALING 120000LBS, COAL BURNER
ONE LOCOMOTIVE EX N°53 GIVEN BY C.V.RY, BUILT AT ST.ALBANS IN 1885, 4-4-0 TYPE, 68 DIA.DRIVERS, 17½x24 CYLS, 140 LBS. PRESSURE, 2850 LBS TRAC.POWER, WT.ON TRUCK 38750LBS; DRIVERS: 56000LBS, TOTALING: 88750 LBS. COAL BURNER.
ALSO C.V.RR No: ONE COMBINATION BAGGAGE-PASSENGER CAR, TWO BOX CARS WERE LEASED FROM THE C.V.RY. FOUR 30 TON CAPACITY BOX CARS, 1 SNOWPLOW AND 1 SCRAPER CAR.

CENTRAL VERMONT RAILWAY INC.
ADIRONDACK and ST.LAWRENCE R.R. LOCOMOTIVES TRANSFERRED TO THE C.V. RY.

A&StL NUMBER	CENT.VT.RY.Nº AS TRANSFERRED	AS OF 1-1-1900	BUILDER	BLDRS Nº	DATE BUILT	TYPE	CYLS	WEIGHT	VALUE	DATE TRANSF'D	REMARKS
1*	9		BALDWIN	5627	1881	4-4-0	10×16	39,300	1500.00	12-6-92	DEMOLISHED 1896
2	20	49	SCH'DY	3515	1891	0-4-0	16×24	66,000	6199.59	NOV.'92	2-27-1924
3*	12	4	BALDWIN		1873	2-6-0	14×18	57,600	2500.00	12-2-92	RET.'92
6	13	42	SCH'DY	828	1871	4-4-0	16×24	68,200		12-10-92	BLT. VALUE '86
11	30	50		3594	1892	4-4-0	17×24	94,000	8046.23	DEC.'92	DEMOLISHED 2-4-92
12	31	51	"	3593	"	"	"		8004.97	JAN.'93	6-14-'92
13	107	102	"	3513	1891	"	"	105,450		APR.'92	2-15-192?
14	108	103	"	3514	"	"	"				11-30-1920
32	116	209	"	3722	1892	4-6-0	19×24	127,000	11088.00	JUN.'93	8-30-1935
33	117	210	"	3723	"	"	"				5-8-1926
34	113	206	RHODE ISLAND	2730	1890	"	"	110,000	9732.00	JAN.'93	2-5-1926
35	114	207	"	2727	"	"	"				10-6-1922
38	112	205	"	2726	"	"	"				6-18-1925
39	115	208	"	2762	"	"	"				
101	129	106	SCH'DY	3878		4-4-0	"	125,500	10830.00	DEMOLISHED 10-13-1928
	110	203	RHODE ISLAND	2760		4-6-0	"	110,000	17700.00	MAY.'92	2-12-1928
	111	204	"	2761		"	"				4-30-1922
116	130	336	SCH'DY	4114	1893	2-6-0	19×26	123,000	9380.00	1893	7-30-1924
117	131	337	"	4115	"	"	"				3-24-1925
118	132	338	*	4116	"	"	"				6-27-1924
119	133	339	"	4117	"	"	"				5-28-1924
120	134	340	"	4118	"	"	"				

* A&StL RR Nºs 1 AND 3 WERE ORIGINALLY NARROW GAUGE ENGINES.
△ A&StL RR Nº 6 MAY HAVE BEEN NEW YORK CENTRAL Nº 339.
IN ADDITION TO THE LOCOMOTIVES THE A&StL TURNED OVER THE FOLLOWING TO THE C.V.RY.
* 6000 29 — LOCOMOTIVE STEAM CRANE (CRAKE INDUSTRIAL WORKS)
2601 29 — LIDGERWOOD DOUBLE HOISTING ENGINE
4500 29 — STEAM SHOVEL
3852 19 — WRECK CAR

CENTRAL VERMONT RAILWAY INC.
OGDENSBURG AND LAKE CHAMPLAIN DIVISION LOCOMOTIVES

TOTAL WEIGHT ENGINE	SCRAPPED	REMARKS
56,300	BETWEEN 1-1-91 AND 6-27-92	
	BETWEEN 6-27-92 AND 5-31-95	LATER RENUMBERED 25
52,500		
52,500		PURCHASED BY RUTLAND AND BURLINGTON
48,700	BETWEEN 1-23-72 BY RUT.& BUR.R.R.	DATE WHEN RENAMED UNKNOWN
52,500	BETWEEN 6-27-92 AND 5-31-95	
52,500	BETWEEN 6-27-92 AND 5-31-95	
53,700		REBUILT 1893
	BETWEEN 6-27-92 AND 5-31-95	CYLINDERS MAY HAVE BEEN 16×24
51,500	NOV.27,1895	WAS BUILT FOR NORFOLK COUNTY R.R. AS THE WATERFORD
56,000		
60,000		REBUILT AT MALONE AND RENAMED 1873
53,000	BETWEEN 6-27-92 AND 5-31-95	REBUILT AT MALONE AND RENAMED 1872
53,200	BETWEEN 1-1-91 AND 4-1-91	LATER RENUMBERED 29
55,000		MAY HAVE BEEN FIRST Nº 7 RE-BUILT
53,000	BETWEEN 1-1-91 AND 4-1-91	

CENTRAL VERMONT RAILWAY INC.
ADIRONDACK AND ST.LAWRENCE R.R. LOCOMOTIVES TRANSFERRED TO THE C.V.RY.

THE ADIRONDACK AND ST.LAWRENCE RAILROAD, WHICH EXTENDED FROM THE MOHAWK TO MALONE, WAS A REORGANIZATION AND EXTENSION OF THE OLD NARROW GAUGE "HERKIMER, NEWPORT AND POLAND" BY DR. SEWARD WEBB. IN 1891 THE MALONE AND ST.LAWRENCE WAS BUILT FROM MALONE TO THE INTERNATIONAL BOUNDARY AND THE ST.LAWRENCE AND ADIRONDACK FROM THAT POINT TO VALLEYFIELD P.Q. AND EVENTUALLY TO ADIRONDACK...

...THESE TWO LATTER ROADS WERE LEASED IN PERPETUITY TO THE CENTRAL VERMONT AND WITH THE A&ST.L. FORMED A THRU LINE FROM THE MOHAWK TO MONTREAL. THE LOCOMOTIVES USED WERE APPARENTLY OPERATED JOINT-LY AND LETTERED BOTH A&ST.L AND C.V.RY. WHILE THE OWNERSHIP OF A CERTAIN NUMBER WAS ASSUMED BY THE CENTRAL VERMONT UNDER A MORTGAGE AGREEMENT. LATER, PROBABLY IN 1894, THE NEW YORK CENTRAL OB-TAINED CONTROL OF THE A&ST.L. AND DR.WEBB ON MARCH 1ST ASSUMED THE M&ST.L. LEASE AS REGARDED INTREST AND PRINCIPAL AND THE ROAD WAS THEN OPERATED BY THE NEW YORK CENTRAL.

ON THE A&ST.L. AS ENGINES WERE DISPOSED OF OTHERS WERE BUILT AND ASSIGNED THE SAME NUMBERS, WHICH ACCOUNTS FOR WHAT OTHERWISE MIGHT BE THAT DISCREPANCIES IN RECORDS. BUILDER'S NUMBERS SHOWN WERE TAKEN FROM BUILDER'S RECORDS AND I.C.C. BOILER FORMS.

A&ST.L ENGINES Nºs 1,3 AND G. C.V.RY Nºs 9,12 AND 13 RESPECTIVELY WERE ORIGINALLY NARROW GAUGE ENGINES OF THE H.N.& P. REBUILT FOR STANDARD GAUGE. THE NYC WAS POSSIBLY EX NYC Nº 339.

A&ST.L ENGINE 101 C.V.RY Nº 129 AND LATER RR Nº 106 WAS BUILT EXPRESSLY FOR SERVICE BETWEEN MALONE AND MONTREAL AND UPON ITS RECEIPT ENGINE 111 THEN ON RUN, WAS RETURNED TO SERVICE BETWEEN MALONE AND HERKIMER TO RUN OPPOSITE 101 WHILE TRACK WAS IN ITS ROUGH CONDITION. THIS HER EXPLICIT INSTRUCTIONS OF DR.WEBB IN NOV. 1892. THIS ENGINE WAS A DUPLICATE OF THE NEW YORK CENTRAL CLASS C ENGINES Nºs 893 TO 898 AND 903 TO 908 BUILT AT SCHENECTADY IN 1891 BUT WAS NOT THE SAME AS THE FAMOUS 999 WHICH LATER ENGINE WAS BUILT AT SCHENECTADY IN 1893 TO SOMEWHAT DIFFERENT DIMENSIONS. ENG 101 HAD 78" DIAM. DRIVING WHEELS AS BUILT.

...REFERED TO THE TWO ENGINES NUMBERED C.V.RY Nºs 116 AND 117 THE FOLLOWING LETTER FROM F.W.BALD-WIN, SUPT. UP TO C.E.FULLER JR. S.M.P. IS EXPLANATORY. "THE PRESIDENT (C.V.RY) HAS AGREED WITH DR.WEBB TO TAKE ENGINES 32 AND 33 IN EXCHANGE FOR COMPOUND ENG'S 30 AND 31. IN ORDER, HOWEVER, THAT THE 32...WILL ALL THE ENGINES PURCHASED FROM DR.WEBB AND COVERED BY THE EQUIPMENT MORTGAGE MARKED WITH THE ORIGINAL NUMBERS SOON AS POSSIBLE. JUNE 26,1893."

SUPPLEMENTARY LIST OF A&ST.L ENGINES TRANSFERRED TO THE C.V.RY. FOR SERVICE ON THE RUTLAND DIVISION AND EVENTUALLY TURNED OVER TO THE RUTLAND RAILROAD

A&ST.L Nº	C.V.RY. Nº AS TRANSFERRED	RUTLAND R.R. LIST Nº OF	BUILDER	BUILDER'S Nº
11	222	50	SCHENECTADY	3510
12	223	67	"	3511
	224	61	"	3512
		60	"	

CENTRAL VERMONT RAILWAY INC.
OGDENSBURG AND LAKE CHAMPLAIN DIVISION LOCOMOTIVES

Nº	NAME OR NUMBER AS OF OCT.15,1852	1874	JAN.1,1891	JUNE 30,1896 MAR. 8,1897	RUTLAND R.R. 1901	BUILDER NAME	NUMBER	DATE BUILT	TYPE	CYL'S	DRIVERS
1	LOREL					AMOSKEAG	16	4-1851	4-4-0	16×20	74
2	MICHIGAU	*J.C.PRATT	301	W.J.RUST		MALONE		4-1851	"	15×20	60
3		G.M.BARNARD	302	W.J.FROST		TAUNTON	62	8-1869	"	14×24	54
	RIDEAU	J.W.PIERCE	303	J.W.PIERCE		ESSEX Cº	471	12-1851	"	16×24	60
4	OSWEGATCHIE	JOHN G.PRATT H.A.CHURCH	304	H.A.CHURCH	303	TAUNTON	435	1868	4-4-0	16×24	60
5						BOSTON	269	4-1850	"	16×24	60
6	DEER					TAUNTON	431	4-1868	4-4-0	16×24	60
7	TRENT	DEWITT C.BROWN	305	D.C.BROWN		KIRK CHURBRIDGE		5-1850		16×20	68
8						MASON	282	6-1868	4-4-0	16×24	60
9	WELLAND	ABRAHAM KLOHS	306	A.KLOHS	306	MASON	286	1868	4-4-0	16×24	"
10		*J.S.FARLOW	307	J.S.FARLOW	74	ESSEX Cº		8-1851	"	15×18	"
11	OTTAWA					TAUNTON	25	11-1850	4-4-0	15×24	"
12	ONTARIO	MALONE	308	MALONE		R.KAY'S ALDUS LOCO.WKS.		1867	"	16×24	"
		OGDENSBURG	309	W.A.SHORT	309	R.KAY'S ALDUS		1867	4-4-0	15×20	"
	ADELE					BOSTON	277	10-1850	"	15×18	"
10		STAGG GEN'L GRANT	310	GEN'L GRANT	310	MANCHESTER		1865	4-4-0	15×24	"
11	SARANAC	FAWN GEN'L SHERMAN	311	GEN'L SHERMAN		BOSTON	270	8-1850	"	15×18	"
12	LAGRASSE	WELLAND	312	WELLAND		MANCHESTER		1866	4-4-0	15×24	"
						BOSTON	276	9-1850	4-4-0	15×20	54
13		ST.LAWRENCE	313		313	MALONE	234	11-1849	"	15×18	60
						BOSTON		1862	4-4-0	15×20	54
	CHAMPLAIN		314		314	ESSEX Cº		2-1852	"	15×24	"
						MALONE		1864	"	15×20	"
						BALDWIN	8309	12-1886	2-6-0	19×24	"
		FAWN	315	FAWN	392	ESSEX Cº		3-1852	"	15×24	"
						MALONE			4-4-0	14×20	60

CENTRAL VERMONT RAILWAY INC.
OGDENSBURG AND LAKE CHAMPLAIN DIVISION LOCOMOTIVES

NAME OR NUMBER AS OF JAN. 1, 1891	JUNE 30, 1896 MAR. 8, 1897	1901 (RUTLAND R.R. N°)	BUILDER NAME	NUMBER	DATE BUILT	TYPE	CYLS	DRIVERS	TOTAL WEIGHT ENGINE	SCRAPPED	REMARKS
316 STAG			BOSTON	400	4-1851	4-4-0	16x24	54			ON 1-1-76 HAD 12x20 CYLS AND 60" DRIVERS
317 ECONOMY			MALONE	294	4-1851	4-4-0	14x20	60	2,000		
RICHELIEU N° 18	317	382	BOSTON		7-1882	2-6-0	18x24	54			
			PORTLAND	456	5-1851		14x20	54	1,800		REBUILT AT MALONE AND RENAMED
			GLOBE			4-6-0	19x24	54			REBUILT AS 91 FOR C.V.RY. RETURNED TO C.V.RY. RENUMBERED 250 SOLD TO N.L.N.RR 9/3/20
318	318	393 153	BALDWIN	10229	9-1890	4-6-0	19x24	54			
			BALDWIN	10238	5-1890	2-6-0	19x26	54	37070		RETURNED TO C.V.RY. RENUMBERED 250
GENESEE			ESSEX C°		5-1851		15x20	60			LATER RENUMBERED 31
319 ENERGY	319	383	MALONE				12x20	60			
			PORTLAND	457	7-1882	2-6-0	18x24	54	31,800		
TURTLE			ESSEX C°		8-1851		15x20	48			
N° 20			MALONE				11x20	48			
320	320	394 122	BALDWIN	10242	7-1884	4-6-0	19x24	54	37000		BUILT AS C.V.RY. N° 33 RETURNED TO C.V.RY. RENUMBERED 220 SOLD TO N.L.N.R.R. 9-3-20
MICHIGAN			ESSEX C°	8310	8-1851		15x20				BUILT AS 300 FOR C.V.RY. BUT APPARANTLY RENUMBERED UPON RECEIPT
321	321		BALDWIN	8310	12-1846	4-6-0	18x24	54	13,000	PRIOR TO 1-1-76	
N° 22 GENESEE DEER			BOSTON	281	10-1849		16x20				BUILT AS C.V.RY. N° 92 RETURNED TO C.V.RY. RENUMBERED 222 SOLD TO N.L.N.R.R. 3-8-20
322	322	346 154	BALDWIN	10236	9-1889	4-6-0	19x24	54	37000		BUILT AS 324 FOR C.V.RY. BUT APPARANTLY RENUMBERED UPON RECEIPT
			BALDWIN	10916	5-1890	2-6-0	19x26				
RIDEAU			MALONE				16x20	60			
323	323	397 155	ERIEGWAY	10917	5-1890	2-6-0	19x24x26	54	37000		BUILT AS 326 FOR C.V.RY. BUT APPARANTLY RENUMBERED UPON RECEIPT
SUPERIOR			BOSTON		10-1849		15x20				
324	324	172	BALDWIN	10124	1840	4-4-0	17x24	66	36000		LATER RENUMBERED 30
			MALONE		5-1851	4-4-0	14x24	54			WAS ORIGINALLY N° 2
325 HURON			THOMSON		1849		14x20	48	7,500	BETWEEN 1-1-91 AND 4-1-91	
326	326	173	THOMSON			4-4-0	16x24	66			

THIS ROAD WAS CHARTERED MAY 14, 1845 ...

THIS ROAD WAS CHARTERED MAY 14, 1845 AS THE NORTHERN R.R. C[O] OF NEW YORK, AND WAS BUILT FROM OGDENSBURG TO
ROUSES POINT, N.Y., 118 MILES. OPENED TO OGDENSBURG ON OCT. 1, 1850. REORGANIZED UNDER FORE CLOSURE, JAN. I,
1858 AS THE OGDENSBURG R.R. AND ORGANIZED AS OGDENSBURG AND LAKE CHAMPLAIN R.R. JUNE 18, 1864. ON MAR.
1, 1870 WAS LEASED TO THE CENTRAL VERMONT FOR 20 YEARS. AND ON JUNE 1, 1886 IN PERPETUITY. THIS LEASE WAS
IN EFFECT UNTILL THE C.V.RY RECEIVERSHIP ON MAR. 20, 1896, WAS OPERATED BY THE RECEIVERS FOR A TIME
AFTER THIS BUT WAS TAKEN OVER BY THE RUTLAND R.R. ABOUT 1900.
THE LAST LOCOMOTIVE LIST SHOWN IN C.V.RY. RECORDS WAS THAT OF MAR. 8, 1897 ALTHO ENGINES
336, 337 AND 338 WERE OBTAINED AFTER THIS DATE. THEY WERE BUILT AS N°263, 51 AND 62 FOR AND USED BY
SMITH AND HANFORD CONTRACTORS ON THE VAN CORTLAND CUT-OFF OF THE PUTNAM DIV. OF THE NEW YORK CENTRAL
R.T.L. WAS N°521[?],2493-2484 BUILT 1893. 14x24" CYLS, 57 DRIVERS. N°339, 340+341 BUILT SCHDY 1897.
51 DRIVERS N°4+2C4[?]-4G47 19x28 CYLS 54 DRIVERS. ROAD N°342 BUILT BY BALDWIN N°4342 IN 1879 14x24 CYL.
BUILDERS N°4 2641-2493-2484 ...
THE ORIGINAL LOCOMOTIVES NUMBERED 1 TO 28 INCL. WERE COPIED FROM REPORT OF THE NORTHERN R.R. (NEW YORK)
TO THE NEW YORK STATE ENGINEER, DATED OCTOBER 15, 1852.
DURING THE PERIOD OF THE LEASE AS TRAFFIC CONDITIONS REQUIRED C.V.RY. LOCOMOTIVES WERE ASSIGN-
ED FOR SERVICE ON THE O. AND L.C. DIVISION. FOR EXAMPLE ON APR. 28, 1893 SUCH ENGINES WERE C.V. RY.
N°S 11, 113, 28, 32, 36, 64 AND 101.
* ENGINES MARKED THUS MAY HAVE BEEN NEW ONES BUILT AT MALONE AS RECORDS SHOW BUT MORE
...KELY WERE OLD LOCOMOTIVES REBUILT AND RENAMED.

CENTRAL VERMONT RAILWAY INC.
OGDENSBURG AND LAKE CHAMPLAIN DIVISION LOCOMOTIVES

NAME OR NUMBER AS OF OCT. 15, 1852	JAN. 1, 1891	JUNE 30, 1896 MAR. 8, 1897	1901 (RUTLAND R.R. N°)	BUILDER NAME	NUMBER	DATE BUILT	TYPE	CYLS	DRIVERS	TOTAL WEIGHT ENGINE	SCRAPPED	REMARKS
SOREL	327 SOREL		76	MALONE		1872	4-4-0	16x24	54	66200		
CHAZY	326 OTTAWA			HINKLEY + DRURY	47	10-1849	4-4-0	11½x20	48			
				MALONE				14x18	60			BUILT FOR OLD COLONY R.R. AS THE MAYFLOWER
LA GRASSE	329 LA GRASSE		398	BOSTON		9-1850		15x18				WAS ORIGINALLY N° 12
SALMON	329 S.R. CARLTON			RHODE ISLAND	1584	1895	2-6-0	14x24	54		PRIOR TO 1-1-76	
GENESEE	330 D.W. LAWRENCE		399	RHODE ISLAND	1585	1885	2-6-0	14x24	54		PRIOR TO 1-1-76	WAS ORIGINALLY N° 25
	331 HOYLE			ESSEX C°		5-1851		16x24	54			WAS ORIGINALLY N° 19. LARGER CYLINDERS APPLIED PRIOR TO 1-1-76
CHATEAUGAY	332 CHATEAUGAY			MALONE	291	1870	4-4-0	16x24	60	73500		WAS C.V.RY. N° 64 BRAINTREE. PURCHASED BY O.+L.C. BETWEEN 1871+1873
ST. REGIS	333 W.J. AVERILL			THOMSON	293	1849		16x24	54	60400		" 65 FAIRFAX
JOHN SCHRIEK	334 JOHN SCHRIEK			"	294	"		16x22	66	61000	BETWEEN 4-27-91 AND 3-31-95	" 62 RICHMOND
V.A. SHORT	335 MAXWELL			"	292	"		16x22	60	62500		" 63 STOWE * DIA WHEELS CHANGED

ON O.+L.C. LIST OF 1-1-91:
ALL ENGINES WERE COAL BURNERS
ENGINES HAVING AIR BRAKE WERE 305 +309, 318, 320, 322, 323, 324, 326, 331, 334+335
" VACUUM " 314, 321+332

ON 5-8-1897 THE FOLLOWING ENGINES WERE IN SERVICE ON THE O.+L.C DIV.
WHOLLY ON O.+L.C. N°S 11, 28, 25, 42, 51, 65, 71
BETWEEN ST. ALBANS AND O.+L.C. POINTS N°S 14, 30, 75, 81, 82, 92, 95, 96, 97, 98

ENB'S N°S 18, 20 AND 22 WERE RECEIVED ON DEC. 7 AND 9, 1889 AND WERE IN SERVICE ON THIS DIVISION ONLY TWO OR
THREE MONTHS BEFORE BEING SOLD TO THE N.L.N.R.R.

ON JAN. 1, 1876 THE O.+L.C. DIV. HAD THE FOLLOWING CAR EQUIPMENT.
17-PASSENGER CARS
9-BAGGAGE-SMOKER   2-SLEEPING CARS   3-MAIL-EXPRESS-BAGGAGE   1-BAGGAGE-EXPRESS
100 3-FREIGHT CARS
702-BOX   241-PLATFORM   32-CATTLE   4-SALOON   4-BOARDING

CENTRAL VERMONT RAILWAY INC.
RUTLAND DIVISION (RUTLAND AND BURLINGTON R.R.) LOCOMOTIVES

ENG. N°	NAME OR NUMBER AS OF JUNE 1, 1855	JAN. 1, 1876	1891	RUT.R OF 1901	BUILDER NAME	NUMBER	DATE BUILT	RE-BUILT	TYPE	CYL'S	DRI-VER	TUBES N°	DIA	L'GT	COST	ENGINE WEIGHTS TRUCK	DRIVER	TOTAL	TEND ER	ENG. AND TEND.	TEND.CAP'Y EMPTY WATER	GAL'S	DATE DEMOLISHED	REMARKS
1	BURLINGTON	BURLINGTON	201 BURLINGTON	62	TAUNTON	213	6-25-41		4-4-0	15x18	68	120	1¾	10-5		6300	34100	50400					1887	ET N°63 STONE REC'D FROM CVRR 10-22-84, CYLS CHANGED 6-11-88, +4C BOILER
2	CHARLOTTE	CHARLOTTE			ST.ALBANS		1872			17x15	68	153	2	11-2	3000°°	7100	34500	71550	69100	134450			10-24-78	LATER IN SERVICE ON M.&P.R.R AS N°2 SARANAC. REC'D AT ST.ALBANS-RET. 10-6 R.R.R
3	VERGENNES	VERGENNES			TAUNTON	50	4-17-50			17x14	54	140	1¾	10-6		6350	32250	42800			1500	1¼	5-1887	
4	NEW HAVEN	NEW HAVEN		37			9-12-44			12x15		100				8000	33000	51000					12-1874	
5	MIDDLEBURY	MIDDLEBURY	202 MIDDLEBURY	35	SOUTHWICK TAUNTON		18-14-51 6-25-44			14x18 15x16	"		2	11-0	7000°°	7000	33000	50000						WRECKED AT TAUNTON - SOLD TO FITCHBURG + WORCESTER AS THE STERLING
6	WHITING	WHITING			MORTIFIED HINCKLEY		8-15-66	10-1870	4-4-0	15x16		120		11-0	808½°°		38100	53100	47300	100600	1300	1½	1831	C.A. REBUILT AT TAUNTON-SOLD TO FITCHBURG + WORCESTER AS THE STERLING
7	BRANDON	BRANDON	203 BENSLIDE		TAUNTON	402	3-1-867		0-4-0	15x22	5A				3500°°		58100							HAD WEST AIR BRAKES APPLIED 6-13-1818
8	PITTSFORD	PITTSFORD		45		49	1-7-50	1852 1877	4-4-0	16x20	57		1¾		7000°°	8500	48500		40000	91500	1000	1	1-1886	C.A. REBUILT AT PITTSFORD NEW AIR BRAKES APPLIED 6-13-1818
9	RUTLAND	(SWEGATCHIE)		32	BOSTON	32	3-18-50 6-11-49 1865			15x18	"	131	"			6610	33450	50060			1½	1500	1-1886	SOLD TO D.C.LINSLEY 6-1881 RENAMED GLENGARY
		204 RUTLAND			RUTLAND		1872					125	1¾			6400	34100	50500					1-23-1872	REBUILT AT RUTLAND IN 1847 TRANSFERRED TO M.+P.R.R. AS N°1 PLATTSBURGH
10	CLARENDON	CLARENDON		63	TAUNTON	46A	7-3-49			16x24	"	149	2	11-4		7000	37500	44500						PURCHASED FROM O. + L.C.R.R WHEN M.+P.R.R. WAS LEASED BY R.+B.R.R
																7000	30900	48700						STILL RUNNING 1872. CHANGED TO COAL 1874, BACK TO WOOD 1875, TO COAL 1878
11	CUTTINGSVILLE	CUTTINGSVILLE			BALLERD	66	3-19-51			15x18	"		1¾	10-0	7250°°	5450	40850	74300	54850	129150				RENUMBERED 204 AFTER PREVIOUS 204 DEM.
			205 L.E.ROYS	64	TAUNTON					16x24	60	120	2	11-0		6540	39900	46340			1500		12-1874	ORIGINAL NAME WAS RED BIRD AS RECEIVED ON LINE
12	MT. HOLLY	MT. HOLLY	GOV. PAGE		TAUNTON	447	11-1868	1866-R		16x24	60	135	2	11-1	7000°°	600	42100	68200	176300		2	2000		WRECKED ON ADDISON R.R. 10-31-76
13	LUDLOW	LUDLOW	MT. HOLLY		TAUNTON	36	11-8-41		4-4-0	16x20	"	133	"	10-3	7800°°	6440	36400	57840			1½	1500	12-1881	KRN ON BUR + LAT VILLE 8-29-78, SOLD TO D.C.LINSLEY 1879
14	CAVENDISH	CAVENDISH	LUDLOW			52	1-28-50			15x18	"	133		10-0		6700	38200	48600			1½	1500		11-5-18 WENT TO BRATTLEBORO TO RUN BETWEEN THERE AND BELLOWS FALLS
15	CHESTER	CHESTER	206 CHESTER		R.NORRIS	77	4-13-51	1865-R	4-4-0	15x22	"	101	2	11-0	7313°°	7000	30000	49000						
16	ROCKINGHAM	ROCKINGHAM			BALLERD TAUNTON		2-26-50 9-12-49	1868-R		15x20	"	101C	2	11-0	7250°°	18100	34700	52800					9-1842	ORIGINAL NAME WAS BLUE BIRD AS RECEIVED ON LINE
17	MOOSALAMOO	MOOSALAMOO	207 MOOSALAMOO		TAUNTON	448	12-1868		4-4-0	16x24	60	135C	1¾	10-0	7000°°	5050	43050	54700	172800		1½	1500	12-1876	WRECKED ON ADDISON R.R. 10-31-76
18	BELLOWS FALLS	BELLOWS FALLS	208 CHAS CLEMENT	65	TAUNTON	34	6-25-49	1873	4-4-0	15x18	"	133C	2	11-1	7000°°	3450	34150	50500			1½	1500		NEW BOILER ST.ALBANS 1880, 16¾ DIA. 156 TUBES, 2-4 11-2; COAL BURNER 11-1887
19	NANTUCKET	(NANTUCKET)	J. BARNES		ST.ALBANS	2	1841			15x24	"	137C	2	10-6	5000°°	21100	34150	72550	63900	136450				CAME's A CONTRACTORS ENGINE
20	VULCAN	KNOW NOTHING	209 OTTER CREEK		BOSTON	549	10-1851 1871		4-4-0	15x24	60	147	"	10-6		TAUNTON R. OWNED BY RUT-BUR. ON FINISH OR CONTRACT FROM BURLINGTON SOUTH								CAMEs A CONTRACTORS ENGINE RENG ...SURG...STROKE 14 FROM NEW
21	GEN. STRONG	GEN. STRONG	210 PICO		HINKLEY	552	8-11-41			16x24	"	134C	2	11-0	2000°°									CAME FROM THE BOSTON AND WORCESTER NOV 1891
22	E.A.BIRCHARD	E.A.BIRCHARD	211		TAUNTON	78	8-26-51	1873		15x20	60	136C	"	10-0		18100	37350	55450			1¼	1700	1893	CHANGED TO COAL BURNER NOV 1891
72		E.A.BIRCHARD	212 E.A.BIRCHARD	66	SCH'DY	3510	8-11-91		0-4-0	15x24	"		"	10-0	8500°°		64800	50400	504000	115200	1½	1500	1891	EY A..0.5.T.L. R.R. N°1
	COL.MERRILL	COL.MERRILL	213 COL MERRILL		AMOSKEAG		8-27-32		4-4-0	16x22		146	"	10-6		25750	62550	66300	7100	135400	2	2000		NEW BOILER ST.ALBANS 1880, 16¾ DIA. 156 TUBES; 2-4 11-2; COAL BURNER 11-1887
	J.L.DAVIS	J.L.DAVIS	214		TAUNTON	4100	1-64		4-4-0	16x20		149	"	11-7	863½°°	24700	36000	64550			1½	2000	1890	COAL BURNER IN 1881
	DUNMORE	DUNMORE	215 DUNMORE		BOSTON	548	10-6-41 9-8-50-R			15x22	"	150	"	10-6½		44400	42600	67000	52600	119400	1¼	1700	BETWEEN 1800 & 1867	COAL BURNER IN 1881

HARLEM EXTENSION DIVISION LOCOMOTIVES of JAN. 1, 1876
1 HILAND HALL   15x22 CYL'S   66 DRIVERS
2 LUTHER PARK   14x24 "   60 "
3 AL. MINER

CENTRAL VERMONT RAILWAY INC.
RUTLAND DIVISION (RUTLAND AND BURLINGTON R.R.) LOCOMOTIVES

ENG. N°	NAME OR NUMBER AS OF JUNE 1, 1855	JAN. 1, 1876	1891	RUT.R OF 1901	BUILDER NAME	NUMBER	DATE BUILT	RE-BUILT	TYPE	CYL'S	DRI-VERS	TUBES N°	DIA	L'GT	COST	ENGINE WEIGHTS TRUCK	DRIVER	TOTAL	TEND ER	ENG. AND TEND.	TEND.CAP'Y EMPTY WATER	GAL'S	DATE DEMOLISHED	REMARKS
26	SAMUEL HENSHAW	216 ETHAN ALLEN			BOSTON	548	10-1851	1871	4-4-0	15x22	60	130C	2	11-1	1720½°°	24400	37400	61900	51500	113800	2	2000	1892	THEY MAY HAVE BEEN NAMED OTTER CREEK AS BUILT
27	KILLINGTON	217 KILLINGTON	67		TAUNTON	354	1-1865	1874	4-4-0	16x24	66	134	2	10-10		27050	40560	67600	55400	123000	2	"	1868	
28	ADDISON	218 ADDISON	68			355	2-1865	1878		16x24	"	134C	2	"		24550	43300	67500	54700	122800	"	"		RENAMED AUG. 1887
29	GOV. UNDERWOOD	219 J.BURDETTE	69			356	5-1865	1877		16x22	60	"				25150	43100	68300	54100	122400	"	"		
30	PETER BUTLER	220 PETER BUTLER	70			480	11-1869	1874		15x22	"	131	2	11-0		25050	43050	68100	55400	123400	"	2070		CHANGED TO COAL BURNER 11-1-91 1888
31	JOHN SIMONDS	221 JOHN SIMONDS	71		ROGERS		4-1870			16x22	"	134C	"	"					55100	126300	"	2000		
32	J.M.HAVEN	222 J.M.HAVEN			BOSTON		10-1852			15x24	"	131	"								"			
33	GEO.B.CHASE	223 GEO.B.CHASE	72		HINKLEY	512	10-1870			16x24	60	138	2	10-7		25750	42550	68200	66300	135400	"	"	7-25-1900	
35	JAS.H.WILLIAMS	225 JAS.H.WILLIAMS				514	1877			17x24	63	150	"	11-0½		24700	43300	67500	58100	126300	"		3-23-1849	EX CVRR N°61 PACIFIC. REPAIRED AND SOLD TO R.R.R 3-13-72
36	LAWRENCE BARNES	226 E.W.HORNER			SCH'DY	3511	18-91			18x24	"		"											
37	J.BURDETT	227 SHELBURNE			BALDWIN	2454	6-20-71		2-6-0	17x24	54	131	"	11-0		23050	47550	74350	54700	129050	"	"		
38	SHELBURNE	228 AMERICA	370		TAUNTON	116	8-8-54		4-4-0	15x24	"	153	1⅛	10-4	1000.	8885	42050	51800	28100	81105	2	1500	6-2-1880	CVRR N°34 STRANGER
39	TICONDEROGA				ROGERS					15x22	64	153	1⅛		5000°°									
40	SALISBURY	229 SALISBURY			BOSTON		10-1852			15x24	"	131	2			20400	33700	54100			2	2072	BEFORE 1-1-76	
41	ROCKINGHAM	230 ROCKINGHAM			HINKLEY		1848			17x24	63	138	"	11-0		9700	38000	57100	41800	105500		1800	1871 ORIG.15-18 CYLS	
42	NEW (RENAMED BRATTLEBORO)	231	182		MASON		1877			18x24	"	150	"	11-0¾		13400	37200	51100	21000	78200		1842		
		232	183			3511	1891									26475	46450	73215	64350	137615				EX A.+S.T.L.R.R. N°11
		233	480			3506																		N°62
		234	481			3505																		
		235																						

MONTREAL AND PLATTSBURGH R.R.

	NAME OR NUMBER																						
1	PLATTSBURGH		3X		TAUNTON		6-11-49	1865-R		15x18	60	106	2	10-0		7000	32500	49500			1½	1500		EX M+B.RR N°9 RUTLAND. TRANSFERRED TO M+P.R.R IN 1869 + RENAMED
2	SARANAC									15x20	66	121	1¾	11-0		8500	31700	50200						RECEIVED WITH M+P.R.R. BY RUT.-BUR.R.R UNDER LEASE DEC.1868

VERMONT VALLEY R.R.

1	PUTNEY				ROGERS		1864-R			14x20	57	134	1¾	10-9		17800	30900	48700			1¾	1680		RECEIVED WITH V.V.RR BY RUT.-BUR.R.R. UNDER LEASE JUNE 1865
2	DUMMERSTOWN						1810-R					135	1¾	10-8		17900	31300	41100						
3	WESTMINSTER									15x22	64	138	2	10-11		17800	30600	48400						
4							1869-R			15x22		153		11-0		20400	33900	54100			2	2072	BEFORE 1-1-76	

HARLEM EXTENSION DIVISION LOCOMOTIVES of JAN. 1, 1876
4 C.G. LINCOLN   14x24 CYL'S   60 DRIVERS   7 VACANT   10 N.Y.B. AND M. I   16x24 CYL'S   60 DRIVERS
5 LEBANON   14x20 "   8 MOUNTAIN BOY   16x24 CYL'S 66 DRIVERS   11 N.Y.B. AND M. 3
6 MANCHESTER   9 MOUNTAIN GIRL

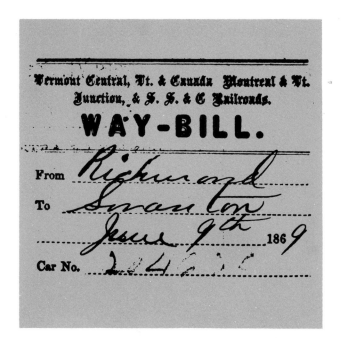

Vermont Central, Vt. & Canada Montreal & Vt. Junction, & J. J. & C Railroads.

WAY-BILL.

From _Richmond_

To _Swanton_

June 9th 186_9_

Car No. _2406_

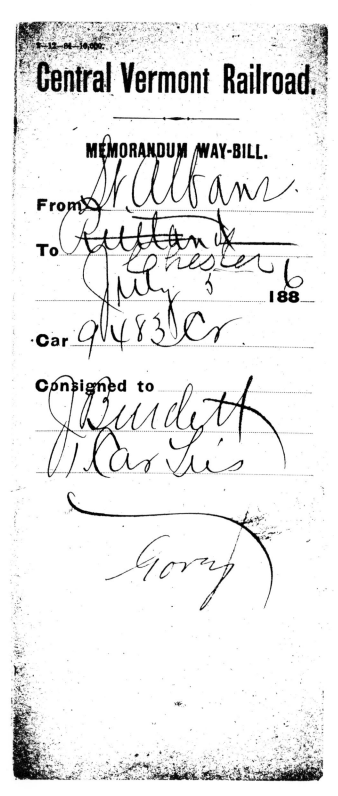

9-12-84-10,000.

Central Vermont Railroad.

MEMORANDUM WAY-BILL.

From _St Albans._

To ~~_Rutland_~~ _Chester_

July 5 188_6_

Car _9483 Cr_

Consigned to _J Burdett_
V Car Lis

Gorry

BIBLIOGRAPHY

This bibliography is intended to represent the major sources used by the author during the preparation of the six volumes that will comprise this series. In addition, the annual reports of the Central Vermont and its antecedent lines were used liberally, as were many other documents and items of correspondence in the railroad's files at St. Albans.

BOOKS

Baker, George Pierce. **Formation of New England Railroad Systems.** Harvard University Press, Cambridge, Mass., 1937.

Carlisle, Lillian Baker, Editor. **Look Around Chittenden County.** Chittenden County Historical Society, Burlington, Vt, 1976.

Forbes, Charles Spooner. "History of the Vermont Central-Central Vermont Railway System, 1843-1933." **The Vermonter**, Nov.-Dec., 1932. Publ. by Charles R. Cummings, White River Jct., Vt.

Harlow, Alvin F. **Steelways of New England.** Creative Age Press, New York, 1946.

Hungerford, Edward. **Vermont Central-Central Vermont. A Study in Human Effort.** Railway & Locomotive Historical Society, Inc., Bulletin. Boston, August, 1942.

Shaughnessy, Jim. **The Rutland Road.** Howell-North Books, San Diego, Calif., 1964.

Stevens, G.R. **Canadian National Railway, Towards the Inevitable.** Volume 2, Chapter 15. Clarke, Irwin & Co., Ltd. Toronto, 1962.

ARTICLES

Boyd, Jim. "Central Vermont Steam," **Railfan & Railroad.** May, 1979.

Rhode, William L. "Border Line," **Railroad Magazine.** August, 1947.

Spaulding, Albert C. "Burlington's Railroad Tunnel," Chittenden County Historical Society **Bulletin.** Volume 5, No. 1 Sept., 1969.

PRINTED SOURCES

Railroad Commissioners' Reports, State of Vermont. Montpelier, Vt. (Published annually for many years)

Report of Masters in Chancery, State of Vermont. **Vermont Central Railroad Accounting.** 1875.

UNPUBLISHED SOURCES

Bottum, Lynn H. Research notes on Grand Trunk/Central Vermont steamboat operations.

Heath, Elwin K. Detailed notes on Central Vermont motive power compiled over a period of many years.

Spaulding, Albert C. "One Hundred Years of Train Travel in Vermont . . . and All Strictly First Class." 8-page paper. Completed in June, 1970.

INDEX

Asterisk (*) After Page Number Indicates Illustration.

Central Vermont Railroad — General Passenger Time-Table.

1876. 1876.

At St. Albans, July 10th, 1876.   Subject to Changes.

Trains are Run by New London Time.

TIME TABLE — GOING SOUTH.

Mls.	STATIONS.	Pass.	Pass.	Pass.
09	Ogdensburg ...Lv	†6.45 am		11.40 am†
	Lisbon	7.30		11.23
17	Madrid {Ar	8.20		11.45
	Norwood {Lv	9.00		12.00
25	Norwood {Ar	8.05		12.08 pm
28	Knapp's {Lv	8.50		12.30
35	Brasher	9.20		12.48
	Lawrence	11.00		
47	Moira	11.45		1.12
49	Brush's Mills	12.05 pm		1.28
55	Bangor	12.40		1.42
61	Malone {Ar	1.10		1.47
	Malone {Lv	1.42	6.00 am†	2.10
69	Burke	2.10	6.35	2.25
73	Chateaugay	2.25	7.10	2.45
	Cherubusco	2.45	7.55	2.52
81	Clinton Mills	2.52	8.10	3.12
83	Ellenburg	3.12	8.56	3.20
89	Dannemora	3.20	9.02	3.29
92	Forest	3.29	9.18	3.35
	Irona	3.35	9.35	3.45
97	Altona	3.45	9.48	3.50
100	Mooer's Falls	3.50	10.08	4.00
105	Mooer's Forks	4.00	10.25	4.10
106	Mooer's Junc. {Ar	4.10	10.55	4.22
114	Perry's Mills	4.22	11.25	4.35
118	Champlain	4.35	11.45	4.50
122	Rouse's Point	4.50	12.15 pm	4.58
126	Alburgh	4.58		5.14
	Alburgh Springs	5.14		5.35
132	Swanton	5.35		6.05
	St. Albans {Ar	6.00		6.18
142	St. Albans {Lv	7.00	8.00 am	6.34
147	North Georgia	7.12	8.14	6.50
152	Georgia	7.24	8.20	7.00
155	Milton	7.30	8.48	7.12
162	Colchester	7.45	8.57	7.24
166	Essex Junc. {Ar	7.55	9.05	7.30
172	Winooski	7.10	9.10	7.45
174	Burlington {Ar	7.22	9.20	7.55
	Burlington {Lv	7.30	9.32	8.00 am
181	Shelburne	7.42	9.42	8.14
186	Charlotte	7.53	9.55	8.20
190	No. Ferrisburg	8.02	10.08	8.48
193	Ferrisburg	8.10	10.35	8.57
195	Vergennes	8.15	10.45	9.05
200	New Haven	8.35	10.50	9.10
205	Brooksville	8.44	12.10 pm	9.20
208	Middlebury	8.57	4.10 am	9.32
219	Salisbury	9.07	4.18	9.42
	Leicester Junc {Lv	9.35	4.26	9.55
232	Brandon	9.42	4.38	10.08
235	Pittsford	9.52	4.47	10.35
	Sutherland Falls	9.55	4.58	10.45
240	Centre Rutland			10.50
241	Rutland {Ar	12.18		12.10 pm
244	No. Clarendon	12.30		12.30
247	East Clarendon	12.40		3.58
251	Cuttingsville	12.49		4.15
254	East Wallingford	12.56		4.42
	Mount Holly			4.58

CONDENSED TIME TABLE.

Mls.	STATIONS.	Going South.		STATIONS.	Going North.		Mls.
25	Ogdensburg ...Lv	†6.00 pm		Philadelphia ...Lv	†11.00 am		556
	Norwood	8.05		New York, via Hudson River	12.00 m / 4.00 pm		521
61	Malone	11.00		New York, via New Haven	2.35 am / 3.00		447
103	Mooer's Junction	1.42 pm		Boston	6.00 / 8.00 am		410
118	Rouse's Point	2.35 am		Hartford	4.00 / 8.20		385
142	St. Albans {Ar	4.00 / 2.50		Springfield	4.35 / 8.54		365
	St. Albans {Lv	4.35 / 3.50		Northampton	5.35		
166	Essex Junction	6.05 / 6.00		New London {Ar	6.05 / 5.00		346
	Burlington	7.10 / 7.00		Norwich	7.10 / 5.32		
174	Rutland	7.30 / 8.20		Norwich & W. Depot	5.40		
241	Manchester, Vt	11.08 / 11.05		Miller's Falls	9.40		434
270	Troy, N.Y.	12.45 am / 12.20 pm		Poughkeepsie	1.03		393
330	Albany	1.00 / 2.25 pm		Hudson	4.43		352
352	Hudson	3.35 / 2.40		Albany	8.00		324
393	Poughkeepsie	4.50		Troy, N.Y.	8.26		
466	New York, via Troy	7.00 / 6.30		Manchester, Vt. {Ar	10.55 / 12.05 pm		270
	White River Junction	12.35 / 1.50 am		Rutland {Lv	1.15 / 1.20		241
262	Concord	3.40 / 2.20		Burlington	4.23 / 4.55		174
330	Manchester	4.22 / 4.45		Essex Junction	4.45 / 5.20		166
348	Nashua	5.05 / 5.00 am		Fall River	5.20 / 3.40 pm		449
363	Boston	6.37 pm / 8.35		Fitchburg	5.55 / 7.05		365
403	Worcester	5.55 / 9.20		Mansfield	7.35 / 8.20		423
409	Providence	8.25 / 4.15		Worcester	4.15 / 8.00		409
453	Fitchburg	8.25 / 6.25		Providence	4.35 / 9.20		403
323	Keene	3.32 / 7.30		Nashua	6.20 / 1.35 pm		348
305	Fitchburg	5.08 / 2.10 pm		Boston	8.05 / 6.05		363
423	Mansfield	7.45 / 9.20 am		Manchester, N.H.	8.59 / 1.10 am		343
381	Fall River / Palmer's Falls	4.34		Concord	1.35 pm		330
346	Norwich	10.53 pm / 6.15		White River Junction {Ar	5.50 / 6.05		262
434	New London	4.31 pm / 8.56		St. Albans {Lv	6.15 / 6.30		142
365	Northampton	5.19 / 9.32		Rouse's Point	7.25 / 8.35		118
385	Springfield	5.43 am / 6.05		Mooer's Junction	8.05 / 10.05		103
410	Hartford	6.20 / 7.15		Malone	10.05 am / 1.55		61
447	New Haven	8.05 / 8.30		Norwood	9.45 / 4.56		25
521	New York, via Springfield ...Ar	12.20 pm / 11.12		Ogdensburg ...Ar	12.05 / 6.45		
556	Philadelphia via Troy	12.05					

† Daily except Sunday.

TIME TABLE — GOING NORTH.

Mls.	STATIONS.	Pass.	Pass.	Pass.	Pass.	Pass.	Pass.
	New London	5.00 am	8.10 am			†1.00 pm	8.00 pm
1	Upper Switch	5.08	8.26			4.00 pm	8.08
3	Waterford	5.15	8.31			4.15	8.16
8	Montville {Ar		8.36			4.34	8.17
	Massapeag {Lv		8.42			4.38	8.21
10	Mohegan		8.45			4.43	8.28
13	Thamesville	5.32	8.48			4.47	8.35
13	Norwich {Ar		8.53			4.56	
15	Norwich & W. Depot		8.59			5.04	
17	Norwich Town {Lv	5.42	9.07			5.13	
20	Yantic		9.15			5.13	
23	Franklin	5.56	9.28			5.25	
26	Lebanon	6.02	9.38			5.37	
29	South Wirdham {Ar		9.40			5.42	
	Willimantic {Lv	6.12	9.52			5.13	
34	South Coventry	6.25	9.56			5.29	
	Eagleville	6.29	10.00			5.33	
36	Mansfield	6.39	10.04			5.37	
38	Merrow	6.39				5.46	
40	So. Willington	6.43				5.59	
42	Tolland	6.47	10.12			6.04	
44	Stafford	7.00	10.25				
49	Orcutts		10.30			6.13	
52	Ellithorpe		10.33			6.22	
53	State Line	7.14	10.39			6.25	
55	South Monson	7.23	10.47				
60	Monson	7.30	10.51			6.34	
62	North Monson		11.00			7.08	
65	Palmer {Ar	7.40	3.00			7.16	
	Three Rivers {Lv	8.20	3.09			7.21	
67	Barretts Junc.	8.26	3.14			7.35	
69	Belchertown	8.31	3.30			7.49	
75	Dwights	8.43	3.44			8.03	
80	South Amherst	8.54				4.09	
82	Amherst {Ar	9.05				4.17	
	North Amherst {Lv	9.11				4.26	
85	Leverett	9.17				4.39	
88	Mount Toby	9.24				4.48	
90	South Montague	9.30				4.56	
95	Millers's Falls	9.42				5.12	
100	Northfield Farms	9.47				5.18 pm	
103	Northfield, Mass.	9.59				10.05 pm	
109	So. Vermon ...Lv	10.07				10.17	
111	Vernon	10.18				11.56	
116	Brattleboro {Ar	10.30				12.13 pm	
121	Dummerston {Lv	10.43				6.50 am	
126	Putney	11.03				7.18	
130	East Putney	11.19				7.50	
138	Westminster	11.25				8.05	
142	Bellows Falls {Ar	11.35				9.10	
146	Bellows Falls {Lv	11.50				9.20	
150	So. Charlestown	12.00				9.35	
154	Charlestown	12.10 pm				9.55	
155	Springfield, Vt.	12.15				10.00	
159	No. Charlestown	12.24				10.15	
163	Claremont Junc	12.35				10.35	
171	Windsor	12.55				11.10	
175	Hartland	1.05				11.30	
179	No. Hartland	1.16				11.48	

† Daily except Sunday.

NORTHERN DIVISION.

GOING SOUTH.

Mls.	STATIONS.	Pass.	Pass.	Pass.
	Montreal ...Lv	†9.00 am	†3.00 pm	
27	St. Johns	10.15	4.00	
29	S. S. and C. Junc.	10.20	4.05	
36	Des Rivieres	10.32	4.20	
42	Stanbridge	10.48	4.37	
46	Moore's	10.55	4.43	
49	St. Armand	11.10	4.59	
52	Highgate Springs	11.20	5.10	
57	East Swanton	11.30	5.21	
64	Swanton Junction	11.36	5.27	
70	St. Albans ...Ar	11.50	5.40	

GOING NORTH.

Mls.	STATIONS.	Pass.	Pass.	Pass.
	St. Albans ...Lv	†6.10 am	†12.35 pm	†6.25 pm
6	Swanton Junction	6.22	1.00	6.40
9	East Swanton	6.29	1.10	6.48
13	Highgate Springs	6.38	1.25	6.57
18	St. Armand	6.50	1.50	7.10
25	Moore's	7.03	2.23	7.25
27	Stanbridge	7.10	2.35	7.32
34	Des Rivieres	7.25	3.08	7.50
41	S. S. & C. Junction	7.38	3.35	8.05
43	St. John's {Ar	7.45	3.35	8.10
	Waterloo {Lv	†5.45	11.50 am	8.26